Date Due
MAY 11 2002
APR 27 1998
W/D
CAT. NO. 23 233
PRINTED IN U.S.A.

D0866422

TEXAS WOMAN'S UNIVERSITY
SCIENTIA LUMEN VITAE

CHARLES KEMBLE,
MAN OF THE THEATRE

Charles Kemble

Portrait by Henry Perronet Briggs. Reproduced by permission of the Governors of Dulwich College Picture Gallery.

CHARLES KEMBLE, MAN OF THE THEATRE

BY

JANE WILLIAMSON

UNIVERSITY OF NEBRASKA PRESS · LINCOLN

Standard Book Number 8032–0727–1

Library of Congress Catalog Card Number 69–19105

Manufactured in the United States of America

To Arthur Colby Sprague

Contents

A section of illustrations follows p. 116.

Acknowledgments

In acknowledging my indebtedness to the many persons who have helped me in the preparation of this book, I want first of all to express my appreciation to the faculty of Bryn Mawr College for awarding me the Fanny Bullock Workman Traveling Fellowship, which enabled me to conduct my research abroad. My research was aided, too, by a travel grant from the University of Missouri–St. Louis.

I am grateful for the cooperation and courtesies extended to me by the following libraries and theatre collections in which I have consulted books, newspapers and periodicals, playbills, promptbooks, and manuscripts: the Bryn Mawr College Library; the Free Library of Philadelphia; the Historical Society of Pennsylvania; the University of Pennsylvania Library; the Washington University Library; the Harvard Theatre Collection; the Boston Public Library; the Theatre Collection of the New York Public Library; the Walter Hampden Memorial Library, The Players; the Folger Shakespeare Library; the Henry E. Huntington Library; the British Museum; the Gabrielle Enthoven Collection of the Victoria and Albert Museum; the London County Council Archives; the Garrick Club Library; and the Shakespeare Memorial Theatre Library. Mr. George Nash, Curator of the Gabrielle Enthoven Collection; Mr.

Philip Knachel, Acting Director of the Folger Shakespeare Library; Mr. Paul Myers, Curator of the Theatre Collection of the New York Public Library; and Mr. Louis Rachow, Librarian, The Players, have been particularly helpful.

I want especially to thank Mr. Roy Plomley of London for sharing with me a letter from Charles Kemble and a receipt for salary signed by Fanny Kemble from his private collection, and Mr. Bertram Shuttleworth of London for permitting me to consult his excellent private collection of early-nineteenth-century theatrical journals.

I owe a special debt of gratitude to Miss Helen Willard, Curator of the Harvard Theatre Collection, and to Miss Sybil Rosenfeld, Honorary Secretary of the Society for Theatre Research, for their help and kindness.

My greatest indebtedness is to Professor Emeritus Arthur Colby Sprague of Bryn Mawr College. Professor Sprague introduced me to stage history and first suggested to me the possibilities for research on Charles Kemble. I have had the privilege of his expert guidance and endless encouragement throughout the various stages in the development of this book. It is scarcely possible to express my debt to him.

CHARLES KEMBLE,
MAN OF THE THEATRE

Prologue

On November 12, 1854, the final curtain descended on Charles Kemble, last survivor of England's most famous theatrical dynasty. As the newspapers and theatrical journals paid their final tributes to "the last of the illustrious line," they were quick to suggest that his death marked the end of an epoch in the history of the English stage. Similar statements were, of course, traditional on such occasions; but in this case they were not without some propriety. As an actor, manager, theatre owner, dramatist, Examiner of Plays, and member of the dramatic family which included John Philip Kemble and the remarkable Sarah Siddons, Charles Kemble had enjoyed for seventy-nine years a life intimately associated with the English stage. Few careers reflect so fully an era in English theatrical history.

As an actor, Charles Kemble's reputation tends to be eclipsed by the fame of his older brother and sister, who have more readily attracted the attention of biographers and stage historians. But although he never equaled the renown of John Philip Kemble or Mrs. Siddons, Charles Kemble won highest praise from English audiences for more than forty years and continued to uphold the Kemble tradition long after John and Sarah had left the boards.

First appearing on the London stage on April 21, 1794,

as Malcolm to his brother's Macbeth and his sister's "fiend-like queen," young Kemble embarked on a long apprenticeship. While his brother and sister remained on the stage he would be overshadowed, and he had to content himself with second place. Gradually, however, this second place he made his own. The critic William Bodham Donne came unreservedly to declare Charles Kemble to be "at all times unsurpassed" in secondary parts;[1] and the son of his rival Charles Young made note: "Whenever he played a second part he made it a first one. Antony, Mercutio, Orlando, Faulconbridge, and Cassio became so in his hands."[2] Certainly many late-eighteenth- and early-nineteenth-century Shakespearean productions displayed a new depth and perfection through the young actor's accomplishments in supporting roles. In fact, his fame in many lesser characters was such that he continued to perform them long after he had succeeded to the leading roles in comedy and tragedy. Donne observed that "at the zenith of his reputation he would undertake characters which inferior actors would have declined as derogatory to them."[3]

Unlike Mrs. Siddons, with succeeding years Charles Kemble greatly extended his range of characters. At the time of his death it was suggested that he played well a greater range of parts than any other actor on record with the exception of Garrick.[4] Indeed, the number and variety of roles undertaken by Kemble during his lengthy career indicates that he was an extremely versatile actor. Still, even

1. William Bodham Donne, *Essays on the Drama* (London, 1858), p. 167.

2. Julian Young, *A Memoir of Charles Mayne Young, Tragedian* (London, 1871), p. 98.

3. Donne, *Essays on the Drama,* p. 163.

4. *Ibid.,* p. 169.

his most enthusiastic admirer could not claim that his personations won uniform applause.

Kemble was least successful in those tragic parts which require an outward display of intense passion, such as Macbeth and Othello. His weakness here had both a physical and a stylistic basis. His speech tended to be imperfect on very high notes; and "the dulcet tones of his voice, which in Romeo and Hamlet went home to the hearts of his audience . . . were less adapted to convey the trumpet notes, the anguish, and the wail of darker passions." Donne noted too a "faintness of colouring in his face and a statuesque repose in his demeanour" which was "unfavourable to the sudden transitions and vivid flashes of emotion which such impersonations require." [5] Moreover, to many who grew to admire the romantic style of Edmund Kean, Charles Kemble's formal acting appeared to lack power and intensity and seemed less suited to the representation of high emotion. The playwright and critic Westland Marston recalled:

> His style in passion was uniformly lofty. There was variety, indeed . . . but it was a variety confined within the limits of what may be called heroic delivery, seldom or never a marked transition from it to colloquial realism. The manner, maintained at the height of feeling, made no such appeals to the many as did Macready and, according to report, Edmund Kean, by those familiar touches which, at times, set before an audience the individual rather than the typical man.[6]

Some unsympathetic critics accused Kemble of being less real in his style of acting than in his costume, of speaking

5. *Ibid.*, p. 172.
6. Westland Marston, *Our Recent Actors* (Boston, 1888) p. 131.

and moving like the creature of an ideal world, while wearing the robes of this;[7] while others proclaimed him to be "more intent on leaving nothing the head can disapprove than presenting anything which the heart can admire."[8]

As the representative of a certain range of characters, however, Charles Kemble was admittedly unsurpassed. Leigh Hunt concisely summarized Kemble's talents when he judged, "Mr. Charles Kemble excels in three classes of character: in the tender lover, . . . in the spirited gentleman of tragedy, . . . and in a very happy mixture of the occasional debauchee and gentleman of feeling."[9] Within these categories fell many of Kemble's greatest roles: his Romeo, which drew from Hunt the comment that in theatric love he was "certainly the first performer on the stage";[10] his Faulconbridge, which through the years became so famous that the mere mention of the name would "instantly evoke the person, the tones, and the looks of Charles Kemble" in the minds of spectators who had seen him;[11] and his Cassio, which time and again was pronounced unrivaled. In comedy Charles Kemble was able to seize on a domain which his brother and sister could never enter with safety to their fame. Declared the "prince of genteel comedy,"[12]

7. William Leggett, "Charles Kemble's Hamlet," New York *Evening Post,* September 18, 1832. Leggett's article is reprinted in *The American Theatre as Seen by Its Critics: 1759–1934,* ed. Montrose J. Moses and John Mason Brown (New York: W. W. Norton and Company, 1934), pp. 50–59.

8. *The Drama; or, Theatrical Pocket Magazine,* May 1824.

9. Leigh Hunt, *Dramatic Essays,* ed. William Archer and Robert W. Lowe (London, 1894), p. 108.

10. *Ibid.*

11. Donne, *Essays on the Drama,* p. 168.

12. *Theatrical Pocket Magazine,* September 1824.

Kemble, in his Benedick, Lovemore, Mirabel, Dorimant, and other gay, buoyant, spirited gentlemen of high breeding, banished all competitors; and as a critic for the *Morning Herald* noted, many such parts which he filled "virtually left the stage when age and infirmity occasioned his retirement into private life."[13]

By the 1820s the applause that greeted Charles Kemble when he crossed the boards of Covent Garden Theatre was warm, steady, and enthusiastic. But behind the curtain, as manager of the theatre from 1822 to 1832 and again briefly in 1842, the younger Kemble found success far more elusive, as he struggled to combat persistent forces which threatened to destroy Covent Garden and more than a century of theatrical tradition. In retrospect the stage historian may conjecture that in the early nineteenth century London's two great patent houses were clearly doomed. But to Charles Kemble, as proprietor and manager, the battle to preserve the fortune, reputation, and rights of the theatre so long associated with his family's name had to be waged.

The problems that beset Kemble as manager were mighty. From the time he assumed the management in March, 1822, Covent Garden was plagued by financial difficulties which reached a peak in the 1829–30 season, when distraint warrants for rates and taxes to the amount of between one thousand and two thousand pounds were issued and the theatre was in the possession of bailiffs. Public subscriptions, voluntary contributions, and, above all, the very successful appearance of Charles Kemble's daughter Fanny helped to retrieve the position of the theatre the following year; but

13. London *Morning Herald,* November 15, 1854.

thereafter heavy debt never failed to weigh "like an incubus"[14] upon Kemble and his family.

Legal difficulties were inextricably intertwined with financial ones. The proprietors of Covent Garden Theatre became engaged in a lawsuit with each other, and finally the whole concern was thrown into chancery. This chancery suit dragged on for more than five years, as Fanny Kemble vividly recalled, "pending, pending, like the sword of Damocles, over our heads, banishing all security for the present or hope for the future."[15]

Financial crises and quarreling partners were not Charles Kemble's only managerial headaches. It was at this period in the history of the London stage that the so-called minor or illegitimate theatres pushed rapidly to the front and for the first time presented a really dangerous threat to the welfare of the "great houses."[16] The end of the theatrical monopoly which the two patent companies had enjoyed since 1660 did not officially come until 1843; but perhaps the greatest battles over patent rights were waged during the period of Kemble's management, and they culminated in 1832 in the investigation and report of the Select Committee on Dramatic Literature of the House of Commons, under the chairmanship of Edward Bulwer.[17]

14. Frances Ann Kemble, *Records of a Girlhood* (London, 1879), I, 57.

15. *Ibid.*, p. 201.

16. Watson Nicholson, *The Struggle for a Free Stage in London* (Boston: Houghton Mifflin and Company, 1906), p. 294.

17. See Dewey Ganzel, "Patent Wrongs and Patent Theatres: Drama and Law in the Early Nineteenth Century," *PMLA*, LXXVI (September, 1961), 384–96. It is to be noted that Ganzel disagrees with E. B. Watson (*Sheridan to Robertson* [Cambridge: Harvard University Press, 1926], p. 49), who says that in 1843 "the monopoly still existed,

Amidst such difficulties Charles Kemble labored to continue and extend the reputation that Covent Garden had enjoyed under his brother's reign as the theatre where the best English plays, especially those of William Shakespeare, were given the most stately, splendid, and perfect representation. At a time when the talents of England's first poets and men of letters seemed ill-suited to writing for the stage and the taste of the public seemed determined to grant trained animals, crude farce, and extravagant melodrama warmest applause, such goals were not easily attained. Kemble's most notable production was his spectacular 1823 *King John*. With its historically accurate costumes, it was the earliest of the archaeological Shakespearean revivals and "initiated a new departure in theatrical art,"[18] giving impulse to the later efforts of Mme Vestris, Macready, and Charles Kean.

Off-stage, one admiring contemporary observed, Charles Kemble was in private life what he was as an artist: "an example of finished excellence, produced by labour and study, working on original nature admirably predisposed to 'fine issues.'"[19] Another recalled: "An evening spent in his society is a bright spot in our memories that nothing can eradicate. [He is] elegant without affectation; learned without pedantry; witty without rancour; humourous without vulgarity."[20]

---

in fact as well as theory, by reason of historical recognition." Ganzel suggests that by 1832 "the monopoly had ceased to be a real factor in English dramatic development."

18. H. Barton Baker, *History of the London Stage: 1576–1903* (London: G. Routledge and Sons, 1904), p. 135.

19. London *Illustrated News*, November 18, 1854.

20. W. Oxberry, *Dramatic Biography and Histrionic Anecdotes*, III (London, 1825), 9.

A large man who shared with his famous brother and sister the classic Kemble features, Charles made a striking appearance in London society. Fanny Kemble referred to her father as "full six feet tall,"[21] and Leigh Hunt mentioned his "winning appearance" and declared him to have had a "most handsome face and a general air of the graceful and romantic."[22] Donne described his form as "noble, his features classical and expressive, his voice . . . remarkably melodious."[23] Both Marston and Donne agreed that Kemble's appearance and manner reminded one of what Marston called a "gentleman of the old school."[24] Donne, writing in 1854, said that "Charles Kemble transmitted to the present age the express image of the English gentleman of the past generation—of the gentlemen whom Reynolds painted, and of whom Beauclerc was the sample and representative";[25] while Marston lamented that "it seemed a wrong to Mr. Charles Kemble's person that he did not, off the stage, wear knee-breeches, silk stockings, and diamond buckles, and that he had survived the time of powdered hair."[26]

The handsome actor was a man of considerable taste and learning. Art, and especially sculpture, he made the subject of earnest study. He spoke several modern languages and reportedly had read widely in their literature. Although he was by no means a classical scholar, he was certainly familiar

21. Kemble, *Records of a Girlhood,* I, 60.
22. Leigh Hunt, *Dramatic Criticism: 1808–1831,* ed. Laurence Houtchens (New York: Columbia University Press, 1949), p. 105.
23. Donne, *Essays on the Drama,* p. 158.
24. Marston, *Our Recent Actors,* p. 133.
25. Donne, *Essays on the Drama,* p. 183.
26. Marston, *Our Recent Actors,* p. 133.

with the masterpieces of ancient Rome.[27] He shared with his brother John a strong interest in philology, a field in which his son later earned a considerable reputation, and as an amusement of his declining years renewed his study of Greek grammar.[28]

When troubles before or behind the curtain grew pressing, Charles Kemble could always seek diversion among his large and notable circle of friends. His house, a contemporary magazine reported, was "at all times the resort of persons distinguished in art and literature."[29] Dinner guests might include Sir Walter Scott, young Alfred Tennyson and his friend Arthur Hallam, William Thackeray, or the American Washington Irving, who were attracted to the Kemble table not only by their eminent and genial host but by other members of a distinguished household as well.

Mrs. Charles Kemble, the former Maria Theresa De Camp, was a most attractive and accomplished wife. An actress and singer, she achieved considerable acclaim until her retirement in 1819. Their daughter Fanny proved a spectacular success in her stage debut in 1829 and remained the rage of English and American society until her marriage to Pierce Butler of Philadelphia in June, 1834. In later years a number of literary men paid Fanny homage: Macaulay, Edward FitzGerald, and Longfellow were among her ardent admirers.[30] John Mitchell Kemble, Charles

27. Donne, *Essays on the Drama,* p. 182.

28. Kemble, *Records of a Girlhood,* I, 83.

29. *Fraser's Magazine,* December 1854.

30. Longfellow, who was a constant attendant at Fanny Kemble's public readings in Boston in the winter of 1849, wrote a sonnet, "On Mrs. Kemble's Readings from Shakespeare," in which he paid warm tribute to her. See *The Complete Poetical Works of Longfellow,* Cambridge ed. (Boston: Houghton Mifflin, 1922), p. 112.

Kemble's eldest child,[31] was destined to become a noted philologist, historian, and pioneer Anglo-Saxon scholar. At Cambridge young Kemble belonged to a brilliant set which included Alfred Tennyson, Arthur Hallam, R. C. Trench, and John Sterling. He was an intimate friend of Tennyson, and his youthful decision to dedicate himself to the ministry inspired the poet's sonnet "To J. M. K." The youngest member of the family, Adelaide, followed her father, mother, and sister to the boards of Covent Garden in November, 1841, to win enthusiastic applause in opera. Ending a short but highly successful career, she married Edward John Sartoris in 1843 and in later years spent much time with her husband in Italy, where, the Brownings agreed with her friend William Thackeray, she "gave quite the pleasantest parties in Rome." [32] Indeed the only member of the household to fail to win public acclaim was Charles Kemble's handsome, dashing, but unstable son Henry. He enjoyed a respectable though undistinguished career in the army, after obtaining a commission purchased by his sister Fanny with money gained from the publication of her first play, *Francis the First*. Still, long after his death, even Henry Kemble gained fame of a sort—when his none-too-flattering love affair with the heiress Mary Ann Thackeray was told to the world in Henry James's novel *Washington Square*.[33]

31. John Mitchell Kemble was the eldest surviving child. The Kembles's first born, Philip, died in infancy.

32. W. M. Thackeray, *Letters and Private Papers*, ed. Gordon N. Ray (Cambridge: Harvard University Press, 1945), III, 340.

33. See Bruce Dickins, "The Story of Washington Square," *Times Literary Supplement*, October 13, 1961; also *The Notebooks of Henry James*, ed. F. O. Matthiessen and K. B. Murdock (New York: Oxford University Press, 1947), pp. 12–14.

I

A Long Apprenticeship

From Brecknock to Drury Lane

The year 1775 was a memorable one for the veteran provincial player and manager Roger Kemble and his actress wife, Sarah. In London, amidst the flourish of Garrick's farewell season, their first child, Sarah Siddons, made her entrance on the stage of Drury Lane. At Brecknock, in Wales, their eleventh child, Charles, was busy, too, with an entrance.

The birth of Charles Kemble on November 25, 1775, was no doubt more orderly than that of his sister Sarah, who in the same town in South Wales twenty years before had reportedly arrived under conditions most trying. On that occasion Roger and his wife had been delighting the rustics of Brecknock with the adventures of Falstaff and Mrs. Ford when Sarah Kemble, suddenly feeling her time had come, was adroitly "conveyed to her lodgings in the very buck-basket the gullible Falstaff had lately concealed himself in."[1]

1. Herschel Baker, *John Philip Kemble: The Actor in His Theatre* (Cambridge: Harvard University Press, 1942), pp. 19–20. Baker repeats the story of Mrs. Siddons's birth as given by Ann Hatton, a sister of Mrs. Siddons and Charles Kemble. For the Hatton account, see "Memoirs of Ann Hatton," MS, Folger Shakespeare Library, Washington, D.C.

Childhood, likewise, was somewhat less difficult for Sarah Kemble's youngest son. "The bitter moments of Roger Kemble's existence had passed," William Oxberry suggested, before Charles Kemble "called him father." At his birth "the parental tree of the Kembles was, though somewhat bowed by time, flourishing in comparative plenty."[2]

Still, life in a family of provincial actors could not have been easy. Charles's father, the son of a barber and periwig maker of Hereford and the founder of England's famous theatrical family, had eloped in 1753 with Sarah Ward, daughter of the manager of a band of strolling performers in which he was engaged. Soon taking over his father-in-law's company, Roger, with his wife and steadily increasing family, year after year toured England's provinces, especially the counties around the mouth of the Severn, acting in inns, barns, and other hired buildings before audiences that were ill-bred and riotous.[3] Thomas Holcroft, who at one point acted with the troop, thought it was "more respectable than many other companies of strolling players," but "not in so flourishing a condition as to place the manager beyond the reach of the immediate smiles or frowns of fortune."[4]

By 1775 the Kembles were probably somewhat more affluent, although precisely what the aging Roger Kemble's circumstances were in that year is not known. In any case, before Charles was ten years old the family's fortunes had considerably brightened. Brothers John and Stephen and

2. W. Oxberry, *Dramatic Biography and Histrionic Anecdotes*, III (London, 1825), 2.

3. Baker, *Kemble*, pp. 3–18.

4. Thomas Holcroft, *The Life of Thomas Holcroft*, ed. Elbridge Colby (London: Constable and Company, 1925), I, 149.

sisters Mrs. Twiss and Mrs. Whitlock had achieved the London stage, and Sarah Siddons was the star of Drury Lane.

Young Charles was thus spared some of the harsher experiences of the precarious life of the strollers which his brothers and sisters had witnessed. Oxberry curiously recorded that as a child Charles was "kept from collision with members of the drama."[5] At thirteen he was sent by his brother John—who from the difference in their ages apparently stood to him as a father[6]—to reap the benefits of a classical education at the English college at Douay, France. Since the reign of Elizabeth the college at Douay had been a popular school for training English Roman Catholics. A noted seventeenth-century ancestor, the Venerable John Kemble, who was seized and executed at the time of the Popish Plot, as well as brother John Philip, who had been sent by his father to undergo the rigorous ecclesiastical training prescribed for the priesthood, had preceded Charles to Douay.[7]

John Philip Kemble, whose own student orations were so impressive that the whole body of fellows and professors are said to have crowded the hall when he spoke,[8] was soon proud of his younger brother's achievements. Indeed, for the next three years the reported attainments of Charles gave him the greatest satisfaction.[9] One report from Douay proved not so welcome, however: John was informed of

5. Oxberry, *Dramatic Biography*, III, 2.
6. William Bodham Donne, *Essays on the Drama* (London, 1858), p. 158.
7. Baker, *Kemble*, p. 22.
8. *Ibid.*, p. 23.
9. James Boaden, *Memoirs of the Life of John Philip Kemble* (London, 1825), II, 48.

Charles's very serious illness. Alarmed, the actor hastened from London to visit his brother, expecting to find him near death. Instead a dramatic meeting ensued. Charles fortunately had recovered and under the care of a friend was making his way home to England. They met upon the road.

> Mr. Kemble was sitting alone in his carriage, reading. As the other carriage advanced in the opposite direction, he raised his eyes from the book and exclaimed, "Charles!"[10]

When the embraces were over, the two brothers returned to London together, and subsequently, at age sixteen, Charles Kemble left Douay for good, taking with him an interest in and a knowledge of language and literature, a "gentleman's education," which in the late eighteenth century was by no means the usual preparation for a theatrical career.[11]

A theatrical career was not prescribed for Charles Kemble, however—at least not by his brother John. Upon leaving Douay he accepted a respectable situation in the post office. Before long "he was removed from one position in it to another," but it seems that "the foreign department proved no more to his taste than the inland."[12] The cause of the young man's restlessness must soon have been apparent. While he had been poring over Terence, Homer, Quintilian, and Cicero, other members of his family had been "reaping the golden harvest of public approbation."[13] Now his brother John was not only the leading actor and "confessed legitimate successor of Betterton, Quinn, and Barry," but

10. *Ibid.*

11. Baker, *Kemble*, p. 24; Boaden, *The Life of Mrs. Jordan* (London, 1831), I, 261.

12. Boaden, *Kemble*, II, 49.

13. Oxberry, *Dramatic Biography*, III, 2.

the manager of Drury Lane; and his sister Sarah Siddons, "in the full majesty of matronly beauty," was the undisputed queen of the English stage.[14] Renewed associations at home could scarcely fail to excite the actor's blood in his veins.

John Taylor, John Kemble's close friend, recalled that he was among those sought out for consultation by "a fine sturdy lad, . . . most anxious to go upon the stage." The advice he gave Charles Kemble was not heartening. "Though he was intelligent and well educated," Taylor observed, "there was such a rustic plainness in his manner" that he thought it best to discourage his theatrical bent.[15] But Charles was not to be dissuaded. Despite all opposition, including his brother's, he "threw off the trammels of restraint" and obtained an offer from a provincial manager who apparently "speculated more on the name than the talent" of the seventeen-year-old youth.[16]

As is often the case with provincial appearances, records of Charles Kemble's earliest dramatic efforts are decidedly obscure. His first regular recorded performance was at Sheffield late in 1792. In writing of the actor more than thirty years later, Oxberry declared, "It is well known that Mr. Kemble had tried his strength in some small company previously, though where, or when, it is now impossible to ascertain," and the author of *The Georgian Era* conjectured that "two or three exhibitions at private theatres" had perhaps preceded the Sheffield engagement.[17] At Sheffield, Charles Kemble's debut was as Orlando in *As You Like It*.

14. Donne, *Essays on the Drama*, p. 166.
15. John Taylor, *Records of My Life* (London, 1832), p. 94.
16. Oxberry, *Dramatic Biography*, III, 2.
17. *Ibid.; The Georgian Era* (London, 1834), IV, 22.

Appropriately, he began with Shakespeare and he ended with him; his farewell was as Benedick at Covent Garden in 1836. In between, his reputation was to a large extent determined by his achievement in Shakespearean roles.

"After inflicting a few first-rate characters on the inhabitants of Sheffield," the gangly young actor went on to Newcastle, Edinburgh, and several other provincial towns, "making unsuccessful attempts at parts far beyond his powers or experience."[18] Nevertheless, a lengthy and arduous probation in the provinces, such as John Philip endured, was not to be this Kemble's fate. His apprenticeship would be a long one, a very long one, but it was destined to be served on the London stage. With scarcely a year's experience Charles Kemble, through the influence of his brother, made his way to the metropolis and to the boards of Drury Lane.

A Strict Probation

Drury Lane had been closed for a major part of the 1793–94 season while a new playhouse was being built. April 21 was the date selected for the gala opening. The new theatre was a magnificent structure. It was nearly twice its former size and was equipped with such modern improvements as an iron curtain and a water tank for protection against fire. "The pit was flanked by eight boxes on either side, above which were two more rows of boxes and two galleries—to say nothing of the elegant new boxes on the sides of the stage. And everywhere were cut-glass chandeliers: the whole huge auditorium, marveled young

18. Oxberry, *Dramatic Biography*, III, 2.

Robert Southey, was lighted as if by the sun at noon."[19] Indeed, the era of the massive theatre had begun. No wonder all London flocked to the box office of Drury Lane before five o'clock that April afternoon and "not a place was to be had in any part, long before the curtain drew up."[20]

The play would befit its palace. *Macbeth* was the offering, with the manager himself as the Scottish tyrant and his sister in her greatest role, Lady Macbeth. It was an elaborate production, boasting many unusual features. William Capon had "devised sets which were dazzling to audiences accustomed to seeing Macbeth, dressed in a British grenadier's uniform, stalk about on a stage adorned with ordinary flats." Grand processions and flashy costumes were the order of the day, and the witches especially were made much of, with "weird costumes and tastefully interpolated songs."[21] The audience was perplexed by at least one Kemble innovation—the absence of Banquo's ghost, which the manager decided should be visible only to the mind's eye of the distracted King and indicated solely by the agitation and horror of the actor.[22] Finally, to top off the evening an occasional epilogue was spoken by Miss Farren as "Housekeeper" showing all the beauties and conveniences of the new stage. Her description was illustrated by magnificent scenery, which a dazzled *Times* reporter suggested reached a peak of splendor when "a boy was introduced rowing a boat on a canal of real water!"[23] But none of these features was what John Kemble selected for

19. Baker, *Kemble,* p. 183.
20. *The Times,* April 22, 1794.
21. Baker, *Kemble,* pp. 185, 186.
22. *Ibid.*
23. *The Times,* April 22, 1794.

notation in his journal entry of that memorable night. Instead, after inserting the receipts (£645 2s.) he wrote simply: "Mr. C Kemble made his first appearance at this theatre in Malcolm the night of the opening."[24]

Newspaper and magazine reporters attached considerably less importance to the debut that evening. What with chandeliers, scenery, and absent ghosts, they scarcely had time to notice the presence of another Kemble on Drury Lane stage. A *Thespian Magazine* critic at least recognized a new face: "A Mr. C. Kemble appeared as Malcolm, which he supported very respectably," he kindly reported.[25] A representative of *The Times* went somewhat further. Catching a glimpse of the family genius, he wrote: "C. Kemble, the younger brother of the manager, is an actor of much promise—his speeches were given with good emphasis and discretion, his tones frequently reminded us of Stephen Kemble and Mrs. Siddons."[26] Later accounts of the performance are hardly as flattering. Oxberry, writing in the 1820s about Charles Kemble, remarked:

> Those who behold his fine majestic figure, and gaze upon his expressive face, now lightened as it is by the warm emanations of genius, can scarcely recognize, as a likeness, the description truth impels us to give. As Malcolm "appeared a tall awkward youth, with what is termed a hatchet face, a figure badly proportioned, and evidently weak in his limbs; his acting was even worse than his appearance."[27]

24. "Professional Memoranda of John Philip Kemble," British Museum Ad. MS 31972.
25. *Thespian Magazine*, June 1794.
26. *The Times*, April 22, 1794.
27. Oxberry, *Dramatic Biography*, III, 3. Oxberry does not indicate the author of the description he quotes here.

Oxberry indeed emphasized that the handsome and statuesque Kemble demeanor had certainly yet to appear. "At this period Mr. Charles Kemble had the most unfortunate pair of legs our readers can well imagine," he continued, "and the facetious Charles Bannister reportedly quipped that 'he, being a Catholic, had received dispensation from the Pope to wear the calf of his leg downwards.'"[28]

Thus a new theatre and a new career were launched. It was certainly no night to compare with September 30, 1783, when John Kemble first won over the town as Hamlet, but the situation was far from the same. Drury Lane was now well stocked with veteran tragedians and comedians; and Charles Kemble, unlike his brother, was still in the rawest state of inexperience when he mounted the London stage. Few could disagree that the young player was guided by the soundest fraternal judgment when he chose not to present himself in one of the arduous characters generally selected for theatrical debuts. As a result he was at least spared the fate of many aspiring London actors, for whom three or four shaky performances at the Theatre Royal were typically followed by a permanent retirement to provincial towns.

Debut over, Kemble settled down to polish his Malcolm and to fill other roles so minor that while they gave him the benefit of experience, they could hardly afford him an opportunity to distinguish himself. It was not that the

28. [John] Doran, *Their Majesties Servants* (London, 1888), III, 213, also writes of Kemble's imperfections on his first appearance: "He had little in his favour but good intentions. He was awkward in action, weak in voice, and ungraceful in deportment." Doran's dates (1807–78) indicate, however, that he could not have witnessed the performance himself, and he does not suggest the basis for his appraisal.

company's manager despaired of his young brother's future success. In fact, James Boaden especially recalled John Kemble's confidence when he first brought Charles to his attention: "Boaden, you will shortly see two young men in the profession in whom I take an interest; one of them is my brother, Charles: *He* will make an actor!" But John Kemble knew that hard work alone would make a player of his favorite brother, and he "compelled him to acquire his art by passing through its gradations."[29] The critic William Bodham Donne suggested that the younger Kemble owed his eventual position to the strict discipline he underwent in his early period under the guidance of his brother, who "imposed upon the young debutant a probation as strict and regular as he was in the habit of prescribing to the least gifted of his associates."[30]

It was to Charles Kemble's credit, Boaden would add, that he "submitted implicitly to his brother's judgment."[31] Hard work, endless hours of rehearsal to perfect second-, third-, or fourth-rate parts, was the prescription; and Charles Kemble followed it diligently. The old actor Walter Lacy related an anecdote suggestive of the new player's spirit. Shortly after Charles's debut John Kemble asked M. Deshyes, whom he had engaged as a tutor, how long it would take his brother to acquire perfect grace of action. The Frenchman replied with a discouraging shrug, "Twenty years, perhaps." Whereupon Charles Kemble arched his brows and calmly announced, "Well, we'll begin!"[32]

29. Boaden, *Kemble,* II, 122.
30. Donne, *Essays on the Drama,* pp. 158–59.
31. Boaden, *Kemble,* II, 122.
32. Walter Lacy, "Old and Young Stager," in *The Green Room,* ed. Clement Scott (London, n.d.), p. 52.

The earlier impressions of an actor who rises gradually in his profession are seldom remarked at the time or remembered afterward, one theatrical writer has wisely observed.[33] The truth of the statement, as applied to Charles Kemble, cannot be denied. Jaques de Boys in *As You Like It*, Cromwell in *Henry VIII*, and Belville in *The Country Girl* followed Malcolm in Kemble's first season, but neither public nor press generally paused to take note. When the critics did remark on the novice's performance, the verdict was often far from encouraging. An unfortunate but inevitable comparison with his brother particularly plagued young Kemble. When John relinquished his role in *Henry VIII*, a typical complaint was to be heard. "The manager has not been so attentive to the cast of this play as *Macbeth*, or he would not have withdrawn himself from the part of Cromwell," a reporter for the *Thespian Magazine* protested. "We had great cause to regret his absence this evening; perhaps if we had never seen him in it, we should have thought Mr. *Charles* Kemble more entitled to commendation."[34] Commendation was later to come. He "was the only Cromwell worthy of the tears and favour of Wolsey," a subsequent critic would boast.[35] But for the moment being a Kemble was at best a qualified blessing.

The popular hit of the spring season was John Kemble's own play *Lodoiska*, a musical spectacle complete with burning castle and a full band of Tartars designed to exhibit the wonders of the new stage. Charles was merely

33. *Fraser's Magazine*, December 1854.

34. *Thespian Magazine*, June 1794.

35. Donne, *Essays on the Drama*, p. 167. John Kemble in his version of *Henry VIII* combined the characters of Cromwell and Griffith to strengthen the role of Cromwell. Thus Charles Kemble, when playing Cromwell, had a rather good part.

one of many Tartars under that greatest of Tartar chiefs, William Barrymore, Boaden recalled; but he "worked every night like a Turk to come at last into broad day-light."[36] Happily, he found special opportunity to shine in the performance of June 21. Barrymore fell sick, and Kemble was hastily assigned to take his part. The stand-in "acquited himself with a tolerable degree of success," even the *Thespian* critic had to concede—but he spoke entirely too loud, the reviewer was also quick to complain.[37]

When summer arrived, the novice turned to the Haymarket to acquire the benefit of two additional months of experience before facing his first full season at Drury Lane. Here he found parts in four productions, including Jemmy in a new "third piece" called *Auld Robin Gray*. "Mr. Charles Kemble was Jemmy, but even the captivating looks of a beautiful Jane could not inspire him with a sufficient share of animation,"[38] a typical critique of the summer season reported.

By autumn practice had by no means made perfect. "In 1795 he was one of the worst performers at either house,"[39] Oxberry bluntly asserted. Certainly the 1794–95 season offered little encouragement to a would-be star. For one thing, Kemble found absolutely no time to polish at least two of his new personations. He had minor roles in an ill-fated revival of *All's Well* in December and in an equally unlucky *Edwy and Elgiva* in March. The former, John Kemble sadly recorded in his diary, "was very dully received";[40]

36. Boaden, *Kemble*, II, 127.
37. *Thespian Magazine*, July 1794.
38. *Ibid.*, August 1794.
39. Oxberry, *Dramatic Biography*, III, 4.
40. "Professional Memoranda of John Philip Kemble," British Museum Ad. MS 31972.

the latter, a tragedy by the famous bluestocking Fanny Burney and cast with the elder Kemble and Mrs. Siddons, was the cause of considerable laughter![41] Both pieces lasted only one day. As the original Count Appiani in *Emilia Galotti,* translated by Benjamin Thompson from Lessing, Charles Kemble was scarcely longer on stage. It was acted only three times, though John Genest thought that it deserved a better fate.[42] For a fourth play, *My Grandmother,* the young performer would have preferred an even shorter run. He had substituted for Bannister in the prominent role of Vapour with little success the previous June. This season he was assigned to repeat the performance, with the most unhappy results. "The Vapour of Mr. Charles Kemble put everybody into the vapours," a *Times* reviewer was quick to pun. "Why will this young man, industrious and indeed decent enough in some characters, keep up a perpetual and unavailing contest with nature?"[43] Evidently it was a performance at which the whole audience groaned, and apparently one man in the pit actually rose to expostulate with poor Kemble on the impropriety of his attempting to enact a part so far beyond his powers.[44]

But the welcome sound of applause was not missing from quite all Charles Kemble's plays. Mrs. Inchbald's comical afterpiece *Wedding Day,* in which he was Young Contest, was "acted with success";[45] and while still storming the castle in *Lodoiska,* he found his way into another popular

41. Baker, *Kemble,* p. 194.
42. John Genest, *Some Account of the English Stage from the Restoration in 1660 to 1830* (Bath, 1832), VII, 180.
43. *The Times,* January 29, 1795.
44. Oxberry, *Dramatic Biography,* III, 4.
45. Genest, *Some Account of the English Stage,* VII, 182.

spectacle. The battles were much the same; but this time instead of a Tartar, he fought as the full-blooded Indian, Zamorin, in the opera *Cherokee*. Finally he heard noticeable cheers in a more somber piece in which his brother John found long-lasting success. On February 28, Drury Lane presented for the first time Cumberland's *Wheel of Fortune*, with Charles Kemble cast at the last minute as Henry Woodville and John Kemble as Penruddock.

On-stage the climate was chilly, but backstage it was sometimes considerably warmer, Charles Kemble was beginning to learn. Certainly one of the more exciting events of the 1794–95 season occurred well behind the curtain. The company at Drury Lane was blessed with its share of charming young ladies, and one of them caught John Kemble's eye. Miss De Camp was of "surpassing beauty," the elder Kemble's biographer explains. Her figure was fine, her face "handsome and strikingly expressive," and the young blades of London were all prostrate before her. But this beauty was matched by conduct most irreproachable—much to John Kemble's dismay. "He must have been drinking that night, and, as the whole town knew, Kemble when drunk was an elfish creature. His passion was not to be denied. The door of the lady's dressing room was flung open: 'he would—she would not—he took hold—she screamed,' and before he knew it the austere manager was surrounded by a crowd of pardonably curious people."[46] It was Charles Kemble who actually effected the rescue, one version would have it; no, it was the young actress's brother who deserved that credit, another would say.[47] In

46. Baker, *Kemble*, pp. 191, 192.

47. Newspaper clippings, in the Garrick Club Library, London. I have not been able to identify the papers or establish their dates.

any case, on January 27 readers found the following interesting announcement in their morning *Times:*

> I, John Kemble, of the Theatre Royal, Drury Lane, do adopt this method of publicaly apologizing to Miss De Camp for the very improper and unjustifiable behaviour I was lately guilty of towards her, which I do further declare her conduct and character had in no instance authorized; but, on the contrary, I do know and believe both to be irreproachable.

"Another scandalous theatrical escapade!" one can hear the pious ladies of London exclaim. "Who would have thought it of stern old Kemble?" someone was sure to note. Fortunately, the excitement was soon forgotten—by all but the Kembles at least. With John, painful memories no doubt lingered a long time, and for Charles the evening carried special import: that disturbingly beautiful actress would one day be his wife!

Meanwhile season followed season, and behind the curtain Charles Kemble's discipline continued severe, and before it, his judges exacting. "The press, which he never courted, repaid his indifference with occasional hostility or general silence," Donne remarked. "He had no declamatory tricks to catch the unwary; he never condescended to play *at* either pit or gallery. And the audience of those days was not easily contented."[48] Still, good parts—at least parts he made good ones—were gradually coming his way; and there were occasional bursts of applause that must have been heartening. In 1795–96 Kemble added to his repertoire several Shakespearean roles which would prove much to his credit. "How full of winning grace and good humour was

48. Donne, *Essays on the Drama,* p. 159.

his Bassanio," Donne recalled, and added that his was "the only Laertes whom it was endurable to see in collision with Hamlet."[49] England's future star Romeo gave a fine performance of Paris this season and somehow even managed a chance to play Hotspur at the Haymarket in *Henry IV*. "Charles Kemble in Hotspur follows his brother, and who can he follow better?" the *Monthly Mirror* of August reported. "Some of the scene with Northumberland was really very well given," it continued, showing a slight note of surprise.

One "Shakespearean" production this year Charles Kemble would have preferred to have missed. Mrs. Siddons indeed refused to act in the spurious *Vortigern*. But Charles Kemble, as Pascentius, was laughed off the stage alongside his brother that infamous night of April 2 when all London turned out to witness the climax of the Shakespeare manuscript hoax.[50] Finally, two stand-in performances this season proved especially worthy of note. In September, Kemble hastily replaced the ailing veteran Barrymore as Carlos in *Isabella*, to win the admiration of his fellow actors as well as the press's acclaim.[51] In May his yeoman service was again called into play. This time it was John Kemble who fell ill, just when he was taking the town by storm as the hero of Prince Hoare's popular opera *Mahmoud*. Charles was called on to supply his brother's place on "so short a notice, considering the length of the part, that nothing but his uncommon facility of study could have enabled him to accomplish it." For the sake of security the young actor was obliged to take the book with him on the stage; "but feeling

49. *Ibid.*, p. 167.
50. Baker, *Kemble*, pp. 204 ff.
51. *The Times*, September 21, 1795.

his confidence strengthened and his emulation awakened by the indulgence of the audience, he soon got rid of the book and of his fears at once, and he performed the character with a spirit and propriety which were at the same moment felt and rewarded."[52]

The next year at Drury Lane, Charles Kemble added a handsome Ferdinand in *The Tempest* and an "elegant" but "rustic" Guiderius in *Cymbeline* to his steadily growing list of Shakespearean characters, and the following season he earned considerable applause as the Prince of Wales in *Henry IV*. Then in 1798–99 he was Claudio in *Measure for Measure* and Richmond in *Richard III*. One of his most memorable performances in Shakespeare at this time, however, took place not at Drury Lane but at his regular summer haunt, the Haymarket. Here on September 4, 1797, he got his first chance to play Cassio. It was still a decidedly second part, Charles Kemble had to admit; but it was one of those that he could make uniquely his own. Make it his own he did. Thereafter no critic could deny that this personation by the younger Kemble, at least, was a masterpiece. Even William Hazlitt, who was never exactly enthusiastic about any of the Kembles, acknowledged that Charles's Cassio was excellent;[53] and the theatrical connoisseur William Robson unreservedly declared of the famous exhibition in the second act: "No drunken scene I ever saw on a stage was comparable to it." He recalled with delight:

> The insidious creeping of the "devil" upon his senses; the hilarity of intoxication, the tongue cleaving to the roof of

52. *The Monthly Mirror*, May 1802.

53. William Hazlitt, *Works*, ed. P. P. Howe (London: J. M. Dent and Sons, 1930), V, 340.

> the mouth, and the lips glued together; the confusion, the state of *loss of self,* if I may so term it, when he received the rebuke of Othello; and the wonderful truthfulness of his getting sober, were beyond description fine—nay real.[54]

In Cassio, Charles Kemble's refusal to play *at* the gallery for once paid off. Perceptive playgoers were pleased to be confronted, for a change, with a drunken man trying to appear sober, instead of a sober man trying to look drunk. Julian Young testified that Kemble's lieutenant was far from the usual "noisy, blustering, sensual, hicupping roysterer" of performers who sought only a clown's applause. While his articulation thickened, his movements grew unsteady, and his perceptions clouded, Charles Kemble did not let his viewers forget that Cassio was a gentleman, reluctantly overtaken by liquor, not an addicted sot.[55] Indeed Leigh Hunt never ceased to marvel how Kemble's Cassio could so thoroughly "amuse us" and at the same time "maintain our respect in intoxication."[56]

Even apart from his favorite Shakespearean roles Kemble was gradually losing his unfortunate reputation for being "a regular stick."[57] In the fall of 1796 it was suggested to Mrs. Siddons that it would be of service to her brother to be brought forward as George Barnwell in Lillo's perennially popular *London Merchant.*[58] Here indeed, the young actor must have sighed, was a first part! In the production of November 28 his sister contributed no inconsiderable

54. William Robson, *The Old Play-Goer* (London, 1846), p. 48.
55. Julian Young, *A Memoir of Charles Mayne Young, Tragedian* (London, 1871), p. 98.
56. Leigh Hunt, *Dramatic Essays,* ed. William Archer and Robert W. Lowe (London, 1894), p. 111.
57. *The Times,* November 15, 1854.
58. Genest, *Some Account of the English Stage,* VII, 287–88.

attraction by her Millwood, but Charles Kemble earned his share of the applause. "Young Kemble in Barnwell appeared to particular advantage," one reviewer encouragingly wrote; "he wants only a firmer voice and a spark of his brother's fire to render him a favorite with the public."[59] That fire was slow in kindling, but nevertheless forthcoming. Three years later when Charles was entrusted with Alonzo in Sheridan's *Pizarro* he rendered his brother John's Rolla and Mrs. Siddon's Elvira extraordinary support. "Charles Kemble displayed so much characteristic animation in his grand scene with the tyrant as to excite the repeated plaudits of the audience,"[60] the press had to report this time. *Pizarro* monopolized the rest of that season as well as most of the next, and Sheridan himself, for one, was ready to acknowledge that he was clearly in young Kemble's debt. For a long time afterward whenever the shrewd author-patentee saw Charles Kemble, he paused to salute "*his* Alonzo" and to pay tribute to his success in the part.[61]

A Playwright's Hopes

The turn of the century signified, in the minds of hopeful young Englishmen, the beginning of a promising new era—and not the least justified of the youthful optimists was Charles Kemble. For one thing, the year 1800 brought him two great new acting successes, one of them in a role which would always continue among his best. The first of these histrionic achievements took place at the Haymarket, where the manager, George Colman, for several seasons had

59. *Monthly Mirror*, December, 1796.
60. *The Times*, May 25, 1799.
61. Boaden, *Kemble*, II, 237.

been treating the fledgling with the utmost courtesy and providing him with opportunities denied him at the winter house. Here on July 2, Kemble appeared as the lead in a spectacularly successful pantomime by Fawcett called *Obi*, with the intriguing subtitle *Three-Finger'd Jack*. A few intellectual Londoners such as James Boaden took the play's unprecedented reception as proof of a long suspected decline in dramatic taste.[62] But night after night, for over a month, the rest of the city flocked to see Kemble portray the terrifying exploits of a famous Jamaican negro robber and to watch breathlessly for the narrow escape of the planter's beautiful daughter who unwittingly became his prey. "An impressive performance indeed!" the audience was always quick to exclaim. The newspapers burst forth with warm praise, and even a would-be poet suddenly found inspiration. A versifier called Azuria scribbled down "Stanzas written on seeing Mr. Charles Kemble in the Pantomime of Obi" and sent them off to the *Monthly Mirror*, which published the piece in its July issue.[63] Unhappily, Kemble's nightly ovations were abruptly cut short while the pantomime was still going strong. At the performance of August 12 an unfortunate accident took place. Kemble made his usual leap from a precipice, but a sluggish stage crew was late with the necessary precautions to break his fall. "The consequence," the *Dramatic Censor* ominously reported, was that "Mr. Kemble received several violent contusions and sprained his back in so dangerous a manner as gives

62. *Ibid.*, p. 269.

63. The manuscript of this poem is in the Enthoven Collection, Victoria and Albert Museum, London. See files of the Haymarket Theatre, 1800. The poem was published in the *Monthly Mirror*, July, 1800.

cause to apprehend that the stage will long be deprived of the benefit of his abilities."[64]

The prognosis was overly pessimistic. While the mishap marked the end of his summer exertions, Charles Kemble recovered in time for the opening of the season at Drury Lane. Here he enjoyed a second and more tasteful triumph not long after his summer reign as toast of the town. On November 20 he was brought forth as Faulconbridge, playing opposite his brother's renowned King John. The performance was not without its detractors: "We have of late . . . been so much accustomed to see C. Kemble overstep the modesty of nature and grasp at things beyond his reach, that we no longer wonder at anything he undertakes,"[65] a confirmed anti-Kemble critic caustically wrote. However, the reviewer for the *Monthly Mirror* thought that the rising actor had contributed considerably to his fame, and a reporter for *The Times* praised the young performer's energetic portrayal.[66] "Mr. C. Kemble does nothing in a finer spirit than the Bastard,"[67] the *Theatrical Inquisitor* some years later would judge; but even now the warm applause of the audience seemed to indicate that in the character of Philip Faulconbridge, Kemble had found one of his strongest roles.[68]

The year 1800 possessed a more striking feature, however, than success in two popular new parts. To Charles Kemble, who was by this time unalterably committed to a life in the theatre, the turn of the century suggested an exciting new

64. *Dramatic Censor,* August 1800.
65. *Ibid.,* January 1801.
66. *Monthly Mirror,* December 1800; *The Times,* November 21, 1800.
67. *Theatrical Inquisitor,* December 1816.
68. *Monthly Mirror,* December 1800.

departure. This year he hopefully turned from his familiar role as actor, to try his hand at becoming a playwright.

That John Kemble's younger brother should make an excursion into the literary world was perhaps only to be expected. Before the curtain Charles's achievements had always been at least partly emulative, and now his famous brother seemed destined to ignite another spark. John Kemble, his biographer maintains, longed for distinction "in the belles-lettres that formed so important an adjunct of every true gentleman's character." In his strolling days he had made early attempts at literary renown in *Belisarius*, a play which was promptly rejected, and in a volume of rather unfortunate verses. Next appeared the none-too-creditable *Lodoiska*, "contrived, as one unkindly critic had it, 'by cutting, pasting, and putting together' materials from French sources." After becoming firmly established in London society, the elder Kemble decided to settle for such scholarly works as an essay on *Macbeth* and numerous alterations of the old dramatists as giving sufficient indication that he was of a literary turn.[69] Thus Charles Kemble's mentor and model was not only London's foremost tragedian, but a "man of letters" as well.

"His muse to-night, / On timorous wings has tried her maiden flight," the attractive Miss De Camp announced to the audience at the Haymarket the evening of July 15, 1800, in the epilogue to the new production *The Point of Honour*. The author in question—Charles Kemble—need not have been timorous, however. His first play proved to be an unqualified success. James Boaden, who had shuddered at the bad taste of *Obi*, after viewing the opening performance

69. Baker, *Kemble*, pp. 187, 211, 212.

recorded: "Charles Kemble redeemed the credit of the theatre by his very clever play called *The Point of Honour*, which was in the first place extremely interesting, and in the second, exceedingly well acted, by *himself* as well as others."[70] Needless to say, the rest of the audience was equally pleased.

Charles Kemble, in all good conscience, had to share his new honors with a Frenchman named Mercier. Fully one-half of the English plays written between 1800 and 1850 must have been suggested by Parisian models, Allardyce Nicoll estimates;[71] and in this respect young Kemble's followed the trend. *The Point of Honour* was, to be exact, an adaptation—or what *The Times* called a "free translation"—of Sébastien Mercier's French play *Le Déserteur*.[72]

Even a cursory glance at the story of the piece suggests something of its dramatic potential. The action takes place in a small town on the German frontier, where French troops have just taken possession. The hero, the handsome and gentlemanly Durimel (Kemble) is in love with Bertha (Miss De Camp), the beautiful daughter of Mrs. Melfort, in whose household he has for some years been employed. Mrs. Melfort is delighted to find a worthy husband for her daughter, and a wedding is about to take place. But Durimel's past is clouded by unmentioned difficulties. He is a deserter from the French army who has fled his regiment to escape punishment for striking an officer. When French troops arrive in the town, the manly integrity of the young man induces him to disclose to Mrs. Melfort his

70. Boaden, *Kemble*, II, 269.
71. Allardyce Nicoll, *A History of Early Nineteenth Century Drama: 1800–1850* (Cambridge: Cambridge University Press, 1930), I, 79.
72. *The Times*, July 16, 1800.

predicament. Unfortunately, his confession is overheard by a ridiculous old dotard and disappointed rival named Steinberg, who seeks revenge by informing on the deserter. Durimel is apprehended and condemned to be shot. His misfortunes then reach an almost unbearable climax when St. Franc, the grave and dignified officer assigned the odious task of signaling the execution, turns out to be his long lost father.

"Here are some impressive scenes!" Charles Kemble must have exclaimed to himself as he first read Mercier; and when he brought them to the Haymarket stage, a tearful English audience was moved to agree. In addition to making a translation, what Kemble accomplished as adapter was basically a twofold task. In the first place, he struggled to condense five wordy acts into a more streamlined three. Second, in the fashion of Nahum Tate, he set out to provide a happy ending to Durimel's distress. In *Le Déserteur* the spectator's worst fears come true. After Durimel and his father are dramatically reunited, blind justice rules the day. Durimel goes off to his prescribed death as a deserter, fortified by the knowledge that, as his wise father tells him, "Tu plongeras dans le tombeau pour te relever immortel." He feels, however, that he dies a hero's death, for St. Franc assures him that as an example to other would-be deserters, his death is of more value to his country than his life: "Si j'ai trahi la loi de mon pays, il n'aura rien à me reprocher; ma mémoire fera sans tache; la réparation aura été plus éclatante que la faute même."[73] Charles Kemble, with respect to the conclusion of the French play, was of the same opinion as a London critic who suggested that to an

73. L. S. Mercier, *Le Déserteur* (Paris, 1770), Act IV, scene iv.

Englishman "such an exhibition would be more offensive than tragic."[74]

In *The Point of Honour* he gives the ending a different turn. Durimel, as in *Le Déserteur,* refuses to attempt an escape, since his custody has been confided to St. Franc with the sacred seal of an oath upon the trust. Here, indeed, lies the point of honor: Durimel will die before he will subject his father to the violation of military duty. In contrast to the French play, however, the execution ceremony is not simply reported, but brought full upon the stage. Durimel is led in, and St. Franc gives the fatal signal. Suddenly the old soldier heroically hurls himself before the body of his son. Before the deadly shots are fired, someone shouts "Hold!" St. Franc's mysterious action is explained and the deserter ultimately receives full pardon for his offense, as mercy—not inexorable justice—reigns supreme. Thus Charles Kemble's tear-stained audience left the theatre wearing a happy smile—all but one avowed enemy from the *Dramatic Censor,* that is. This perpetual thorn in the young actor's side departed, as usual, wearing a heavy frown. It is a dangerous play, he wrote next day, "that palliates the crime of desertion!"[75]

The success of *The Point of Honour* extended far beyond its Haymarket run. In London's winter houses, provincial theatres, and even the United States it enjoyed periodic revivals for the next forty years. Meanwhile the publication of at least eight editions helped to keep alive its fame. Indeed, to a modern reader the popularity of the piece is enough to confirm all doubts about early-nineteenth-century popular dramatic taste. The situation admittedly

74. *Monthly Mirror,* August 1800.
75. *Dramatic Censor,* July 1800.

holds interest; but the sentimentality is staggering, and the constant attempts at poetic dialogue are almost beyond belief. The following exchange between mother and daughter is only too typical:

> *Mrs. Melfort.* Dispel the smallest cloud which threatens to obscure the sunshine of your peace. . . .
>
> *Bertha.* I see no clouds, nor do I dread a storm; the sun of happiness shines full upon me, and brightens all my prospects.[76]

To Charles Kemble, however, there seemed no need to blush at melancholy metaphors. The reception awarded his play represented a heartwarming confirmation of his appraisal of dramatic appeal, and to the hopeful young man of the theatre it seemed to betoken a brighter day.

Old Patterns with Variations

Despite the promising omens of 1800, to relate the events of Charles Kemble's theatrical career for the next twelve years would be largely to repeat the past. The rigorous daily rehearsals and nightly performances—usually still in second parts—unhaltingly continued, as Kemble worked to polish and to perfect. Occasionally, of course, an especially hopeful note was sounded, as in 1803 when Charles Kemble first played Hamlet, or in 1805 when John relinquished to him Hastings (*Jane Shore*) and Jaffeir (*Venice Preserved*). The Hamlet performance of May 19, 1803, marked Kemble's first leading role in Shakespearean tragedy, and on that occasion the *Monthly Mirror* encouragingly wrote:

76. Charles Kemble, *The Point of Honour* (London, 1800), Act I, scene i.

> Mr. Charles Kemble played Hamlet for the first time, for his own benefit, and has greatly increased his reputation, before deservedly high, by his chaste and animated performance.[77]

The significance which the young actor himself attached to this opportunity is suggested in his later confession to a friend: "The fame of my brother John in tragedy caused me for long to avoid trespassing upon his ground. To give up Hamlet, however, would have been a sacrifice beyond me."[78] It was fortunate for Charles Kemble that he did not make that sacrifice, for, as Westland Marston observed, Hamlet proved in later years to be "the one Shakespearean character in tragedy in which the excellence of the actor was unanimously admitted."[79] For the moment, however, the chance to play Hamlet was only a welcome exception, and minor roles continued to be the rule.

Among seasons characterized by sameness, 1803–1804 was destined to stand out. For the first time in his nine years in London, Charles Kemble, along with his brother and sister, made his entrance on an unfamiliar stage. John Kemble, it seems, deemed it prudent to make a change. Admittedly, at Drury Lane he enjoyed the highest status, for he was leading actor and manager as well. But relations with the theatre's strong-willed chief patentee had never been exactly the best. According to James Boaden, Kemble, as manager, was kept firmly under Richard Brinsley Sheridan's ruling thumb.[80] Sheridan, moreover, not only

77. *Monthly Mirror*, June 1803.

78. Quoted by Westland Marston, *Our Recent Actors* (Boston, 1888), p. 120.

79. Marston, *Our Recent Actors*, p. 120.

80. Boaden, *The Life of Mrs. Jordon*, I, 137. Also Baker, *Kemble*, p. 123.

imposed his opinions; he was annoyingly slow to pay his debts. At one point he owed his star actor some £1367 in back salary![81] At the end of the 1795–96 season an open rupture between Kemble and Sheridan took place. Kemble angrily threw up the management, only to be wooed back to his old position in 1800–1801. When he resumed his role as manager, however, he had still higher prospects firmly in his mind. He made a tentative agreement with Sheridan to become a sizable partner in the affairs of Drury Lane. Then the negotiations unexpectedly fell through; and after the spring of 1802, John Kemble left the house that had brought him all his fame—taking with him his prestige, his sister, and a rejected investment of ten thousand pounds.[82]

But the crown of theatrical ownership was not to be denied. At the rival Covent Garden Theatre John Kemble and his money found a more enthusiastic reception than they had met with at Drury Lane. In 1803 he purchased—reportedly for twenty-three thousand pounds[83]—a one-sixth share in Covent Garden, a portion which many years later would pass into his younger brother's hands. Meanwhile, Charles Kemble remained for one more season at Drury Lane—and "very awkward it was to remain, in a concern where his duty compelled him to serve a cause, which his family were considered to have deserted."[84] Then the following year, in line with family loyalty, he too left the familiar house. After a summer respite in Europe he returned to London to join his brother and sister on the

81. Baker, *Kemble,* p. 226.
82. *Ibid.,* p. 239.
83. Boaden, *Kemble,* II, 374. Baker, *Kemble,* p. 274, indicates that the purchase price was twenty-two thousand pounds.
84. Boaden, *Kemble,* II, 326.

Covent Garden stage. He was rewarded by cheers the opening night as he appeared as Henry in *Speed the Plough;* and just a week later, for the first time, John Kemble wrote in his journal: "Charles was very much applauded in Romeo."[85] Still, competition for the young actor had by no means been lessened by the move; instead, it had decidedly increased. For Charles now had not only his brother to claim the first parts, but Covent Garden's imposing regular star, George Frederick Cooke.

The 1809–10 season proved to be another that Charles Kemble would long remember—though it was certainly one he would try hardest to forget. This was the year of the notorious "Old Prices" riots, which marked the nadir of the Kemble family's fame. The trouble all started in the ominous pre-dawn hours of September 20, 1808. John Kemble, in one sentence in his diary, tells the disastrous tale: "This morning between four and five o'clock a fire broke out in Covent Garden Theatre, which in less than two hours time consumed it to the ground."[86] There was no alternative: a whole new theatre had to be built. In the details of the construction that followed, however, the choices made were not always the best. It seems that the "massive, squat building, put up at a 'hand-gallop, without check, without control, without superintendence' while Kemble was luxuriating in Ireland," pleased no one.[87] Certainly the new Covent Garden was absurdly large, all discriminating persons agreed. There were further complaints when it was learned that the proprietors were

85. "Memoranda of John Philip Kemble," British Museum Ad. MS 31974.
86. *Ibid.*, Ad. MS 31975.
87. Baker, *Kemble*, p. 295.

reducing the galleries to provide for twenty-six private boxes. Finally when, about a week before the gala opening, the public heard that there was to be an increase in the prices of admission (from 6s. to 7s. for the boxes and from 3s. 6d. to 4s. for the pit) and that a foreign singer, Mme Catalani, had been engaged for the spectacular sum of £75 a night, their outrage reached fever pitch.[88]

"The theatre opened under the most inauspicious circumstances," Genest recorded with supreme understatement; "a riot began on the first performance and lasted till the sixty-seventh night."[89] Indeed on September 18 when John Kemble stepped on stage to speak an occasional address, he was greeted with volleys of hoots, groans, and catcalls. Soon the cry of "Old Prices!" resounded through the house, as banners and placards were angrily waved. The play itself—*Macbeth,* with Kemble and Mrs. Siddons in their usual roles and Charles cast as Macduff—followed; but it proceeded largely in pantomime, for "scarcely a word was heard." Night after night the same amazing scene of confusion continued, while reasons and explanations from the management were offered to no avail. John Kemble became the symbol of oppression and the target of almost unbelievable abuse, while the O. P.'s conduct toward Charles Kemble "was, if possible, still worse, as they did not even pretend that he had given them any personal offence—but he was to be insulted for no reason upon earth, but because he was John Kemble's brother."[90] While John was subjected to defamatory O. P. songs under his windows at home and nightly "mobs gathered omin-

88. *Ibid.,* pp. 295–99.
89. Genest, *Some Account of the English Stage,* VIII, 169.
90. *Ibid.,* 169, 170, 171.

ously before his door,"[91] neither he nor his sister Mrs. Siddons dared to attempt to act on the stage. Charles Kemble alone braved the audience those days. Finally, on December 15 a truce was accepted: John Kemble was forced to concede to the rioters' demands. The harassments abruptly ended, and the nightmarish experience was at last at a close. John Kemble could scarcely muster a smile, however—not even one of relief. He emerged from all this, Professor Herschel Baker has suggested, a bitter, disillusioned old man;[92] while his younger brother Charles had witnessed a scene which, despite subsequent glory, he could never quite forget.

In 1808 just before the gloomy days of the fire and the O. P. calamities, Charles Kemble had twice repeated his bid for a playwright's fame. Although they never matched the applause of his promising first play, *The Point of Honour,* two new adaptations, *The Wanderer; or, the Rights of Hospitality* (produced at Covent Garden, January 12, 1808) and *Plot and Counterplot; or, the Portrait of Michael Cervantes* (produced at the Haymarket, June 30, 1808) achieved what might be termed "respectable" success.

The Wanderer represented Kemble's concession to an amazing vogue in England for the writings of the German dramatist Augustus von Kotzebue. Between 1790 and 1810 there were approximately 170 English editions of Kotzebue's works, a total which E. F. Thompson estimates was "equal in number to the aggregate of all other German writers translated at that time."[93] The popularity of *The Stranger*

91. Baker, *Kemble,* p. 309.
92. *Ibid.,* p. 316.
93. E. F. Thompson, *Kotzebue: A Survey of His Progress in France and England* (Paris: Champion, 1928), p. 55.

and *Pizarro* alone, however, would have been sufficient to suggest to Charles Kemble that for a translator or adapter the German dramatist offered especially fertile soil. *The Wanderer* is an adaptation of Kotzebue's *Eduard in Schottland,* which, curiously, is itself a translation of Alexander Duval's French piece *Edouard en Ecosse*. The play relates an adventure of Charles Edward Stuart, the Young Pretender. Escaping from his pursuers after a harsh defeat at Culloden, the weary, bedraggled, and starving Prince throws himself upon the mercy of a noble household and temporarily finds humanitarian refuge with a Scots family who cannot deny "the rights of hospitality."

Interestingly, both Duval and Kemble in their attempts to produce the play found themselves faced with a similar problem. Duval's *Edouard en Ecosse* was forbidden by Napoleon, who was understandably sensitive about plays that presented fugitive monarchs in a sympathetic light. Charles Kemble's *Wanderer,* upon its first submission to the office of the Lord Chamberlain, likewise met with a veto "from a notion that the recollection which it revived of the 'Young Chevalier' might be dangerous to the public tranquility." [94] Kemble, however, was not to be discouraged. He simply altered the setting of the piece from Scotland to Sweden, whose history, he remarked in a preface to the 1808 edition, "furnished me with a hero under circumstances similar to those of the Pretender." An island in southern Scotland becomes the isle of Oeland and Charles Edward, grandson of James II, becomes Sigismund, son of John, the late King of Sweden. Thus the wanderer was, as Kemble put it, "attired in Swedish garb, and the drama was licensed

94. *The Times,* November 27, 1829.

and acted with great pleasure."[95] It should be noted that twenty-one years later the English Examiner of Plays was not so squeamish; Kemble's *Wanderer* was revived in 1829 with its hero the original Scot.

Apart from the alteration of location, Charles Kemble's 1808 production boasted several other "improvements" on its German counterpart. As in *The Point of Honour*, the first chore was to streamline. Kemble condensed verbose German speeches and omitted the multiplicity of scene divisions to give the action a freer flow. Next, much to the dismay of some purists, music and spectacle were added to liven up the somber piece. A tremendous storm scene reminiscent of *The Tempest* was introduced to open the play. An attention getter, it provided occasion for elaborate scenery and some stirring songs by a shipwrecked crew. Most creditable to a dramatist's talents, however, was the development of a delightfully comic servant called Ramsay, who somehow was allowed not only to retain a Scots name, but a highland accent as well. The servant Tom in Kotzebue is the stock faithful retainer, but the proud, blunt, good-hearted Ramsay in Charles Kemble's hands proved a considerably more rounded characterization. His refreshingly homely speech provides welcome relief from the stilted dialogue of noble Sigismund; and although Kemble himself played the hero, one suspects John Fawcett as Ramsay might easily have stolen the show.

The Wanderer, on its first production, played to contented audiences at Covent Garden for sixteen nights, and five months later *Plot and Counterplot* enjoyed a somewhat

95. Charles Kemble, Preface, *The Wanderer; or, the Rights of Hospitality* (London, 1808).

longer run at the Haymarket. The latter piece is an adaptation of *Le Portrait de Michel Cervantes*, a French comedy by Michel Dieulafoy. *Plot and Counterplot* is a rollicking farce based on the numerous contrivances of two intriguing lovers, each assisted by a roguish servant, seeking access to a closely chaperoned Spanish maiden. The señorita is the daughter of an eminent painter, Hernandez, who in turn is engaged in an intrigue of his own in an attempt to paint a portrait from the dead body of the celebrated author Michael Cervantes. The complications multiply so rapidly that the audience must have struggled to keep pace, as "dead" bodies amazingly rise up in their shrouds and lovers seem to "pop out of every hole."[96] *Plot and Counterplot* represents a much closer translation than Charles Kemble's two earlier works. There is no rewritten ending or original characterization—not even a change in locale. Still, as adapter Kemble did eliminate some long-winded, slow-moving passages to create a constant atmosphere of excitement and urgency—perhaps no insignificant contribution to a farce in which humor depends greatly on tempo. Unfortunately, on the opening night at the Haymarket the excitement and urgency was not confined to the stage. As in the proverbial manager's nightmare, a leading actor suddenly became ill. Charles Kemble was called to the rescue, and this time he saved his own play. He took over the role of Don Fernando, one of the scheming lovers, and "by reference to the book when off stage," reportedly "performed it letter perfect."[97]

96. Charles Kemble, *Plot and Counterplot* (London, 1808), Act II, scene i.

97. Oxberry, *Dramatic Biography*, III, 6.

A Playwright's Dismay

Following *Plot and Counterplot,* three more adaptations, one original farce, and an interesting abridgment of Shakespeare's *Henry VI* plays completed Charles Kemble's playwriting career.[98] To his dismay the former, which were

98. In addition to the plays mentioned here, one more drama seems to have become erroneously linked with Charles Kemble's name. A farce called *A Budget of Blunders,* which was taken from French sources, was produced at Covent Garden Theatre, February 16, 1810. As contemporary reviewers and John Kemble attest, it was the work of a gentleman with the strange name of Greffulhe. The play met with notable success in London and subsequently found its way to the United States. Here it was published in Philadelphia in 1823; but instead of the author Greffulhe's, the edition bore Charles Kemble's name. The evidence for the authorship of *Budget of Blunders* is as follows: John Kemble in his "Professional Memoranda" (British Museum Ad. MS 31975) wrote in the entry for February 16, 1810, "Mr. Greffulhe," after inserting the title of the play *A Budget of Blunders* as he customarily did to indicate the author of a new piece. As manager of the theatre John Kemble seems to be the one person most likely to know the author of a new play, since he no doubt negotiated its purchase. W. C. Oulton (*A History of the Theatres of London* [London, 1818], II, 144) attributes *Budget* likewise to Greffulhe, and Genest simply records: "Oulton attributes it to Greffulhe." The *Monthly Mirror* of February, 1810, reports that the author of *Budget* is "Mr. Greffulhe," who it further informs us is a foreigner in London who "gives the profits of his dramatic productions to the fund for the relief of decayed actors." The *Monthly Mirror* states that Greffulhe is also the author of *Is He a Prince?* and *The Portrait of Cervantes.* The fact that the latter play bears the same title as the subtitle of *Plot and Counterplot* and like Kemble's play is an adaptation from Dieulafoy's *Le Portrait de Michel Cervantes* probably led to the later confusion of Kemble and Greffulhe. The *Biographia Dramatica* states merely that *Budget* is reportedly by the author of *Is He a Prince?* and *Portrait of Cervantes,* as does *Johnson's Sunday Monitor and British Gazette,* February 18, 1810. *Budget* was published in Philadelphia by Mathew Carey in 1811, and the title page bore the words "by the author of Plot and Counterplot etc. etc." Another edition, published by Thomas H. Palmer in Philadelphia in 1823, bore the words "by Charles Kemble." It seems

never published, were promptly hooted off the stage, while the latter, probably his most creditable literary effort, never reached the boards.

The "melting" of the three parts of *Henry VI* into "one piece" was a task which John Philip Kemble had once proposed to undertake. The elder Kemble had discussed such a scheme with his fellow *littérateur* Horace Walpole in 1789.[99] His plan was soon forgotten however, and had long been laid aside when his brother, years later, decided to revive the project.

Shakespeare's trilogy was almost unknown when Kemble set out to fashion his abridgment. Since the Restoration there had been a single performance of the First Part (at Covent Garden, March 13, 1738), while the Second and Third Parts had never been given. Kemble's effort to rework the Henry VI material, however, was not unique. There had been two Restoration versions by John Crowne, which boasted Betterton in the cast; and both Ambrose Philips and Theophilus Cibber had borrowed from Shakespeare for Henry VI plays in 1723. Later, Edmund Kean had an adaptation of *Henry VI* written specifically for him by John Herman Merivale, which was performed seven times in the 1817–18 season at Drury Lane.

Kemble's method in *Henry VI* was, happily, far different from that employed in the Kean-Merivale version. The

---

to me most likely that the first Philadelphia publisher confused Greffulhe's *Portrait of Cervantes* and Kemble's *Plot and Counterplot; or, The Portrait of Michael Cervantes,* and that Palmer, the second publisher, identifying *Plot and Counterplot* as being by Charles Kemble, simply mistakenly inserted Kemble's name.

99. Horace Walpole, *Letters,* ed. Peter Cunningham (London, 1859), IX, 215.

latter, judged by George C. D. Odell to be "about the worst mélange . . . in the entire course of our history of Shakespearian alterations,"[100] consisted mainly of events from Shakespeare's *2 Henry VI,* but began with *1 Henry VI,* Acts IV and V, and incorporated passages from such diverse sources as Chapman's *Bussy d'Ambois,* and *Byron's Conspiracy,* Webster's *White Devil,* and Marston's *Antonio and Mellida.* Kemble, in contrast, drew for his adaptation entirely from the three parts of *Henry VI,* with the exception of seven passages from *Richard II* amounting to about thirty-five lines and two passages from *Richard III* comprising about fifty-eight lines. When his abridgment was complete, Kemble's play revealed comparatively few lines which were not Shakespearean; there was, of course, some alteration of words and phrases and occasional rearrangement of line sequence and transference of speeches from one character to another.

To shorten and unify merely through omission was Kemble's basic plan. Of the three plays of Shakespeare, *1 Henry VI* is the most severely curtailed. The action in the abridgment takes place entirely on English soil; the subject of Talbot and the fate of the English forces in France is left out. In addition, the Gloucester-Winchester feud is given less scope, the scene between York and dying Mortimer is omitted, and Exeter, with his choruslike prophecies of trouble, is deleted from the cast. *The Second Part of Henry VI* forms a more integral part of Kemble's version. Still, Eleanor is omitted as a character; the scenes of Gloucester's debunking the miracle of "blind" Simpcox, the quarrel

100. George C. D. Odell, *Shakespeare from Betterton to Irving* (New York: C. Scribner's and Sons, 1920), II, 130.

between Horner and his apprentice, the death of Cardinal Beaufort, and the killing of Cade by Iden are removed; the Margaret-Suffolk relationship is quite undeveloped; and the horrors of the Cade rebellion are considerably curtailed. With respect to *3 Henry VI*, the battles are telescoped, and the scenes of the murder of Rutland, the stabbing of York, Henry on the molehill, and Henry's murder in the tower are all cut out.

What remains is a fairly unified play on the political struggle of the House of York to gain the throne. It opens with the Temple Garden scene and the beginning of the York-Lancaster dispute; it ends with Edward seated on the throne following victory at Tewksbury. In Act I the Temple Garden scene is succeeded by a brief one in which Plantagenet's and Somerset's followers continue the quarrel. Next Henry restores Richard Plantagenet to his place as Duke of York after momentarily quelling a Winchester-Gloucester outburst and just before Suffolk enters with Margaret, Henry's bride. By the end of Act I, Buckingham has suggested that the time is ripe to cast off the Lord Protector, and York has clearly enunciated his ambitions: "A day will come when York shall claim the crown." In Act II the good Duke of Gloucester, the first obstacle in York's path to power, is removed, and York plots to manipulate the Cade rebellion as he sets off to crush the Irish revolt. The third act reveals a rapid advance in the fortunes of York. Following the Cade uprising, York is victorious at St. Albans in a scene which shows considerable adaptation at Kemble's hands. He transfers the agreement to permit York's heirs to succeed in exchange for Henry's rule for life to the scene of battle, which is embellished too by a number of lines from *Richard II*. York, for example, sights Henry, echoing Bolingbroke's famous lines:

> See, see, King Henry doth himself appear,
> As doth the blushing discontented sun,
> From out the fiery portal of the east. . . .

Kemble's telescoping makes the opening scene of Act IV seem somewhat awkward. Having ended Act III with the peace through compromise, he abruptly begins Act IV with a messenger bringing news to Edward and Richard of the deaths of York and Rutland. In this act York's sons take up the family's claim, and after defeating the Lancastrian forces, Edward makes his unwise decision to marry Lady Grey. The final act is made up largely of scenes from *3 Henry VI,* Acts IV and V. It comprises the desertion of Clarence and Warwick, the capture and rescue of Edward, and various battles climaxed by the encounter at Tewksbury. Here Kemble turns briefly to *Richard III* for embellishment, as Margaret, after witnessing the stabbing of Prince Edward, delivers curses from the latter play. The final scene is taken from *3 Henry VI,* Act V, scene vii, and shows Edward on the throne, surrounded by his family, with Richard secretly plotting to "blast his harvest."

Frank Marshall, who published Kemble's abridgment of *Henry VI* in an edition entitled *The Works of William Shakespeare,* which he coedited with Henry Irving, called Kemble's version a "very ingenius piece of mosaic; evincing a thorough knowledge of Shakespeare, a conscientious regard for the integrity of his text—as far as the requirements of the stage will permit—and a thorough sympathy with the spirit of his work."[101] But even the most favorable

101. Frank Marshall, Introduction, *Henry VI: A Tragedy in Five Acts Condensed from Shakespeare,* in *The Works of William*

critic would have to admit that the total effect of his adaptation differs considerably from Shakespeare's plays. The scope of Shakespeare's treatment has been greatly diminished, and the complexity and richness of both meaning and style sacrificed. Instead of a trilogy exploring in its many ramifications the theme of discord, disorder, and chaos in a nation's history, Kemble's abridgment is a play focused rather narrowly on a particular political struggle. With respect to style, much of the dramatic liveliness and feeling of closeness to events remains; the strain of formalism and stylization, the close patternings, the archaic quality of the morality, which come side by side with it in Shakespeare, are gone. Gone, too, is much of the interest in and depth of characterization. Eleanor is completely omitted, and with her go two scenes in which the characterization of Gloucester is partially achieved; indeed the good Duke Humphrey, one of the more interesting figures in Shakespeare's plays, remains rather flat. Margaret is considerably softened —possibly in line with supposed contemporary taste; she is no longer the "tiger's heart wrapt in a woman's hide!" Henry, too, is but a shadow of his Shakespearean self.

An adapter, of course, cannot expect to achieve the same depth and fullness in plot or characterization in five acts as in fifteen. Kemble set out to condense and unify a trilogy persistently believed to be deficient in certain dramatic requirements, and to a considerable extent he succeeded in his task. His *Henry VI,* while lacking certain merits of the original, is not a bad play—indeed, it is probably quite an

Shakespeare, ed. Henry Irving and Frank A. Marshall (London 1890), II, 203. Marshall and Irving published Kemble's play from "the only copy known," a manuscript in Irving's private library. There is no evidence that it had ever been published before.

actable one, although no audience had opportunity to judge it.

Charles Kemble would have been spared some painful moments if, instead of *Henry VI*, his last three foreign adaptations and especially his original farce had failed to achieve production. In 1811 he borrowed again from Kotzebue for a three-act drama called *Kamchatka; or, The Slave's Tribute*,[102] only to learn that by then the enthusiasm for the German dramatist had passed. Omitting a number of scenes and adding some original verses for "glee and chorus," Kemble turned Kotzebue's *Graf Benyowsky* into a musical spectacle with such features as a melodramatic pantomime of a bear nearly devouring a prisoner and an elaborate ceremony in which Russian captives present their tribute of skins to the governor of Kamchatka. But neither scenery nor spectacle could atone for a plot which critics and audience agreed offended British taste. Count Benjowski, the heroic leader of a group of Polish confederates exiled to Kamchatka, unexpectedly wins the favor of the governor and the steadfast love of his daughter Athanasia. Nevertheless he plots a successful escape in which he leaves behind his betrothed with the chilling news that he already has both wife and child. "We cannot recognize a hero without a heart," The *Times* critic indignantly stormed in his review of the Covent Garden production of October 16. Chiding

102. The play was first called *The Day of Tribute* and the manuscript copy (Larpent MS 1691, Huntington Library) bears this title. When produced at Covent Garden Theatre, October 16, 1811, however, the play was announced as *Kamchatka; or, The Slave's Tribute* and playbills use the latter title. The spelling of the Russian region Kamchatka varies in the manuscript, playbills, and newspaper reviews. The spellings in these sources include, besides *Kamchatka*, *Kamtschatka*, *Kamschatka*, and *Kamtchatka*.

Kemble for reworking "the worst play of the worst writer of the worst dramatic school in Germany," he decreed that Kemble had failed to improve a "worthless original": he neither "retrenched the superfluous," "softened the rude," nor "elevated the low."[103]

After *Kamchatka*'s failure, Kemble's next dramatic venture, *The Brazen Bust*, which opened at Covent Garden on May 29, 1813, was a marked attempt to cater to popular taste. It was a full-fledged melodrama drawn from French sources; but like the outdated adaptation from Kotzebue, it achieved only a discouraging four-night run. Henry Bishop, the regular composer for Covent Garden, supplied no fewer than twenty-two separate pieces to accompany such exploits as the wild pursuit of the fugitive hero to the summit of a rocky cliff, followed by a horrendous leap into the raging Danube below, or the mysterious descent of the hero into a secret subterranean vault by means of a trap door ingeniously concealed beneath a brazen bust.[104] Kemble indeed followed faithfully the usual recipe for successful melodrama: the dialogue was kept meager but florid ("Hush! moderate these transports, I conjure you," a friend cautions the embracing lovers);[105] the action was fast-moving and exciting; the characters were flat and undelineated; and the ending was crowned with happiness for all as well as a favorite moral tag, "Beware youthful follies." But success was not forthcoming. *The Times*, in this case, was almost complimentary. Praising the "mechanical

103. *The Times*, October 17, 1811.

104. The musical score for *The Brazen Bust* is preserved in British Museum Ad. MS 27706. The play itself is preserved in Larpent MS 1771 at the Huntington Library.

105. *The Brazen Bust*, I. i.

merit" of the plot and the skill in "theatrical effect," it judged: "This little piece does all which it pretends to do."[106] But the audience evidently expected more, and Kemble's melodrama was speedily withdrawn.

A third adaptation, billed as "a serious drama in three acts" and entitled *Proof Presumptive; or, The Abbey of San Marco*, appeared on the Covent Garden stage October 20, 1818.[107] Based on a French source, it presented the chilling story of Alberto (Charles Kemble), a young Italian nobleman who under pressure of gambling debts is persuaded by his evil companion, Romani (William Macready), to assist him in a robbery which unexpectedly leads to murder. Alberto's brother-in-law is unjustly accused of the crime, and a compelling trial scene precedes the ultimate unraveling. An interesting, suspenseful, carefully plotted piece with dialogue characterized by relatively natural conversation, *Proof Presumptive* reveals a spark of talent and some artistic advance over earlier dramatic attempts. Effective sets and excellent acting by Kemble and Macready certainly enhanced the production. Macready noted that his part "afforded me opportunities which I did not neglect,"[108] and his performance as Romani earned him the typical praise: "He yields to no one in the delineation of the cool and crafty yet bold and determined villain."[109] Still, some felt the play to be too long and protracted, while others complained that

106. *The Times*, May 31, 1813.

107. The play was first called *Proof Presumptive; or, The Secret Marriage* and the manuscript copy (Larpent MS 2049, Huntington Library) bears this title. Upon production the subtitle was changed to *The Abbey of San Marco.*

108. William Macready, *Reminiscences*, ed. Frederick Pollock (New York, 1875), 125.

109. *The Times*, October 21, 1818.

"gloom and horror pervaded every scene."[110] Ultimately *Proof Presumptive* proved to be "too gloomy to become popular," as the *Theatrical Inquisitor* had accurately predicted.[111]

Finally, the reception of *The Child of Chance*,[112] an afterpiece and Charles Kemble's one venture at an original play, was such that he never made a second attempt. Although not an adaptation, the hastily composed farce displayed nothing that could be termed new: the plot, puns, and characters had been seen a hundred times before. Young Henry Volatile resorts to all the traditional ruses to court his ladylove, Sophia, who, typically, is contracted at the insistence of her father to Tony Luff, the son of his good friend. Forged letters, disguise, mistaken identity, and the antics of impudent and intriguing servants contribute to the hustle and bustle before Jack wins Jill. Not much worse than many such farcical afterpieces, Kemble's creation nevertheless apparently omitted sufficient ear boxing and similar slapstick and included too much artificial conversation and too many old jokes to suit the galleries. A reporter present at the Haymarket on July 8, 1812, tells the result in one sentence: "A new farce, entitled *The Child of Chance*, was stillborn at this house on Wednesday night."[113]

110. *Theatrical Inquisitor*, October 1818; *The Times*, October 21, 1818.

111. *Theatrical Inquisitor*, October 1818.

112. The play was first called *Love's Error; or, The Child of Chance* and the manuscript copy (Larpent MS 1723, Huntington Library) bears this title. When it was produced the name was changed to *The Child of Chance*.

113. Newspaper clipping in the files of the Haymarket Theatre for 1812 in the Enthoven Collection of the Victoria and Albert Museum, London. I have not been able to identify the paper or to establish the exact date.

Thus during the first two decades of the new century the young actor had a grand total of six adaptations and one original play to his credit, apart from the undated abridgment of *Henry VI*. But prospects for his future as a playwright were not exactly fair. Instead of improving, each new piece seemed to draw less applause than the last. By 1818 and *Proof Presumptive*, the once hopeful writer was pretty well forced to concede that further efforts as a dramatist were unlikely to enhance his fame.

Off-Stage Roles

Meanwhile, away from the theatre during these apprenticeship years, Charles Kemble was enjoying a busy life. Dashing suitor, proud husband, and doting father were three new off-stage roles in which he was cast, and his leading lady in each case was none other than John Kemble's old friend, Maria Theresa De Camp.

Miss De Camp was born in Vienna in 1774 and was brought to England as a child by her family, a group of French musicians and dancers. At the age of six she was already dancing Cupid in Noverre's ballet at the London Opera House, and from a childhood of singing and dancing she made her way to the legitimate stage. She had not quite entered her teens when on October 24, 1786, she made her debut at Drury Lane as Julie in *Richard Coeur de Lion;* and for the next thirty years she was one of the most familiar figures on the London boards. A fine dancer, a charming though not powerful singer, and a wonderful pantomimist, she excelled in melodramatic characters, sprightly parts, and genteel comedy; indeed, she was reportedly one of the best representatives of chambermaids and abigails in her day.[114]

The unfortunate dressing room siege by John Kemble possibly first served to draw Charles Kemble's attention to the pretty young actress who had so excited his brother's interest. In any case, not long after, he and Maria De Camp became fast friends as they worked opposite each other in play after play. When Kemble first undertook the gallant Charles Surface, his Lady Teazle was the beautiful Miss De Camp; when, black-faced, he terrorized the Jamaicans in *Obi,* the captive planter's daughter was his future wife. By the summer of 1797 affairs between the two had already taken the obvious turn. That August, Charles Kemble was cast as Vivaldi and Maria De Camp as Ellena de Rosalva in Boaden's adaptation of a romance by Mrs. Radcliffe called *The Italian Monk*. "It was not very difficult at this time to see the strong interest which he felt in the success of my heroine," Boaden remarked, "and the green room at the Haymarket arranged, by anticipation, the union that some years after took place between him and Miss Decamp."[115]

In 1800 the betrothal was announced; but the ensuing courtship was far from smooth, as the diary of Jane Porter, a close friend of the couple, attests. Whatever feelings John Kemble harbored after his encounter with the attractive actress, they were such that he firmly opposed her becoming his brother's wife. "John Kemble was violent against it," Jane Porter, speaking of the engagement, recorded; and "the rest of Charles's relations soon joined John, and on pain of their everlasting displeasure, they adjudged him not to marry her." As might be expected, a heated contest

114. Doran, *Their Majesties Servants,* III, 216–18.
115. Boaden, *Kemble,* II, 202.

ensued, and finally, Miss Porter noted, "it was reduced to this—that all visiting at her house should be laid aside; but that if they continued in the same mind when he was thirty, then the consent of his brother etc. should be given."[116]

Needless to say, this agreement did not meet with very enthusiastic approval from the newly engaged pair, but it seems neither Charles nor Maria wished to risk a marriage "under the displeasure of all his friends." So somehow the strange probation was endured—probably only because Maria confessedly "could never form an idea of being happy with any other man than Charles Kemble."[117] In any case, by 1806 the onerous conditions had been fulfilled: the handsome actor was now thirty years old, and both he and Maria "continued in the same mind." John Kemble kept to his bargain, and the *Morning Herald* of July 3 tells the happy end of the colorful tale:

> Yesterday morning a marriage long expected in theatrical circles took place at St. George's, Bloomsbury, between Mr. Charles Kemble and Miss De Camp. Mr. John Kemble was present at the ceremony and gave the bride away.

A postscript perhaps should be added to attest that despite the ominous beginning this proved to be a marriage that prospered and endured. Within a year a child was born, and within eight years three more; Charles Kemble settled down to the pleasures of a proud husband and father, and Maria De Camp to those of a contented mother and wife.

116. "Diary of Jane Porter, 1801–1803," MS, Folger Shakespeare Library, Washington, D.C.

117. *Ibid.*

By 1813 the apprenticeship of Charles Kemble had continued long beyond what anyone—least of all the actor himself—could have expected. He had nearly twenty years' experience on the London stage, but he was yet to achieve the coveted position of a star. To his professional colleagues and to the public as well he was still "the younger Kemble," a fine supporter of his famous brother and other leading actors of the day.

Viewing this situation, he understandably grew discontented. If he was ever to advance, the thirty-eight-year-old performer strongly felt, his career would have to undergo some drastic change. The previous season Kemble, confessing that "my future prospects entirely depend upon the estimation in which I am to be held for the next [few] years," had gone so far as to consider a move back to Drury Lane.[118] In the summer of 1812, however, this plan suddenly fell through. Now in 1813 the actor tried a different tack in a desperate attempt to shift his public image and to emerge at last from the rut of supporting roles. To everyone's surprise he quit his job at Covent Garden. With his wife, Maria, he left the theatrical capital and set out for the provinces, where for two years he not only enjoyed engagements in first parts, but pretty steadily achieved a warm acclaim.

The remedy proved at least partly a success. When Kemble returned to London in the fall of 1815, it was to

118. Charles Kemble to an unidentified official at Drury Lane Theatre, letter dated June 17, 1812, in the Enthoven Collection, Victoria and Albert Museum. In this letter concerning a possible engagement at Drury Lane, Charles Kemble stresses that salary is "but a secondary consideration." His main concern is for an agreement to his "claim to a certain line of characters"; that is, he is anxious to be assured of more than secondary parts.

play Hamlet, Macbeth, and Romeo in addition to his usual secondary roles. Of course he was never to achieve the stature of his brother. And the appearance of Edmund Kean in London during his absence dealt a severe blow to the whole Kemble school. Still, for Charles Kemble, after twenty years the long apprenticeship was over; for the next twenty he would at least rank among the masters who labored for applause.

II

A Master Performs: Hamlet, Mercutio, Faulconbridge

Hamlet

It was on a hot and sultry Monday night, the seventeenth of September, 1832, that an American audience had its first and eagerly anticipated look at Charles Kemble. An enthusiastic audience crowded into the Park Theatre in New York. The play was *Hamlet,* and Kemble was cast as the Danish prince, a role in which he had received acclaim ever since his first performance of it during his apprenticeship at Drury Lane nearly thirty years before. "It was my dear father's first appearance in this new world," Fanny Kemble recorded in her *Journal,* "and my heart ached with anxiety. The weather was intensely hot, yet the theatre was crowded; when he came on, they gave him what everybody here calls an immense reception; but they should see our London audience get up, and wave hats and handkerchiefs, and shout welcome as they do to us. The tears were in my eyes, and all I could say was, 'They might as well get up, I think.'"[1] George Odell concluded that

> it must have seemed like a dream to imaginative souls, to sit in that theatre, watching the playing of an actor who

1. Frances Ann Kemble Butler, *Journal* (Philadelphia, 1835), I, 93.

> was so large a part of the glory of the English stage during the first quarter of the Nineteenth Century. The spirits of John Kemble and of his famous sister, Mrs. Siddons, must have been invoked in talk, if not in memory. How many present had seen that other sister, Mrs. Whitlock, who for a season had played leading rôles on the Park stage, now so many years ago? Who recalled Mrs. Hatton, still another sister, whose Tammany had created a stir before the last century died? And here was another of the noble clan—the only survivor of that generation still in active service—appealing for the suffrage of an American audience who could hardly have hoped ever to see this excellent brother of the great, great Siddons. It must have been almost as if time had turned backward in his flight![2]

The expectations of the audience were fulfilled. Despite the "intolerable heat" and nervousness and the fact that "he was not well dressed," Kemble played with his "usual excellence," and the audience was delighted.[3] The critic William Leggett, although he himself disagreed at times with Kemble's interpretation of Hamlet and also noted that "his school of declamation is not the one we have been most accustomed to admire," writing in the New York *Evening Post* the next day, reported, "Indeed we have seldom seen an audience more delighted—or *better* delighted, for they were louder in their praises after the play had been seen through, than they were disposed to be at first"; and the *American* of September 18 declared of Kemble's performance:

> He created a sensation in the house to which it has long been a stranger, and, an hour after the play was over, you might

2. George C. D. Odell, *Annals of the New York Stage* (New York: Columbia University Press, 1927–49), III, 603–04.
3. Butler, *Journal,* I, 94.

> see many an earnest group in the lobbies, comparing their opinions, and dwelling with delight upon the pleasure they received.

William Bodham Donne, in reviewing Charles Kemble's accomplishments on the stage, concluded that his performance of Hamlet was perhaps his "greatest achievement as an actor." He observed that Hamlet's "form, his voice, his demeanour, his power of expressing sentiment, his profound melancholy, his meditative repose, were all strictly within the range of his physical and intellectual endowments, and had all been anxiously trained up to the highest point of precision and harmony."[4] The reception accorded Kemble at the Park Theatre would suggest that many New Yorkers would have concurred with this English critic's judgment. "It appeared to be generally conceded," the reviewer for the *American* noted, "that Mr. Kemble is the first Hamlet we have ever had in this country." And, he continued, "For our own parts we may say, that he is the only actor who, on our stage, realized our conception of the romantic and philosophic Dane."[5] Of course one spectator, at least, felt that the fifty-six-year-old performer, though still handsome, looked somewhat too old for his character. "Notwithstanding a characteristic wig," James Hackett complained, "his features denoted his age to be far in advance of the 'thirty years' which the grave-digger reports Hamlet to have attained at the time when the fifth act of the tragedy has commenced."[6] But Fanny Kemble thought that her

4. William Bodham Donne, *Essays on the Drama* (London, 1858), p. 175.
5. New York *American*, September 18, 1832.
6. James Henry Hackett, *Notes, Criticisms and Correspondence upon Shakespeare's Plays and Actors* (New York, 1863), p. 174.

father "looked wonderfully young and handsome" on this September night, and William Leggett was amazed by the actor's "exterior of five and twenty."[7]

As the comments of Leggett, Fanny Kemble, and Hackett suggest, certain impressions of a theatrical performance inevitably vary with the eyes of the beholder. Add to this axiom the realization that no two performances by an actor are identical, and hopes of recapturing the art of an actor from the past grow dim indeed. Despite such limitations, however, by reviewing the many comments on Charles Kemble's appearances as Hamlet during the thirty-seven-year period in which he played the part, by examining a studybook of *Hamlet* which bears the note that it was "marked from Mr. C. Kemble's promptbook,"[8] by observ-

7. Fanny Kemble, *Records of a Girlhood* (London, 1879), III, 241; William Leggett, New York *Evening Post,* September 18, 1832. Leggett's review is reprinted in *The American Theatre as Seen by Its Critics, 1752–1934,* ed. Montrose J. Moses and John Mason Brown (New York: W. W. Norton and Company, 1934), pp. 50–59.

8. This studybook is Folger Shakespeare Library promptbook *Hamlet*, 44. It apparently belonged to the American actor J. B. Roberts; it bears his name on the title page. On the page preceding the beginning of the text, it bears the note "Marked from Mr. C. Kemble's promptbook." I have not been able to determine when or by whom it was copied. It may have been marked from Kemble's promptbook during his American visit in 1832–34. It is a Cumberland edition with interleaves. The book has been marked by two different pens: one with black ink, the other with brown ink. The black ink markings are those of the principal annotator and include, in addition to the notation of ownership, indication of stresses in Hamlet's speeches, cuts, restorations, diagrams, and a great deal of stage business. These markings in black ink are in an extremely neat and regular hand. The brown ink markings are in a rather careless hand and include only a few stage directions, primarily near the end of the play for characters other than Hamlet. The natural assumption would be that the full markings in black ink represent the copying of "Mr. C. Kemble's

ing R. J. Lane's notations of Kemble's accents in the text used in his public readings,[9] and by noting the text and stage directions in Cumberland's acting edition of *Hamlet* (c. 1829), which professes to record productions in which

promptbook," and that the few brief notes in brown ink dealing with characters other than Hamlet were made at some later date. It should be remarked, however, that the notation itself that this book is "marked from Mr. C. Kemble's promptbook" appears in brown ink. This notation is somewhat neater than the other brown ink markings, but could be by the same hand. I am inclined to think that Roberts himself may have recorded, after the fact, that the book was originally marked by a copyist from Kemble's book, and then that Roberts also added a few quick notes (in brown) himself. Because of the richness of the regular annotations in black ink (which are, indeed, consistent with all information I have been able to discover about Kemble's performances from other sources), I have included reference to them in the discussion of Kemble's Hamlet which follows. However, I must advise the reader to accept these references with some caution because of the unknown origin of this promptbook. (I do not refer to any brown ink markings, which do not deal with Hamlet in any case.) I shall hereafter refer to this promptbook as Folger 44.

9. *Charles Kemble's Shakespere Readings*, ed. R. J. Lane (London, 1870), Vol. I. Lane indicates whenever possible the accents and stresses employed by Kemble in his public readings at Willis's Rooms in May, 1844. In his preface he notes that he had assisted Kemble in preparing a suitable reading text and had given him "a copy of Hanmer's quarto, in order that he might mark the scenes and passages that were to be omitted; and, happily, his marks were extended to the *accentuation* of words, and an occasional *syllabic* stress; to which my experience of his reading has enabled me to add emphatic marks, which Mr. Kemble had not thought it necessary to insert in a book prepared for his own use." I have included reference to *Kemble's Shakespere Readings* in the discussion of Kemble's Hamlet which follows, although it must be admitted that a reading text is not precise evidence of stage performance and may occasionally record certain subtleties that a stage performance would not permit. Still, the Kemble style of acting attached so much importance to the singling out of emphatic words and to subtle stresses that Lane's notations seemed to me to be worthy of inclusion.

the actor appeared,[10] it is possible to reconstruct to some extent his characteristic performance of the role, and hence to imagine, at least partially, what it must have been like to have viewed his portrayal of the Danish prince at the Park Theatre that warm night in 1832.

Among the more general qualities of Kemble's Hamlet which were impressive to the Park Theatre crowd—qualities which had long been admired by London audiences—were his princely courtesy, his grace and dignity, his tenderness, and his refinement.[11] As Westland Marston was later to remark of his appearance at the Haymarket in the summer of 1835, "beauty of treatment, indeed (as contrasted with what is commonly known as power of treatment . . .) was the feature of the performance." Invariably Kemble's interesting "contrasts of impetuosity and inaction, of pensiveness and passion, of amiability and irony, all harmonized and made lifelike,"[12] and his veracity, which, like the advice to the players, "never once o'er steps the 'modesty of nature,'"[13] were favored aspects of his personation.

10. This Cumberland edition of *Hamlet* professes to print the text "from the acting copy," and to include a description of costume, cast of characters, and record of stage business "as now performed." The cast which it publishes is for the Covent Garden productions of 1829, with Charles Kemble as Hamlet. It may be noted that this edition forms the basis for the promptbook, Folger 44, and that the annotator of Folger 44 regularly underlines the printed stage directions of the Cumberland edition to indicate their retention.

11. Butler, *Journal*, I, 94.

12. Westland Marston, *Our Recent Actors* (Boston, 1888), pp. 115, 119.

13. Charles Rice, *The London Theatre in the Eighteen Thirties*, ed. A. C. Sprague and Bertram Shuttleworth (London: Society for Theatre Research, 1950), p. 75.

One element of his performance which his New York audience failed to admire, however, was the use of the long pause. It was also singled out for comment by James Musgrove when he saw Kemble a few weeks later in Philadelphia. "He has the fault, and a fault it surely is, because it tires the audience, which induced the small wits of the London papers to give a greater actor than himself the nickname of 'Long Pause,'" Musgrove observed. "This he carried so far in some of the early scenes, that he wore out the patience of several who would have admired and applauded him in subsequent passages."[14]

Attention to the minutiae of presentation, to the most fleeting shades of character, to the most intricate subtleties and refinements, which was always a dominant characteristic of Charles Kemble's acting, was particularly evident in New York. Fanny Kemble, after watching her father on this occasion, noted in her *Journal:* "My father looked well, and acted beyond all praise; but oh, what a fine and delicate piece of work this is! there is not one sentence, line, or word of this part, which my father has not sifted grain by grain; there is not one scene or passage to which he does not give its fullest and most entire substance, together with a variety that relieves the intense study of the whole with wonderful effect" (I, 93).

Kemble's extreme attention to detail again became a topic for comment in his daughter's *Journal* after she had witnessed a similar first night in Philadelphia a month later. On this occasion, however, she voiced some doubts about the value of this refined style which is so firmly associated with

14. James Musgrove, quoted by Charles Durang, *The Philadelphia Stage from the Year 1749 to 1855* (Philadelphia, n.d.), chap. 23. The "greater actor" Musgrove referred to is William Charles Macready.

all the Kembles; and she seemed, this time, to have missed the variety which earlier she felt relieved the intense study. She remarked of her father's acting that in one respect his "very minute accuracy and refinement renders it unfit for the frame in which it is exhibited. Whoever should paint a scene calculated for so large a space as a theatre, and destined to be viewed at a distance from which an audience beholds it, with the laborious finish and fine detail of a miniature, would commit a great error in judgment" (I, 143–44). Fanny Kemble realized that many, if not most, of the "fine tints" upon which her father put so much emphasis, and which enchanted her personally, passed unnoticed and uncomprehended by the public.[15] Her remarks in her *Journal* on her father's Hamlet, inspired by his performance in Philadelphia, stand as perhaps the most effective criticism of Charles Kemble's acting available:

> Now the great beauty of all my father's performances, but particularly of Hamlet, is a wonderful accuracy in the detail of the character which he represents; an accuracy which modulates the emphasis of every word, the nature of every gesture, the expression of every look; and which renders the whole a most laborious and minute study, toilsome in the conception and acquirement; and most toilsome in the execution. But the result, though the natural one, is not such as he expects, as the reward of so much labour. Few persons are able to follow such a performance with the necessary attention, and it is almost as great an exertion to see it *understandingly*, as it is to act it. The amazing study of it requires a study in those who are to appreciate it, and, as I take it, this is far from being what the majority of spectators are either capable or desirous of doing; the

15. Butler, *Journal*, I, 94.

> actor loses his pains, and they have but little pleasure. Those who perform, and those who behold a play, have but a certain proportion of power of exciting, and capability of being excited. If, therefore, the actor expends his power of exciting, and his audience's power of being excited upon the detail of the piece, and continues through five whole acts to draw from both; the main and striking points, those of strongest appeal, those calculated most to rouse at once, and gratify the emotions of the spectator; have not the same intensity of vigour, that they would have had, if the powers of both the actor and audience had been reserved to give them their fullest effect. . . . All things cannot have all their component parts equal, and "nothing pleaseth but rare accidents." This being so, I think that acting best, which skillfully husbands the actor's and spectator's powers, and puts forth the whole of the one, to call forth the whole of the other occasionally only; leaving the intermediate parts sufficiently level, to allow him and them to recover the capability of again producing, and again receiving such impressions. (I, 144–46)

Fanny Kemble's very perceptive analysis, which no doubt Edmund Kean would have appreciated, is, in effect, a basic criticism of the Kemble style, a style which lies behind James Hackett's remark, concerning the Park Theatre performance, that Kemble's reading "though artistical, was prosy and measured; his action and gestures were graceful, but never seemed impulsive, and his manner . . . studied and mechanical," as well as Donne's subsequent feeling that the one thing left to be desired in his interpretation of Hamlet was that "occasionally the harmony of the execution had been broken by the disturbing forces of passion."[16]

16. Hackett, *Shakespeare's Plays and Actors,* p. 173; Donne, *Essays on the Drama,* p. 175.

The refinement and the flawless execution, which had become the hallmarks of Kemble's performances, were evident from the moment the curtain rose in the second scene and the New Yorkers caught their first glimpse of the English actor. To the accompaniment of a "flourish of trumpets" Hamlet, displaying "the 'dejected 'haviour' which a rooted sorrow brings,"[17] entered at the end of a procession which included Polonius, King Claudius, Queen Gertrude, and various lords and ladies of the court.[18] A sense of isolation and loneliness were among the first traits suggested, as Hamlet stood somewhat apart and to the left of the stage.[19] "Nothing could exceed his picture of loneliness of soul as he stood encircled by the Court of Denmark," Donne remarked of Kemble's opening.[20] Then, when he began to speak, Hamlet's first aside and his reply to his uncle,

> Not so, my lord; I am too much i' the sun,

were not said with the customary scorn or sarcasm. On the contrary, Marston recalled that he was struck by a kind of "graceful, pensive idling" of the brain which "made them

17. New York *American*, September 18, 1832.

18. Cumberland edition; Folger 44 indicates the order of the entrance with "Hamlet last." Folger 44 is an annotated Cumberland edition (Covent Garden cast of 1829, with Charles Kemble as Hamlet) and makes use of the printed stage directions (which are underlined and occasionally elaborated or qualified) as well as those inserted by hand in ink. In subsequent notes I shall cite Cumberland edition when the reference is to printed stage directions in this promptbook and Folger 44 when the reference is to directions entered by hand. Of course, where these two sets of directions are not complementary and handwritten directions in Folger 44 change in any way printed directions, I shall make this clear.

19. Cumberland edition.

20. Donne, *Essays on the Drama*, p. 176.

seem tricks of fence to ward off approach to his deeper nature. Though they had their touch of causticity, they were thrown off with an air of courtly ease and respect widely different from the intense and scornful significance employed by some actors, who have thus disclosed, at the very outset of the play, Hamlet's loathing for the King." He noted that "Charles Kemble's fine instinct taught him the unseemliness of launching bitter sarcasms at Claudius before his courtiers. The subdued and delicate irony of his manner might be understood by those whose guilt gave the key to it. To the rest it was the mere humour of the moment, or play upon words."[21]

Subsequently in his response to Gertrude, who, reminding her son that death is common, inquires, "Why seems it so particular with thee?" Kemble emphasized strongly the contrast between appearance and reality, between what seems and what is:

> Seems, madam! Nay, it IS; I know not seems.
> 'Tis not alone my inky cloak, good mother,
> Nor the dejected 'haviour of the visage,
> No, nor the fruitful river in the eye,
> Together with all forms, moods, shows of grief,
> That can denote me truly: These, indeed, SEEM.[22]

According to the stage directions in Folger promptbook *Hamlet* 44, which bears the note that it was "marked from Mr. C. Kemble's promptbook," Hamlet "turns quick to Queen" and then pauses a moment just before he begins this reply. R. J. Lane's notations of the words Kemble stressed

21. Marston, *Our Recent Actors*, pp. 113–14.

22. *Kemble's Shakespere Readings*, I, 56. Folger 44 also indicates the stress on *seems* and *is*.

in his public readings indicate that, in his reading performances at least, another marked effect produced by word emphasis followed shortly in Hamlet's response after both the King and Queen have urged him to remain in Denmark:

I shall in all my best obey YOU, madam.[23]

Here the stress fell upon the word *you*, accentuating the strong distinction Hamlet makes between his mother and his uncle.

The King pronounces Hamlet's decision to be "a loving and a fair reply," and with a flourish of trumpets the court exits ceremoniously.[24] Folger 44 notes that Hamlet "retires a little up, looks after them, then comes down LH" as he begins his first soliloquy, "O, that this too, too solid flesh would melt." Further stage directions here call for Hamlet to glance once more after the King and Queen upon his reference to "things rank and gross in nature" and to speak in an especially "plaintive tone" in the latter part of this passage. Indeed with Charles Kemble the predominant tone in this soliloquy was one of melancholy. Marston remarked that he had heard it often rendered with "greater bitterness, with more passionate denunciation of the Queen's inconstancy, with a fiercer recoil from the King, but never . . . with so much pathetic beauty. There was, of course, indig-

23. *Kemble's Shakespere Readings*, I, 57. Whether Kemble customarily made such a pointed effect in his stage performances as well as in his readings is not clear. It would seem to be somewhat out of keeping with the "subdued and delicate irony of his manner" with respect to Claudius which Donne noted. Folger 44 does not record the stress on *you*.

24. The Cumberland directions indicate further that in this exit Polonius departs first, "with a White Rod, formally leading the way; 2d, the King and Queen; 3d, Laertes; 4th male and female Attendants."

nation," he confessed, "but the predominant note was that of melancholy. You heard a wail over human instability, conveyed by a music of delivery which, skillfully varied in its tones, insinuated, rather than forced its way, and made sorrow lovely:—

> Why, she would hang on him,
> As if increase of appetite had grown
> By what it fed on! And yet, within a month,—
> Let me not think on 't;—Frailty, thy name is woman!

These last words seemed to float away in a very melody of sadness. The fitful and wilder grief that preceded them had sunk into a sigh."[25] If Kemble's voice was unsuited for expressing the violent and tumultuous passions, it was apparently particularly appropriate for the rather melancholy tone which he made dominant in this soliloquy. So well did he read here, and in fact in the whole scene, that Marston was inspired to comment: "I never imagined there could be so much charm in words as mere sounds."[26]

In Hamlet's meeting and conversation with Horatio a spirit of joy suddenly replaced the preceding melancholy. "What a gleam of joy beamed forth in his welcome of Horatio!" Donne observed. "Now at least he has one faithfull counsellor and friend; he is no longer all alone."[27] The transition was skillfully marked in Kemble's reading of

25. Marston, *Our Recent Actors*, pp. 114–15.

26. *Ibid*, p. 113. It might be noted that the only omissions in this speech, as indicated by the Cumberland text, were the parenthetical exclamation, "(O God! a beast that wants discourse of reason / Would have mourn'd longer)" and the reference to the incestuous nature of the marriage, "O, most wicked speed, to post / With such dexterity to incestuous sheets!" both of which call for a particularly intense or passionate response from Hamlet.

27. Donne, *Essays on the Drama*, p. 176.

Hamlet's first words in reply to Horatio's greeting, "Hail to your lordship!" Kemble's Hamlet seemed unconscious that his friend was present when he spoke the line

I am glad to see you well.

These words were uttered apparently "more out of courtesy than friendship—but slowly raising his eyes he throws off his melancholy stupor, explaining in the most cordial manner—

Horatio—or I do forget myself,

evidently chiding himself for his indifference of reply before he knew by whom he had been addressed."[28]

Kemble, it seems, emphasized a distinction in this scene between Hamlet's attitude toward Horatio and toward the other witnesses to the strange apparition, Marcellus and Bernardo—a distinction which prepared here for his business later in the Ghost Scene, where, as Hamlet is about to confide in his friend Horatio, he is prevented from speaking out by some distrust of Marcellus. Folger 44 suggests that Hamlet, in his greeting of his friend and his initial query, "And what make you from Wittenberg, Horatio?" speaks "with familiar warmth until he sees Marcellus." Subsequently in his reading of the question addressed to Horatio concerning the Ghost, "Did you not speak to it?" Charles Kemble followed in the tradition of his brother and accented the word *you*—"Did YOU not speak to it?"—again marking a distinction between Horatio and the others.[29]

28. Rice, *The London Theatre in the Eighteen Thirties*, p. 76.

29. *Kemble's Shakespere Readings*, I, 59; Rice, *The London Theatre in the Eighteen Thirties*, p. 76; and Folger 44 all indicate this reading of the line.

His reading at this point, Charles Rice noted, was criticized by at least one reviewer on the grounds that Horatio's words,

> I saw him once; he was a goodly King,

indicate that Horatio's acquaintance with the elder Hamlet was such that he would have no more reason than the other officers to address the spirit. Rice, of course, defended Kemble by pointing out that Horatio is Hamlet's intimate friend and a scholar, and hence much more likely to have spoken to the Ghost than Marcellus or Bernardo; and he observed that Horatio's reply,

> My Lord, I did; but answer it made none,

confirms Hamlet's basis for singling out his friend.[30] The warmth of the friendship between Hamlet and Horatio was apparently further reinforced in this scene by Hamlet's action on two separate occasions of clasping Horatio by the hand. When Hamlet replies, "In my mind's eye," to Horatio's startled query about where he thinks he sees his father, the stage directions in Folger 44 note that Hamlet "takes Horatio's hand"; he repeats the gesture when, startled himself, he responds to Horatio's information that the Ghost "wore his beaver up" with the anxious question, "What, look'd he frowningly?"

Kemble's scenes with the Ghost always ranked among the high points in the play. His Hamlet entered in scene iv followed by Horatio and Marcellus and proceeded to pace back and forth in nervous expectation during the conversation

30. Rice, *The London Theatre in the Eighteen Thirties*, p. 76.

with his fellow watchers.[31] When finally the Ghost appeared from the left and Horatio exclaimed, "Look, my lord, it comes!" Hamlet stood alone at right center, with Horatio "about two yards from the back of Hamlet" and Marcellus "about the same distance from Horatio up the stage."[32] Whatever the degree of his initial "start,"[33] the predominant attitude on Hamlet's part during the apostrophe to the Ghost was not terror, as with Garrick, nor bravado. It was, instead, a combination of awe, filial trust, and reverence. Marston referred to Kemble's voice as subdued and awe-struck. "When Horatio and Marcellus would fain restrain him from following the spectre, what grace mingled with the energy of his struggles, how picturesque was his figure, how fraught with filial trust and reverence! There was about him," Marston declared, "an air of elevation and trust in his spiritual visitant when he broke from his companions, which seemed to speak him of a different and higher nature—as one who had kinship with supernatural life which they might not comprehend. The house sat breathless to see him glide off after his father's spirit, which magnetically and irresistibly drew him."[34] Both his daughter

31. Folger 44. This practice of pacing was a common one. A. C. Sprague (*Shakespeare and the Actors: The Stage Business in His Plays: 1660–1905* [Cambridge: Harvard University Press, 1944], p. 137) suggests that John Kemble apparently paced, as well as Macready and others.

32. Cumberland edition.

33. A notation in Folger 44 reads: "Alarm. Starting" before "Angels and ministers of grace defend us!"

34. Marston, *Our Recent Actors*, pp. 115–116. Folger 44 indicates that after the Ghost first beckons, Horatio and then Marcellus move one step forward toward Hamlet. According to these notes they subsequently take Hamlet by the hand, then later by the arm to restrain him. As Hamlet says to them, "Unhand me, gentlemen," the

Fanny and the critic Donne were especially enthralled by the way in which he spoke the line

Go on, I'll follow thee

to the Ghost. "The full gush of deep and tender faith, in spite of the awful mystery, to whose unfolding he is committing his life, is beautiful beyond measure," judged Fanny Kemble. "It is full of the unutterable fondness of a believing heart, and brought to my mind, last night, those holy and lovely words of scripture, 'Perfect love casteth out fear.'"[35] Donne praised Kemble's performance throughout both the scenes with the Ghost, saying:

> We have seen actors who fairly scolded their father's spirit, and others who quailed before it; but, except in Charles Kemble, we have never seen one whose looks and tones accorded with the spirit of that awful revelation of the prison-house and the concealed crime and its required purgation, and expressed at once the sense of woe endured, anticipated, and stretching onward through a whole life.[36]

One piece of business which Kemble adopted in the fifth scene especially impressed Rice when he saw him. While other actors, including Garrick, had occasionally bowed upon the Ghost's words, "I am thy father's spirit,"[37] Charles Kemble at this point dropped to his knee. Rice, in commenting on this business, noted that "Hamlet had before

---

direction "entreaty" is inserted, which would seem to suggest a rather polite manner on Hamlet's part in breaking away from his restrainers.

35. Butler, *Journal*, I, 148.

36. Donne, *Essays on the Drama*, p. 176. The attitude of Kemble toward the Ghost perhaps most closely resembles Betterton's, and Donne's remarks are reminiscent of Colley Cibber's famous description of Betterton.

37. A. C. Sprague, *Shakespeare and the Actors*, p. 142.

judged the spirit to be that of his father but by ocular demonstration, but as soon as he is convinced of the fact by the above expression of the apparition, he falls at his feet, as to his living sire, in reverential awe."[38] Subsequently as Hamlet listens to the Ghost's commands and disclosures his voice and expression register a feeling of mounting horror, the notations in Folger 44 suggest. Indeed when the Ghost first indicates that Hamlet is bound not only to hear but to revenge, Hamlet's reply, "What?" bears the descriptive notation "Horror!" A few lines later, when he learns that he must revenge a "foul and most unnatural murder," Hamlet's response carries the direction "Horror burst."

The Ghost concludes his revelations and disappears; Hamlet vows to remember; and Horatio and Marcellus excitedly call out to Hamlet from within before entering.[39] Kemble's Hamlet then seems to have struggled with the question of whether or not to reveal his news and finally decided to remain silent because of a distrust of Marcellus. According to Folger 44, at Horatio's request to "tell it," Hamlet acts "as if he would tell—and sudden pause—looks at Marcellus" before replying, "No; you will reveal it." With his next line he is again "doubtful as if to reveal"; but after remarking, "There's ne'er a villain dwelling in all Denmark," Hamlet displays a "sudden resolution not to tell" and crosses over to Marcellus as he concludes, "But he's an arrant knave."[40] Later, however, after Horatio has remarked about his "wild and whirling words," Hamlet

38. Rice, *The London Theatre in the Eighteen Thirties,* p. 76.

39. Cumberland edition. Folger 44 indicates that the Ghost exits through the "front trap."

40. Folger 44.

once more draws near to his friend and "takes his hand" as he confesses,

> Touching this vision here—
> It is an honest ghost, that let me tell you.[41]

The swearing on the sword which follows was the least impressive aspect of the Ghost scenes in the opinion of the American critic William Leggett. Leggett was happy to see that Kemble, in his appearance in New York, followed Young in his choice of sword styles. (Young had introduced the cross-shaped handle, instead of the more modern black-hilted dress sword.) He felt, however, that the actor did not make the most impressive use of the sword: "Why did he not use it as we have every reason to fancy it should have been used?—as enjoined by the institutions of chivalry, in which pagan savageness and religious sublimity are so strangely and so wildly mingled?" Leggett lamented that Kemble imposed the oath "more with the flippancy of the robber hero of melodrama, than the solemnity of a Prince under an injunction direct from another world, to bind those he was deeply interested to impress, by the most terrible responsibility which can be imposed in this."[42] The swearing finally completed, Hamlet declares, "Rest, rest, perturbed spirit!" Then, a notation in Folger 44 indicates, "repressing his feelings," he takes the hands of Horatio and Marcellus and "attempts to rouse himself" before uttering his final lines and departing with his two companions.

In the second act Kemble's skillful treatment of Hamlet's madness exhibited during his conversation with Polonius,

41. Cumberland edition.
42. New York *Evening Post,* September 18, 1832.

which is interrupted first by his encounter with Rosencrantz and Guildenstern and later by the arrival of the players, was one aspect of his presentation which particularly won the praise of a French reviewer who saw him in Paris in September, 1827. Here, indeed, the younger Kemble seems to have surpassed his brother, who apparently found the sudden adjustments of manner somewhat beyond his powers.[43] J. L. Borgerhoff, citing an article in *La Réunion* of September 13, noted a French critic's admiration for Charles Kemble's ability to master the swift transitions which so often appear grotesque.

> C'est pendant la folie simulée d'Hamlet que l'acteur a été tout à fait admirable. Il y a là un ensemble de nuances confondues très difficiles à rendre; or Kemble les a interprétées de façon "à faire disparaître les transitions grotesques qu'offre nécessairement un tel rapprochement." Dans cette partie du rôle, le tragique est porté jusqu'à l'exaltation, le comique y descend jusqu'au cynisme, et l'acteur s'est tiré avec une maîtrise consumée de tous ces changements à vue d'oeil.[44]

Kemble's Hamlet entered in Act II, scene ii—reading, of course—just after the King and Queen had departed, leaving Polonius behind to "board him presently." The stage directions in Folger 44 indicate a number of quick shifts in attitude on Hamlet's part during the initial conversation with Polonius, with Hamlet at one moment ignoring the meddlesome courtier, the next exhibiting a sudden start of attention or interest. For example, when Hamlet remarks

43. A. C. Sprague, *Shakespearian Players and Performances* (Cambridge: Harvard University Press, 1953), p. 48.

44. J. L. Borgerhoff, *Le Théâtre anglais à Paris sous la Restauration* (Paris: Hachette, 1913), p. 94.

that he wishes Polonius were "so honest a man" as a fishmonger and Polonius replies quizzically, "Honest, my lord?" the stage directions suggest that Hamlet reacts abruptly to the old man's repetition of the word *honest* and "turns to him quickly" as he proclaims, "Ay, sir! to be honest, as this world goes, is to be one man picked out of ten thousand," and then proceeds to cross over to him. A few lines later he walks away and begins reading, and he does not even look up at Polonius as he replies, "Words, words, words," to the question about what he is reading. But when Polonius asks, "What is the matter, my lord?" Hamlet jerks to attention and "turns quickly, expressing wonder" as he inquires, "Between who?" Oxberry interestingly discloses that Kemble's expression frequently revealed a rather melancholy smile during this scene with Polonius, a smile which he felt was "worth a volume of elocution."[45]

Another distinctive feature of Kemble's portrayal of Hamlet's "antic disposition" was the extent to which he refrained, for the most part, from exhibiting a tone or manner of bitter insolence or blatant rudeness toward Polonius. R. J. Lane's record of the words which Charles Kemble stressed when giving his readings of *Hamlet* at Willis's Rooms in the spring of 1844 gives the impression that in these performances Hamlet's quips with Polonius, who is trying to tell him of the player's arrival, were perhaps not so much spoken with the spirit of insolence, as many actors have done, as with the spirit of courtly jesting. To Polonius's

My lord, I have news to tell you,

45. W. Oxberry, *Dramatic Biography and Histrionic Anecdotes,* III (London, 1825), 11.

Hamlet follows by repeating his words:

My lord, I have news to tell you.

Kemble, however, did not utter this reply in simple mimicry of Polonius, but changed the emphasis by laying stress on the word *you:* "My lord, I have news to tell YOU."[46] Instead of heightening the possibilities for rudeness in Hamlet's speeches and business, Kemble indeed seems occasionally to have affected an air of comic politeness toward Polonius. Leggett, in his review of the performance at the Park Theatre, noted with pleasure the novelty of Kemble's "courtly deference" as he turns to Polonius, asking him whether it shall be a passionate speech from the players, "instead of the usual way of bidding the player speak a passionate speech, without consulting the pleasure of anyone present but himself."[47] Earlier in the scene, just before the arrival of Rosencrantz and Guildenstern, Polonius tells Hamlet, "I will most humbly take my leave of you," and Hamlet replies, "You cannot, sir, take from me anything that I will more willingly part withal, except my life, except my life, except my life." Folger 44 suggests that Hamlet here takes the edge off his brusque retort by walking up to Polonius "very ceremoniously" and thus offering him a most courtly dismissal.

In the interview with Rosencrantz and Guildenstern, Charles Rice found Kemble to be "particularly happy."[48] After an exchange of cordial greetings with his school friends, Kemble's Hamlet seemingly began rather quickly to suggest suspicion of the two visitors. Much of the initial

46. *Kemble's Shakespere Readings,* I, 76.
47. New York *Evening Post,* September 18, 1832.
48. Rice, *The London Theatre in the Eighteen Thirties,* p. 76.

dialogue between Hamlet and Rosencrantz and Guildenstern was regularly omitted in Kemble's performances, and the two friends have scarcely been welcomed when Hamlet begins to probe the reason for their visit.[49] Kemble's manner of reading the lines in which Hamlet attempts to get his friends to admit that they were sent for must have been especially effective, and his emphasis here was frequently praised:

Ham. Were you not SENT for? Is it your own inclining? is it a free visitation? Come, come, deal justly with me: come, come; nay, speak.

Guil. What should we say, my lord?

Ham. Anything but to the purpose. You WERE sent for; and there is a kind of confession in your looks. I KNOW the good king and queen have sent for you.

Guil. To what end, my lord?

Ham. That YOU must teach ME.[50]

The famous soliloquy concluding the second act, "O, what a rogue and peasant slave am I," was one which, rather surprisingly, Charles Kemble sometimes cut, leaving

49. The Cumberland edition omits approximately forty-five lines of the opening dialogue between Rosencrantz and Guildenstern and Hamlet. Nine lines after their entrance, Hamlet is asking the two friends, "Were you not sent for?"

50. *Kemble's Shakespere Readings*, I, 74. In general, a similar reading is suggested by Folger 44, and the emphatic words marked by Lane are noted for stress in Folger 44. However, Folger 44 tends to give a more detailed notation of emphasis than Lane. It thus distinguishes between heavy stress and lighter stress, while Lane generally only notes the most emphatic words. In addition to the emphasis noted by Lane in the passage cited, Folger 44 indicates the following stresses: OUR OWN INCLINING . . . FREE visitation . . . ANYthing—but to the urpose . . . CONFESSION in your LOOKS . . . the GOOD KING and UEEN.

only the last eighteen lines.[51] Such an omission, which would have the effect of diminishing any sense of Hamlet's delay and deemphasizing his tendency to introspection, can hardly have found favor with his more romantic viewers. Rice noted, however, that when he did hear him give this speech, it was with "great energy."[52] Lane's record of Kemble's emphatic markings suggests his exploitation here of the contrasting words connoting cowardice and bravery:

> Am I a COWARD?
> . . . for it cannot be
> But I am PIGEON-LIVER'D, and lack GALL
> To make oppression bitter; . . .
> Why, what an ass am I? This is most BRAVE;
> That I, the son of a dear father murder'd
> Prompted to my revenge by heaven and hell,
> Must fall a cursing like a very drab,
> A scullion![53]

On the occasion of the performance at the Park Theatre which Leggett witnessed, Kemble, much to Leggett's dismay, chose to omit this soliloquy and proceeded at once to the passage

> I have heard
> That guilty creatures, sitting at a play,
> Have by the very cunning of the scene
> Been stuck so to the soul, that presently
> They have proclaim'd their malefactions.

Leggett took exception to Kemble's reading of the passage, declaring that he uttered the lines "as if in that moment the

51. Rice, *The London Theatre in the Eighteen Thirties*, p. 76; Leggett, in the New York *Evening Post*, September 18, 1832.

52. Rice, *The London Theatre in the Eighteen Thirties*, p. 76.

53. *Kemble's Shakespere Readings*, I, 79.

idea of the play had *first* arisen, although every arrangement about it had been previously made." Leggett complained: "His asking the players sometime before the soliloquy, if they could play the murder of Gonzago, and study the addition he proposed to make, certainly denotes 'a foregone conclusion.' It therefore appears to us that the mention of his project in the soliloquy afterwards is only a part of the artifice of the poet to explain his view more fully to the audience, and to express the misgiving so characteristic of Hamlet, on which the intended trial is founded. To accomplish this, we look for a different emphasis from that given by Mr. Kemble." [54]

Kemble's performance of the third act, including the interview with Ophelia, the play within the play, and the closet scene with Gertrude, invariably inspired a wide range of comment. In the "To be, or not to be" soliloquy, in addition to the general excellence of elocution, theatregoers found several effects to be noteworthy. One viewer remarked on how Kemble, in making his reference to the "bare bodkin," illustrated his speech by a "contracted nicety of the finger and thumb, as if holding the nominated implement." [55] Another noted with pleasure that the conclusion at which Hamlet arrives, that to die is but to sleep, and then the sudden overturning of his conviction with the words, "To sleep—perchance to dream," "were pourtrayed by an emphasis which completely precluded the possibility of mistaking the meaning of Shakespeare." [56] Kemble's Hamlet apparently was alone on the stage during the major

54. New York *Evening Post*, September 18, 1832.
55. *Hull Dramatic Censor*, February 24, 1827, quoted by A. C. Sprague, *Shakespeare and the Actors*, p. 151.
56. Rice, *The London Theatre in the Eighteen Thirties*, p. 77.

portion of the soliloquy; Ophelia was not present to distract the audience's attention from his speech.[57] After being coached by Polonius where to walk and after receiving her book, Ophelia moved up-stage and retired. She re-entered just before Hamlet's line, "Thus conscience does make cowards of us all," and was first observed by Hamlet as he concluded his soliloquy and remarked, "Soft you, now! The fair Ophelia."[58]

The meeting with Ophelia drew highest praise from most members of Kemble's audience, including Donne, Marston, and perhaps his most judicious critic, his daughter Fanny. Among the New York spectators who found something to criticize in the performance of September 17, however, was again William Leggett. Leggett had to admit that the acting was of the highest order, but his quarrel was with the interpretation which Kemble seemed to give. Leggett felt that Hamlet was never really mad, that here as elsewhere he only counterfeited his "antic disposition"; and he thought that Charles Kemble failed in this scene with Ophelia because he appeared to play it as if Hamlet were genuinely mad. "He seemed to have taken the side of those who imagine Hamlet to be really and permanently mad, and therefore to have thought he might play what pranks he liked," Leggett protested. "Under this conception . . . his manner of giving most of it was admirable. He began in confusion and ended in raving; but softened throughout by a pitying gentleness towards her he loved, which looked

57. Cumberland edition. It might be noted, too, that the King's conscience-stricken aside which follows Polonius's directions to his daughter and immediately precedes Hamlet's entrance here was regularly omitted.

58. Cumberland edition.

somewhat rational. Still, much as we admire Mr. Kemble's skill in expressing his impression, and his policy in, at the same time, so qualifying it as to take away all it involves of the repulsive, we quarrel with the conception."[59] Interestingly, Fanny Kemble, writing in her *Journal* five days before her father's opening in New York, went to great pains to justify the interpretation of Hamlet as mad:

> I am surprised at anybody's ever questioning the real madness of Hamlet: I know but one passage in the play which tells against it, and there are a thousand that go to prove it. But leaving all isolated parts out of the question, the entire colour of the character is the proper ground from which to draw the right deduction. (I, 73)

She went on to note the elements of Hamlet's character, including his gloom, despondency, sorrow, thoughtfulness, uncertainty, and "pulseless" love, and the effect of the strange circumstances upon such a nature. She then concluded: "If these do not make up as complete a madman as ever walked between heaven and earth, I know not what does." There nevertheless remain some doubts about Charles Kemble's intended meaning in the scene with Ophelia. At least in other performances, such as the one praised by the French reviewer who wrote of Kemble's "folie simulée,"[60] Kemble does not appear to have given the impression that he was interpreting Hamlet as actually mad; and many accounts of the scene seem at some variance with Leggett's response. Perhaps the most accurate analysis of Kemble's treatment of Hamlet's madness comes from the critic for the New York *American*, who viewed the same performance as Leggett. He described Kemble's Hamlet as

59. New York *Evening Post*, September 18, 1832.
60. Borgerhoff, *Le Théâtre anglais à Paris*, p. 94.

one who "assumes the madness while actually hovering upon the verge of lunacy."[61]

The qualities which Charles Kemble most clearly emphasized in the encounter of Hamlet with Ophelia were compassion, pity, anguish, despair, tenderness, and conflicting love and distrust. The "passionate anger"[62] with which his brother read the lines evidently did not play a very significant part in his personation. Indeed he seems to have been closer in conception to Kean than to his brother here. Marston illustrated Kemble's complex presentation of distrust striving with love, overcome by it, and reasserting itself, and again overwhelmed, by the simile of an ebb tide. "I will venture to say that this scene vividly suggested to me a shore at ebb-tide," Marston declared, "now bare, now for a moment revisited, even flooded, by the returning wave, which, as it once more recedes, chimes its own plaintive, lingering farewell."[63] Donne noted the "tenderness of voice" with which Charles Kemble delivered "even the harsh and bitter words of reproach and self-scorning," and praised "his forlorn and piteous look" which "seemed labouring to impart the comfort which he could not minister to himself. Every mode or change of expression and intonation came with its own burden of anguish and despair."[64] Fanny Kemble gave witness to the infectious nature of her father's all-pervading grief in the scene with Ophelia. She recorded in her *Journal:*

> I have acted Ophelia three times with my father, and each time, in that beautiful scene where his madness and his love

61. New York *American,* September 18, 1832.
62. A. C. Sprague, *Shakespearian Players and Performances,* p. 49.
63. Marston, *Our Recent Actors,* p. 117.
64. Donne, *Essays on the Drama,* pp. 176–77.

> gush forth together like a torrent swollen with storms, that bears a thousand blossoms on its troubled waters; I have experienced such deep emotion as hardly to be able to speak. The exquisite tenderness of his voice, the wild compassion and forlorn pity of his looks, bestowing that on others, which, above all others, he most needed, the melancholy restlessness, the bitter self-scorning; every shadow of expression and intonation, was so full of all the mingled anguish that the human heart is capable of enduring; that my eyes scarce fixed on his ere they filled with tears; and long before the scene was over, the letters and jewel cases I was tendering to him, were wet with them. . . . O, it made my heart sore to act it. (I, 148–49)

Indeed Kemble's meticulous and formal style at its best seems not to have been without power to command the profoundest emotions in his observers.

It should be noted, finally, that according to Folger 44 the staging of this scene included the traditional business of Hamlet's suddenly catching a glimpse of Polonius and the King eavesdropping, but this discovery came relatively late. At Hamlet's line, "Ha, Ha! are you honest?"—a point where many Hamlets have detected Polonius thrusting forth his head or dropping his staff[65]—directions in Folger 44 read: "Pause, look at jewels, at the time Polonius appears." Apparently the audience, but not Hamlet, saw Polonius here. It is not until later when he suddenly asks, "Where's your father?" that the directions in Folger 44 indicate that Hamlet "perceives King and Polonius." Following this discovery Hamlet seems to have registered his increased agitation in part by a series of sudden exits and reentrances. Ophelia says that her father is at home, and

65. A. C. Sprague, *Shakespeare and the Actors*, p. 152.

Hamlet responds, "Let the doors be shut upon him, that he may play the fool nowhere but in's own house. Farewell," and "runs off L." Then Ophelia's line, "O, help him, you sweet Heavens!" is followed by Hamlet "running back to her" as he cries out: "If thou dost marry, I'll give thee this plague for thy dowry."[66] Concluding this speech with the command, "To a nunnery, go!" Kemble's Hamlet again hastened off, right,[67] and returned moments later to continue his attack: "I have heard of your paintings too, well enough."

The Play Scene lacked, to some extent, the skill and power of the Nunnery Scene, if one can accept the opinion of Westland Marston, who felt it was not given "with all the breadth and fire of which it is capable."[68] Still, it possessed a number of the subtle refinements to which Kemble devoted so much attention. One such refinement elicited the praise of William Leggett, the reviewer who was in so many instances critical of Kemble's performance. As the King, Queen, Ophelia, and the numerous courtiers await the beginning of the play, Hamlet "calls Polonius to him"[69] and proceeds to question the garrulous old counsellor about his experiences as an actor. When Polonius proudly recalls that he "did enact Julius Caesar" and "was killed i' the Capitol" by Brutus, Hamlet's pun, "It was a brute part of him," was broken by Kemble "so as to take off its rudeness." Leggett observed that "Kemble tells Polonius 'it was a brute part,' and then walks away, chuckling to himself over the re-

66. Cumberland edition.

67. The printed stage direction in Cumberland reads, "Hastens off L." Folger 44, however, bears the correction "R. Kemble."

68. Marston, *Our Recent Actors*, p. 117.

69. Folger 44.

mainder of the joke—'to kill so capital a calf there,' affording a trait of character in a lesson of politeness."[70] His delivery of Hamlet's answers to the King and Queen during this scene also reflected the Kemble polish. The undermeanings, Marston noted, "could scarcely have been better conveyed; they were polished, but keen as arrows."[71]

Kemble employed two contemporary items of stage business in the Play Scene, one of which seems a rather unhappy choice. As the players enacted the murder of Gonzago (without the dumb show) on a raised stage, the King and Queen were seated in state chairs, left, with Polonius standing just behind them, while Ophelia and Horatio watched from positions opposite them at stage right.[72] Kemble's Hamlet lay down at Ophelia's feet when he quipped, "Lady, shall I lie in your lap?" Subsequently, like several other eighteenth- and nineteenth-century tragedians, Kemble proceeded to amuse himself with her fan and made skillful use of it in order to hide his close observations of the King.[73] Dumas was so impressed by this when he saw him that he referred to the Play Scene as "la scène de l'éventail."[74] The second and less tasteful piece of business adopted by Kemble was Hamlet's crawling from the feet of Ophelia to the King while the poisoner is pouring the poison into the sleeper's ears and his subsequent ranting into the King's ears:

> He poisons him i' the garden for his estate. His name's Gonzago; the story is extant, and written in very choice

70. New York *Evening Post,* September 18, 1832.
71. Marston, *Our Recent Actors,* p. 117.
72. Cumberland edition.
73. Borgerhoff, *Le Théâtre anglais à Paris,* p. 78.
74. Dumas, *Mes Mémoires,* 10 vols. (Paris, 1894–1900), IV, 280. Cited by Sprague, *Shakespeare and the Actors,* p. 158.

> Italian; you shall see anon, how the murderer gets the love of Gonzago's wife.

James Musgrove, as well as the critic for the *Courrier Français,* lamented this "roulant par terre," which was scarcely appropriate for an otherwise dignified and graceful Prince.[75] It might be added that prior to this moment when he crawled over to the King, Kemble apparently made a practice of repeatedly "rapping the stage with his knuckles," a device which the reviewer for the *American* judged to be "a little mechanical."[76]

Kemble's representation of Hamlet's reaction when the King rushes from the room involved a combination of indignation and grief, rather than the "fierce and ringing tones of exaltation" which Macready employed. The "conflict of indignation with grief," which was "aided by the actor's grace of delivery and princely bearing," is said by Marston to have "captivated rather than excited the house."[77] However, when he saw Kemble in New York, Leggett observed that this was one of the "situations" which was especially applauded "and perhaps seldom so well acted."[78]

Kemble's manner in the subsequent rebuke of the spies, Rosencrantz and Guildenstern, was unsurpassed, Marston felt, by any other actor he had witnessed. He observed that the dignity of the prince was never lost under the weight of the sarcasm. "His sarcasms, though given incisively, were so free from violence, and his disdain had such lofty quietude

75. James Musgrove, quoted by Durang, *The Philadelphia Stage,* chap. 23; *Courrier Français,* quoted by Borgerhoff, *Le Théâtre anglais à Paris,* p. 78.

76. New York *American,* September 18, 1832.

77. Marston, *Our Recent Actors,* p. 117.

78. New York *Evening Post,* September 18, 1832.

and such a suggestion of melancholy at the worldliness and insincerity of men, as to reconcile the displeasure of the Prince with the elevation both of manner and feeling."[79] The critic for the New York *American*, however, perceived a somewhat different aspect to Kemble's performance here. While the dignity of the Prince still remained to some extent beneath the sarcasm and disdain, he detected a new bitterness underlying the "assumed levity" as Hamlet unmasked his treacherous schoolfellows. This critic, indeed, felt that a considerable change in Hamlet's manner and attitude was registered in this scene. He noted that "when the story of his father's wrongs have had time to work their full effect upon his soul" and "above all, when the black development is brought home in all its truth to his mind by the scene of the play, then the Hamlet of the platform becomes a different being. Except so far as his mother is concerned, he feels a bitter joy in the task he before had shrunk from, and even revels in his assumed levity when they would 'fool him to the top of his bent.' "[80] Kemble's technique of emphasizing the word *you* in order to make a distinction between characters was witnessed again in this Recorder's Scene. After Rosencrantz declares that he is unable to play upon the pipe, Kemble's Hamlet addressed his next line to Guildenstern, saying: "I do beseech YOU."[81] A final Kemble touch here, one which Leggett singled out for comment, was the utterance of a bitter laugh in dismissing Rosencrantz and Guildenstern. Exclaiming, "Leave me,—friends," he mixed it with the last word. Leggett found it "new and effective" and noted that it "takes off the

79. Marston, *Our Recent Actors*, p. 117–118.
80. New York *American*, September 18, 1832.
81. *Kemble's Shakespere Readings*, I, 89.

impolicy of forgetting the mask of courtesy he has worn so long and so warily, by the usual expression of contempt and disgust."[82]

An extremely brief scene in which the King directs Rosencrantz and Guildenstern to convey Hamlet to England and Polonius reports that he is on his way to the Queen's chamber regularly preceded the Closet Scene in Kemble's performances. The King's soliloquy and vain attempt to pray and Hamlet's speech upon seeing the kneeling King were generally omitted.[83] In the Closet Scene with Gertrude, as in the scene of his first encounter with the Ghost, Kemble stressed filial affection—this time for his mother as well as his father. James Musgrove remarked that he was "earnest and impassioned, without going too far; and what we never observed in any other Hamlet, constantly made us remember that filial affection and duty were the feelings that controlled and guided all his designs and acts."[84] Marston indeed thought that Kemble somewhat overemphasized the gentleness of Hamlet's nature here: "Grief and filial tenderness prevailed, perhaps unduly, over the sternness which, however restrained, should still, I think, be in the ascendant."[85]

The staging of the Closet Scene as suggested by notations in Folger 44, by the printed directions in the Cumberland acting edition, and by the comments of reviewers of course proves interesting. Hamlet enters his mother's

82. New York *Evening Post,* September 18, 1832.

83. Cumberland edition. The two moments of conscience-stricken confession by Claudius (here and III. i) were thus deleted.

84. Musgrove, quoted by Durang, *The Philadelphia Stage,* chap. 23.

85. Marston, *Our Recent Actors,* p. 118.

closet from the right with "sword on and picture" just after Polonius "conceals himself behind the arras, L.S.E."[86] He begins to upbraid the Queen; and when she declares, "Nay, then I'll set those to you that can speak," and apparently starts to walk away from him, "Hamlet stops her."[87] When presently the Queen becomes frightened and calls for help, Polonius's echo from behind, "What ho! help!" is followed by a curious direction for Hamlet in Folger 44: "Pause a little, as surprised, then assume the pretended madness." Hamlet of course draws and stabs Polonius. The Cumberland edition (c. 1829), which lists Charles Kemble as Hamlet, indicates simply that "Hamlet draws, and makes a pass through the arras"; and Polonius, after crying out, "Oh! Oh! Oh!" "falls and dies, L." Folger 44, however, bears a note which suggests that Hamlet draws and "goes off LH 2nd E," and then enters again, no doubt shaken, as he replies, "Nay, I know not," to the Queen's anxious question, "What hast thou done?" Subsequently, Folger 44 indicates that Hamlet once more "goes off L," presumably to determine whom he has killed, while the Cumberland text carries the stage direction: "Takes a candle, lifts up the arras, and sees Polonius." Whatever procedure Kemble's Hamlet followed here, he clearly seated himself shortly afterward, as did the Queen.[88] Upon sighting the Ghost, Kemble's Hamlet was momentarily overcome by fear. Leggett observed that Kemble was much applauded when he sprang

86. The phrase *sword on and picture* is in a notation inserted in Folger 44; the direction "conceals himself behind the arras, L.S.E." is a printed stage direction in Cumberland edition.

87. Folger 44.

88. Leggett, in the New York *Evening Post*, September 18, 1832; Cumberland edition; Folger 44.

from his chair and stood "petrified in the presence of the Ghost," exclaiming,

> Save me, and hover o'er me with your wings,
> You heavenly guards![89]

The filial affection so evident earlier on the platform soon reappeared, however, and Folger 44 suggests that Hamlet kneels before his father's spirit, while the Queen stares at him with her back to the Ghost. After the Ghost has delivered his message, Hamlet rises and becomes concerned about his mother's strange response. The Ghost "steals away" through a left stage door, and Hamlet turns to the Queen to implore her to

> Lay not that flattering unction to your soul,
> That not your tresspass, but my madness, speaks.

When the Queen tells her son that he has "cleft [her] heart in twain," he "slightly advances" to her, after cautioning her to "throw away the worser part of it." But Folger 44 also suggests that when he bids his mother good night, it is with considerable reserve. As Hamlet says, "So, again, good night!" the Queen "appears desirous to embrace, he in action coldly refuses."[90] The Queen then exits right, and Hamlet, uttering the couplet,

> I must be cruel, only to be kind:
> Thus bad begins, and worse remains behind,

departs in the opposite direction.[91]

89. New York *Evening Post,* September 18, 1832.

90. Folger 44.

91. Cumberland edition. Hamlet's very harsh final speech of advice to the Queen in which he warns her not to "let the bloat King tempt you again to bed," as well as any efforts on his part to dispose of Polonius's body, to "lug the guts into the neighbour room," were thus omitted.

Charles Kemble apparently found particularly good opportunities to assert his elocutionary skill in the "noble passages with which this scene abounds." One can almost imagine the actor with the "elocution so finished that its art seemed nature"[92] glorying in such distinctions as occur in Hamlet's displaying the pictures:

> This WAS your husband.—Look you now what follows:
> Here IS your husband; like a mildew'd ear,
> Blasting his wholesome brother;

or in his cautioning his mother:

> ASSUME a virtue, if you HAVE it not.[93]

While his reading throughout the scene was generally commended, Kemble's employment of a bitter laugh after the stabbing of Polonius drew at least one rebuke. Leggett, who had praised the scornful laughter used earlier in the dismissal of the two spies, found it inappropriate here. "His sly chuckle in asking his mother 'Is it the King?' after he had slain Polonius, was a failure," the *Post* critic judged.[94]

The Churchyard Scene appears to have made a varying impression on Kemble's critics.[95] After the Gravediggers have entertained the audience with their initial gossip and antics, Hamlet and Horatio enter and "stand behind the grave, C." The First Gravedigger "sings while digging," tosses up numerous skulls and bones, and answers Hamlet's

92. Marston, *Our Recent Actors*, p. 118.
93. *Kemble's Shakespere Readings*, I, 94, 96; Folger 44.
94. New York *Evening Post*, September 18, 1832.
95. Act IV, it should be noted, was frequently cut sharply in early-nineteenth-century productions of *Hamlet*. The scene of Hamlet's encounter with Fortinbras (IV. iv) apparently was always omitted in Kemble's performances. It might be added that there was no mention of Fortinbras in Act I, and he did not appear at the end of the play.

queries with equivocations.[96] Marston observed nevertheless a feeling of tender beauty in the scene and noted that the interchanges with the Gravediggers were characterized by a "vein of wandering reverie" as Kemble "followed the quaint, half-humorous speculations of the part with such nice perception as never to disturb the prevailing gravity which they relieved."[97] The First Gravedigger finally unearths the skull of Yorick. He "pats the skull with his hand" as he remembers how the king's jester "poured a flagon of Rhenish on my head once" and then "gives the skull up to Hamlet R. at the end of the grave."[98] "This?" Hamlet questions as he points at the skull. At "Alas! poor Yorick," a note in Folger 44 cautions Hamlet: "Don't stir until you repeat the line 'Alas' etc., then advance C, a tear of sorrow." Folger 44 then indicates that as Hamlet recalls, "Here hung those lips that I have kissed I know not how oft," he "looks at skull"; and when he asks Horatio whether he thinks Alexander "looked o' this fashion i' the earth," he "holds the skull with the LH extended." Horatio says, "E'en so," and Hamlet gives the skull to Horatio after exclaiming, "And smelt so? pah."[99] When he saw Kemble at Covent Garden in 1836, Rice thought the only weakness in the scene was a poor reading of the speech that follows, in which Hamlet traces "the noble dust of Alexander" until he finds it "stopping a bung-hole." Here, he declared, Kemble was "very monotonous."[100]

Considerable tolling of a bell seems to have preceded and

96. Cumberland edition.
97. Marston, *Our Recent Actors,* p. 118.
98. Cumberland edition.
99. Folger 44.
100. Rice, *The London Theatre in the Eighteen Thirties,* p. 77.

accompanied the entrance of a rather extensive funeral procession, complete with lords, ladies, and priests, in Kemble's performances.[101] The Cumberland edition indicates that "attendants, with torches, stand up the L. side of the stage. King and Queen stand C. beyond the grave. Priest at the R. end. 1 Gravedigger at the L. end." Horatio and Hamlet have retired, right; and Hamlet appears "surprised" as he recognizes Laertes, who is at stage left.[102] Even greater surprise, of course, must come when he perceives that the grave is for "the fair Ophelia." The Queen scatters her flowers, and Laertes "leaps into the grave."[103] At this point Marston recalled that Kemble "lacked the overmastering impulse of Macready."[104] Apparently he followed his brother in avoiding the melodramatic leap into the grave to lay hands upon Laertes. Instead, it seems, Laertes leaped out of the grave to grapple with Hamlet.[105] Interestingly, Musgrove, who saw Kemble in Philadelphia, felt that the best passage of the play, one in which he "could not detect a fault" and in which he "could note more beauties than we now have space to set down," occurred here at the grave's edge. "The single speech 'I loved Ophelia' etc. would have sufficed to prove him a tragedian of extraordinary feeling, taste and intellect," Musgrove thought. "And who could fail to remark the mode in which, without any apparent

101. The Cumberland edition indicates that the bell tolled three times during Hamlet's speech on Alexander and the subsequent entrance of the procession; Folger 44 calls for six tollings of the bell.

102. Folger 44.

103. Cumberland edition.

104. Marston, *Our Recent Actors*, p. 118.

105. The stage direction in the Cumberland edition reads, "Leaping out of the grave, and grappling with him" after Laertes's line, "The devil take thy soul!"

effort, he gave an emphasis to the word 'brothers' [I loved Ophelia; forty thousand BROTHERS / Could not, with all their quantity of love, / Make up my sum] which made that inimitable passage tell with tenfold effect upon the hearts of those who are accustomed to read Shakespeare with devotion."[106]

Kemble never let his audience down in the final moments of the play, if one may judge by the remarks of playgoers Marston, Rice, and Musgrove. He particularly excelled in the banter with the fawning Osric, which usually constituted a brief but separate scene just before the fencing match.[107] Not only was Kemble proficient in "the display of graceful melancholy," but also "in the art of enhancing its effect by momentary reliefs of fancy"; and the excellence of "his manner of rallying from weighty cares to accommodate himself to the fantastic levities of Osric" won special applause.[108] In the final scene trumpets sounded as the curtain rose to reveal the King and Queen seated, up stage center, flanked by various guards and courtiers on their left and right.[109] Hamlet and Horatio enter and, according to Folger 44, there is a "flourish till Hamlet bows." Hamlet asks Laertes's pardon, Laertes accepts his "offer'd love," Osric provides the foils, the King calls for the cups and drinks to Hamlet, "Drums and Trumpets sound—Cannons shot off within,"[110] and finally the "brother's wager"

106. Musgrove, quoted by Durang, *The Philadelphia Stage,* chap. 23.

107. Cumberland edition.

108. Marston, *Our Recent Actors,* p. 119.

109. A diagram in Folger 44 illustrates the arrangement for the opening of this scene. The printed directions in the Cumberland edition suggest a similar staging.

110. Cumberland edition.

begins. In the fencing match Kemble's grace and skill invariably earned him acclaim. Marston, especially, commended him here for his "gentle bearing" in the match with Laertes—"the smiling, subdued grace of one only conscious of 'the yoke of inauspicious stars.'"[111] The pace of the action increases. The Queen drinks from the poisoned cup, Laertes wounds Hamlet, and "while struggling, they exchange rapiers." Hamlet wounds Laertes, the Queen swoons and is led off, and ultimately Hamlet "stabs the King on the throne."[112] Throughout all this action Kemble won Rice's praise for his "elegant acting" and Musgrove's admiration for the manner in which he "acted feelingly and earnestly, without rant."[113] Finally, denying Horatio the privilege of the "antique Roman," Hamlet implores his friend to tell his story. Hamlet exclaims:

> Oh! I die Horatio!—
> The potent poison quite o'erthrows my spirit—
> The rest is silence.

The rest was silence in Kemble's performances. There was a brief pause in which the audience received a final glimpse of Hamlet, and then the curtain descended.[114] Westland Marston was only one of many who long remembered "the tender beauty" of Kemble's "dying—fitly and softly led to the sleep which 'rounded' his princely life."[115]

There seems little doubt that in Hamlet, Charles Kemble found the one leading role in tragedy for which his talents

111. Marston, *Our Recent Actors,* p. 119.
112. Cumberland edition.
113. Rice, *The London Theatre in the Eighteen Thirties,* p. 77; Musgrove, quoted by Durang, *The Philadelphia Stage,* chap. 23.
114. Folger 44.
115. Marston, *Our Recent Actors,* p. 119.

seemed completely suited, the one major role in which he could at least match, if not exceed, the perfection which characterized so many of his secondary parts. One can see, indeed, a legitimate basis for James Boaden's appraisal, "It is now I believe clear that his Hamlet never ought to have yielded unless to his brother's,"[116] even if one disagrees. The fact that the judicious Fanny Kemble, who was by no means blind to her father's weaknesses, could remark: "I think that it is impossible to conceive Hamlet more truly, or execute it more exquisitely than he does,"[117] says a good deal for Charles Kemble's ability in the part, as does the concession by the basically hostile critic William Leggett, who admitted of Kemble's New York performance: "If he did not express *our* conception of Hamlet, he expressed his own with great ability. . . . We doubt if our stage has ever before witnessed so fine a picture of unaffected courtliness; of the gallant and finished gentleman."[118]

Mercutio

William Macready called Charles Kemble "a first-rate actor in second-rate parts."[119] The judgment of this temperamental tragedian could scarcely be termed impartial; still, taken in the strictest sense, his appraisal is one with which both Kemble's critics and his admirers could agree. Many of his critics felt that Kemble was never really a first-rate actor in leading roles, at least in tragedy; his

116. James Boaden, *Memoirs of Mrs. Siddons* (Philadelphia, 1893), p. 415.

117. Butler, *Journal*, I, 94.

118. New York *Evening Post*, September 18, 1832.

119. W. C. Macready, *Reminiscences and Selections from His Diaries and Letters*, ed. Frederick Pollock (New York, 1875), p. 57.

admirers, however, would argue that certainly his Hamlet and his Romeo were among the best. But praise of his achievements in secondary parts was nearly unanimous.

Among his secondary roles Mercutio was one of his finest. It was the favorite of many of his viewers. That avid playgoer Charles Rice, who was inexhaustible in his praise of Kemble's Hamlet, gave the edge to his Mercutio. "Although Mr. Kemble's Hamlet ranks very high in my estimation," Rice declared, "I must give the palm of supremacy to his Mercutio."[120] The American actor Charles Durang, writing of Kemble's eighteen-night engagement in Philadelphia in the fall of 1832, proclaimed: "Mr. C. Kemble's Mercutio crowned his fame; it was deemed even richer and more highly wrought than his Benedick, excellent as that performance was. It was called by all the *ne plus ultra* of high comedy."[121]

Both Durang and another actor, Francis Courtney Wemyss,[122] gave vivid accounts of the success of Charles Kemble's November 3 performance in Philadelphia, which was the first time he played the part in America. Durang wrote: "It was the topic of conversation throughout the city the next morning. 'Did you see Kemble's Mercutio last night?' 'You lost a treat.' 'We had no conception of the character before,' and so went the gossip."[123]

Kemble indeed had won similar acclaim as Mercutio from the time of his first appearance in the part on October 5, 1829, at Covent Garden, which was the occasion of his

120. Rice, *The London Theatre in the Eighteen Thirties,* p. 79.
121. Durang, *The Philadelphia Stage,* chap. 24.
122. Francis Courtney Wemyss, *Twenty-Six Years of the Life of an Actor and Manager* (New York, 1847), I, 211.
123. Durang, *The Philadelphia Stage,* chap. 24.

daughter Fanny's stage debut. By this date, of course, he had long been playing leading roles in tragedy and had achieved great success as Romeo. But for his daughter's opening night he chose a second part, that of Mercutio. Walter Lacy recalled with pleasure how "the matchless Romeo, after taking the dying hand of so many Mercutio's from the 'Starry Lewis' to 'Gentleman Jones' first taught the town how the part should be performed, when his famous daughter Fanny . . . made her debut as Juliet."[124] Fanny Kemble, always a keen critic, immediately perceived her father's excellence in the new role. She noted later in her *Records of a Girlhood:*

> My father not acting Romeo with me deprived me of the most poetical and graceful stage lover of his day; but the public, who had long been familiar with his rendering of the part of Romeo, gained as much as I lost, by his taking that of Mercutio, which has never since been so admirably represented, and I dare affirm will never be given more perfectly. The graceful ease, and airy sparkling brilliancy of his delivery of the witty fancies of that merry gentleman, the gallant defiance of his bearing towards the enemies of his house, and his heroically pathetic and humorous death-scene, were beyond description charming. He was one of the best Romeos, and incomparably *the* best Mercutio, that ever trod the English stage.[125]

Leigh Hunt, upon viewing the personations of father and daughter, was disappointed in Fanny's Juliet, but he too saw the fineness of Charles Kemble's portrayal: "The best performance in this piece is decidedly Mr. Charles Kemble's

124. Walter Lacy, "Old and Young Stagers," *The Green Room,* ed. Clement Scott (London, n.d.), p. 52.

125. Kemble, *Records of a Girlhood,* II, 16–17.

Mercutio."[126] One feature which especially impressed him was the actor's "abundance of vivacity."

After 1829, whenever he appeared with his daughter Fanny, Charles Kemble played Mercutio rather than Romeo, with the exception of a few performances in the United States; and his excellence in the role continued throughout the remainder of his acting career. Significantly, Mercutio was among the characters undertaken by him when he temporarily returned to the stage in 1840 at the request of Queen Victoria. Walter Lacy recorded an anecdote concerning this command performance which suggests the esteem which the actor earned in the part. "The night 'that gallant spirit had aspired the clouds,' Charles Mathews rushed into the cozy Garrick Club in King Street, and addressing that old and respected member Mr. Francis Fladgate, exclaimed, 'Oh! My dear Frank, I've had such an escape! I was going to play Mercutio myself, and I've just seen Charles Kemble play it! What an escape I've had!'"[127]

Charles Rice saw Charles Kemble in *Romeo and Juliet* at Covent Garden, December 17, 1836, and declared his Mercutio to be unique.[128] From a careful piecing together of the comments of such perceptive observers as Leigh Hunt, William Bodham Donne, George Vandenhoff, Westland Marston, and Rice himself, it is possible to develop a fairly clear impression of Kemble's personation of Romeo's lively friend and, consequently, to gain some idea what was meant by Rice's use of the word *unique*.

Kemble's Mercutio was, first of all, a spirited character of

126. Leigh Hunt, *Dramatic Essays*, ed. William Archer and Robert Lowe (London, 1894), p. 151.

127. Lacy, *The Green Room*, p. 51.

128. Rice, *The London Theatre in the Eighteen Thirties*, p. 78.

high comedy. The *Gentleman's Magazine,* in an article published shortly after Charles Kemble's death, reviewed the contributions of the veteran performer and emphasized that he "restored Petruchio and Mercutio from the region of bullies and fops to that of high comedy."[129] It had not been uncommon to present Mercutio as essentially a blustering bully or fop or rake, full of enmity and possessing a propensity for merciless ridicule. But this was not Kemble's conception. The general impression conveyed by his personation was of a "gallant, courtly, soldier-like high gentleman."[130] Donne suggested that Kemble "restored Mercutio to his proper position as a humorous, high-minded, and chivalrous gentleman, such as in its most palmy days maintained the honour of Verona, and figured in Titian's pictures, or in Villani's pages."[131] Leigh Hunt, speaking generally of Charles Kemble's talents as a comedian, once noted that when he "acts comedy, he gives you the idea of an actor who has come out of the chivalrous part of tragedy. It is grace and show that are most natural to him."[132] In the case of Mercutio this air of the chivalrous gentleman was, indeed, an integral part of the interpretation. Chivalry combined with a playful humor, an overflow of animal spirits, and a keen, restless enjoyment of life in the Mercutio which so captivated Charles Kemble's London and American audiences.[133]

Westland Marston, who saw Kemble as Mercutio in his

129. *Gentleman's Magazine,* January 1855.
130. George Vandenhoff, *Leaves from an Actor's Notebook* (New York, 1860), p. 60.
131. Donne, *Essays on the Drama,* p. 178.
132. Hunt, *Dramatic Essays,* p. 216.
133. Vandenhoff, *An Actor's Notebook,* p. 60.

last stage appearance in the role, a performance which included James Anderson as Romeo and Miss Emmeline Montague as Juliet, noted that the spontaneity of his Mercutio was what first struck the audience. "The art that conceals art had done its work to perfection," he observed. "Besides that ease and distinction which set him apart, even from actors conventionally graceful and spirited, there was in Kemble that freshness which arises when an actor seems to speak from the impulse of the moment, and when his utterances are apparently as fresh to himself as the listener."[134] This impression of freshness or spontaneity was the key to his excellence in his first long speech, the fanciful description of Queen Mab. His recitation of the Queen Mab passage was, without doubt, one of the high points in his performance. The actor George Vandenhoff, who was once fortunate enough to have Kemble read the lines for him on a chance meeting in the Green Room, testified that his delivery of this passage alone made him undisputed master of the part.[135]

The first line,

> Oh, then I see, Queen Mab hath been with you,

Marston claimed, "was uttered without a touch of formal rhetoric or *pose*—by no means as a prelude to a set description, but as a simple, whimsical thought springing from mere buoyancy of heart,"[136] which suggests that Kemble, although noted for his formal style, was not without ability to win praise for naturalness. "The thought uttered,"

134. Marston, *Our Recent Actors,* p. 121.
135. Vandenhoff, *An Actor's Notebook,* p. 62.
136. Marston, *Our Recent Actors,* p. 122.

Marston continued, "you saw that it gave birth to another equally unpremeditated—

> She is the fairies' midwife, and she comes
> In shape no bigger than an agate stone;

until, pursuing the image, he had described her journey—

> Athwart men's noses as they lie asleep.

Then came another sudden burst of fancy, born of the first, gaining fresh strength and impetus in its course, till the speaker abandoned himself to the brilliant and thronging illustrations which, amidst all their rapidity and fire, never lost the simple and spontaneous grace of nature in which they took rise." Charles Rice had been struck, too, by the Queen Mab lines when he had heard them four years earlier and had called Kemble's presentation "one of the finest pieces of elocution the stage can boast."[137]

The Queen Mab speech, it should be remarked, regularly occurred in the third scene of the first act in the early-nineteenth-century productions of *Romeo and Juliet* in which Charles Kemble appeared. In these productions there were some rather notable manipulations of Shakespeare's text in Act I, with respect to both scene divisions and the assignment of speeches.[138] The first scene customarily

137. Rice, *The London Theatre in the Eighteen Thirties*, p. 78.

138. Cumberland's acting edition of *Romeo and Juliet*, which professes to print the play "as now performed" and which lists the Covent Garden cast of June 6, 1831, including Charles Kemble as Mercutio and Fanny Kemble as Juliet, shows the manipulations of Shakespeare's text referred to here and in the following discussion. John Kemble's acting edition of 1811 is identical to Cumberland's in the arrangement of the first act, which indicates that these changes in the text originated before Charles Kemble took over the part of Mercutio. (In 1811 Charles Kemble regularly played Romeo.) Indeed many of the changes go back to Garrick's alteration.

ended with the conversation between Benvolio and old Montague, which follows the exit of the Prince and the various participants and spectators at the brawl. Romeo's entrance was postponed until the third scene, and the opening scene concluded with Benvolio telling Montague that he and Mercutio, who were "most near" to Romeo, would "attempt upon his privacy" and endeavor to discover "from whence his sorrows grow." The second scene consisted solely of a brief conversation between Capulet and Paris. In the third scene, set in "a wood near Verona,"[139] the audience finally met Romeo (who was lovesick for Juliet, not Rosaline), as well as his witty friend Mercutio. The dialogue for this scene combined speeches from the latter parts of scenes i, ii, and iv in Shakespeare's text. The fourth scene consisted of the conversation between Lady Capulet, Juliet, and the Nurse; the fifth was the feast at Capulet's.

In general, the effect of the various manipulations in the acting text was to increase Mercutio's part, while condensing the act as a whole. In the script used in Kemble's performances the first meeting and conversation between Romeo and Benvolio (which occurs in Act I, scene i, in Shakespeare's text) becomes a conversation between Benvolio, Romeo, *and* Mercutio. Indeed it is Mercutio, gaily dressed in "scarlet jacket and panteloons embroidered, russet boots, round black hat, and white plumes,"[140] who first sees Romeo as he "crosses through the Wood," and who declares to Benvolio:

139. The Cumberland edition thus describes the location for scene iii.

140. Mercutio's costume is thus described in the Cumberland edition.

See, where he steals.—Told I you not, Benvolio,
That we should find this melancholy Cupid
Lock'd in some gloomy covert, under key
Of cautionary silence, with his arms
Threaded, like these cross boughs, in sorrow's knot?[141]

A few lines later it is again Mercutio who pursues the conversation as he draws near the unhappy lover:

Tell me, in sadness, who she is you love.
Rom. In sadness, then, I love a woman.
Mer. I aim'd so near, when I supposed you loved.

When Romeo confesses that "'tis a hopeless love," Mercutio offers his friend advice:

Be ruled by me; forget to think of her.
Rom. O, teach me how I should forget to think.
Mer. By giving liberty unto thine eyes:
Take some new infection to thy heart.
And the rank poison of the old will die:
Examine other beauties.

After Romeo protests, "Thou canst not teach me to forget," and moves away from his adviser, Mercutio continues by appropriating a number of Benvolio's lines from Act I, scene ii:

I warrant thee; if thou'lt but stay to hear.
To-night there is an ancient splendid feast
Kept by old Capulet, our enemy,
Where all the beauties of Verona meet.
Rom. At Capulet's?

141. Quotations from *Romeo and Juliet* are from the Cumberland edition (Covent Garden cast of June 6, 1831, with Charles Kemble as Mercutio) unless otherwise noted.

Mer. At Capulet's, my friend:
Go there; and, with an unattainted eye,
Compare her face with some that I shall show,
And I will make thee think thy swan a crow.

Rom. When the devout religion of mine eyes
Maintains such falsehood, then turn tears to fires,
And burn the hereticks! All-seeing Phoebus
Ne'er saw her match, since first his course began.

Mer. Tut, tut, you saw her fair, none else being by,
Herself poised with herself; but let be weigh'd
Your lady-love against some other fair
And she will show scant well.

Rom. I will along, Mercutio.

However, in this scrambled version Romeo suddenly changes his mind and declares, "I will not go to-night." Such a textual manipulation permits a quick shift to passages from Act I, scene iv, and sets up the Queen Mab speech. To Romeo's refusal Mercutio inquires:

Why, may one ask?

Rom. I dreamt a dream to-night.

Mer. Ha! ha! a dream?
O, then, I see, queen Mab hath been with you.

Later, in the scene at Capulet's feast, Mercutio, who is silent in Shakespeare's script, once again borrows lines, this time from Romeo rather than Benvolio. Since Romeo already loves Juliet and knows her to be a Capulet when he arrives at the festivities, Mercutio is the one who asks the Nurse, "What is her mother?" and who subsequently offers the startled query, "Is she a Capulet?" to her reply. The result of all these changes is, of course, to give added importance to the figure of Mercutio. The increase in his lines, combined with the compression of the first act as a whole, makes him a central figure in the early part of the play. It is interesting to note that a text which similarly emphasizes the character of Mercutio was used by Kemble in his public readings, where indeed he "played" all the parts.[142]

Kemble's Mercutio of the second act was a young man whose "overflow of life, with its keen restless enjoyment, was embodied with infectious spirit."[143] The lines omitted in the Covent Garden performances suggest, further, that Kemble played down Mercutio's propensity for bawdy repartee. In the first scene, for example, in which Mercutio and Benvolio search for Romeo in "an open Place, adjoining Capulet's Garden,"[144] the pun about the "medlar tree" is excluded. After Benvolio's remark, "Blind is his love, and best befits the dark," Mercutio simply concludes with:

> Romeo, good night!—I'll to my truckle-bed,
> This field-bed is too cold for me to sleep!
> Come, shall we go?

Mercutio's mimicries of Tybalt and the fops and his encounter with the Nurse and Peter in the fourth scene were, of course, the highlights of the act. Here the irrepressible wit of Kemble's Mercutio was particularly evident. It was consistently a playful wit, however, never a bitter or scornful one. Marston observed that whenever Kemble's Mercutio was "betrayed into the indulgence of ridicule, it

142. *Kemble's Shakespere Readings*, II, 367 ff.
143. Marston, *Our Recent Actors*, p. 122.
144. The Cumberland edition thus describes the location for Act II, scene i.

was the spirit of mirthful humour that overcame him."[145] He emphasized that there was no gall in his makeup.

Leigh Hunt, like Marston, especially delighted in the take-off on the fops. Kemble's "*pardonnez moi* seemed at once a joke on the coxcombry it nicknamed, and a kick into the bargain," he declared.[146] R. J. Lane's notations of Kemble's accents and pronunciations in his Willis's Rooms readings show some of the refinements which characterized his delivery of this passage in those performances:

> O! he is the courageous captain of compliments. He fights as you sing prick-song, keeps time, distance, and proportion; rests me his minim rest, one, two, and a third in your bosom: the very butcher of a silk button, a DUELLIST, a duellist; a gentleman of the very first house,—of the first and second cause; Ah, the immortal passado! the punto reverso! the hai!
>
> *Ben.* The what?
>
> *Mer.* The plague of such antick, lisping, affecting fantasticoes; these new tuners of accents! A VERY GOOD BLADE! A VERY TALL MAN! A VERY GOOD WENCH! Why, is not this a lamentable thing, grandsire, that we should be thus AFFLICTED with these strange flies, these fashion-mongers, these PARDONNEZ MOYS?[147]

With the appearance of Romeo, Mercutio continues his merriment:

> Signior Romeo, BON JOUR! there's a FRENCH salutation for you.

145. Marston, *Our Recent Actors*, p. 122.
146. Hunt, *Dramatic Essays*, p. 151.
147. *Kemble's Shakespere Readings*, II, 389.

The Lane edition interestingly suggests that Mercutio kisses Romeo after this emphatic BON JOUR.

After a lively greeting of his friend, Mercutio takes Romeo's arm[148] and teasingly chides him for giving his companions "the counterfeit fairly last night"; but he finds little opportunity to pursue his raillery before the arrival of the Nurse and Peter. The texts used by Kemble in his stage performances and in his public readings skip quickly from Mercutio's greeting of Romeo to the entrance of the Nurse and Peter, omitting the ribald exchanges between Romeo and Mercutio. The effect, no doubt, was to minimize the coarser side of Mercutio's character; but, unhappily, much of the flavor of his wit must have been sacrificed. Subsequently in the brief conversation with the Nurse, Kemble's gallant and courtly humorist carefully avoided giving any impression of cruelty or bitterness in his jesting. In his reply to the Nurse's request that Peter give her her fan, for example, Mercutio said only, "Do, good Peter, to hide her face," omitting the harsher jibe, "for her fan's the fairer face." Marston particularly noted this lack of harshness and remarked: "I have seen Mercutio derisively cruel in their banter of the Nurse. With Charles Kemble it was the sport of the encounter that drew him on. He assumed a grave, though somewhat exaggerated, courtesy towards the 'ancient lady,' as if to mask his ridicule from her, while enhancing it towards his comrades. It was only as the jest wore to its close that his enjoyment overmastered him, and showed him as a 'saucy merchant' to the offended domestic."[149] Several of Mercutio's cruder witicisms at the Nurse's expense were excluded, including the "hare song,"

148. Cumberland edition.
149. Marston, *Our Recent Actors*, p. 123.

but Romeo's playful kinsman built up to a fairly "saucy" exit. He departed here mimicking the Nurse and her earlier call for her fan:[150]

> Farewell, ancient lady.—Peter, my fan.—Farewell, lady.

Fanny Kemble, in speaking of Mercutio's final scene, called it a "heroically pathetic and humorous death-scene."[151] Charles Kemble seems to have mastered well this mixture of pathos and humor in his portrayal. His chivalrous Mercutio, it should first be noted, was initially led into the duel of words with Tybalt "even more by the love of excitement than by enmity."[152] Strong anger was not conveyed in his reply to Tybalt's "A word with one of you":

> And BUT one WORD with one of us? Couple it with something; make it a word and a BLOW.[153]

Mercutio's eagerness for an exchange with this "villain that fights by the book of arithmetic" mounts as Tybalt suggests that he "consort'st with Romeo":

> CONSORT! what, dost thou make us minstrels? an thou make minstrels of us, look to hear nothing but DISCORDS: here's my fiddlestick; here's that shall make you dance. 'Zounds, CONSORT![154]

With this speech Mercutio is already "laying his hand on his sword," but Benvolio dissuades him from drawing and the encounter is temporarily averted. When Tybalt spies Romeo

150. Cumberland edition.
151. Kemble, *Records of a Girlhood,* II, 17.
152. Marston, *Our Recent Actors,* p. 122.
153. *Kemble's Shakespere Readings,* II, 396.
154. *Ibid.*

and remarks to Mercutio and Benvolio, "Well, peace be with you, sirs,—here comes my man," Mercutio indeed "retires up the stage" as he quips, "But I'll be hanged, sir, if he wear your livery."[155] Here Mercutio watches the conversation that ensues and receives the crowning provocation for the duel when he imagines Romeo's honor has been wounded by "dishonourable, vile submission." At this point a complete change of attitude was suddenly suggested in Kemble's personation. How startling was his change of tone, Marston observed, "after he deemed Romeo disgraced by his forbearance with Tybalt!" He displayed "no more the reckless light-hearted aptness for the stimulant of quarrel, but the stern swift scorn, the lightning-like retaliation of one whose heart has been pierced, whose person and cause have been humiliated in his friend."[156] As this scene was staged in Kemble's performances, both Romeo and Tybalt leave the stage, going their separate ways, whereupon Mercutio comes forward proclaiming: "O calm, dishonourable, vile submission." He then draws his sword and cries out to Tybalt to get him back:

> Ha! *la stocatta* carries it away—Tybalt!—you rat-catcher!

Tybalt immediately returns, and Romeo reenters just as Tybalt, drawing, declares: "I am for you sir."[157] "Scarcely has Tybalt parried [Mercutio's] furious thrust, when Romeo's intervention gives him his chance, and Mercutio has his mortal wound. 'I am hurt,' he exclaims, at first scarcely realizing his disaster; then, feeling its deadly effect,

> A plague o' both your houses!—I am sped:

155. Cumberland edition.
156. Marston, *Our Recent Actors*, pp. 123–24.
157. Cumberland edition.

Charles Kemble as Hamlet

From an engraving by R. J. Lane. Courtesy of the Folger Shakespeare Library.

Charles Kemble as Mercutio

From an engraving by R. J. Lane. Courtesy of the Folger Shakespeare Library.

Fanny Kemble

After a painting by Thomas Lawrence. Courtesy of the Harvard Theatre Collection.

47

Theatre Royal, Covent Garden,

This present MONDAY, 24*th* NOVEMBER, 1823,

Will be revived, *Shakspeare's* Tragedy of

KING JOHN

With an Attention to COSTUME

never before equalled on the English Stage. Every Character will appear in the precise

HABIT OF THE PERIOD:

The whole of the Dresses and Decorations being executed from indisputable authorities, such as

Monumental Effigies, Seals, illuminated MSS., &c.

The Dresses by Mr. PALMER, Miss EGAN, and Assistants.

The BANNERS, SHIELDS, and other Properties, by Mess. BRADWELL and SON, &c.

King John, Mr. YOUNG,

Prince Henry, Master C. PARSLOE, Earl of Pembroke, Mr. MEARS.
Earl of Essex, Mr. HORREBOW, Earl of Salisbury, Mr. CONNOR.
Hubert, Mr. BENNETT,
Faulconbridge, Mr. C. KEMBLE,
Robert Faulconbridge, Mr. PARSLOE, English Herald, Mr. LEY,
James Gurney, Mr. AUSTIN, Executioner, Mr. NORRIS,
Philip, King of France, Mr. EGERTON,
Lewis, the Dauphin, Mr. ABBOTT
Prince Arthur, Master HOLL, *(his first appearance on the stage)*
Archduke of Austria, Mr. COMER,
Cardinal Pandulph, Mr. CHAPMAN, Chatillon, Mr. BAKER,
French Herald, Mr. HENRY, Citizens of Angiers, Mess. Atkins, Collet, &c.

Queen Elinor, Mrs. VINING,
The Lady Constance by Mrs. BARTLEY,
Blanch, of Castile, Miss FOOTE,
Lady Faulconbridge, Mrs. PEARCE.

Authorities for the Costume.

KING JOHN's EFFIGY, in Worcester Cathedral, and His Great Seals.
QUEEN ELINOR's EFFIGY, in the Abbey of Fonteveraud.
EFFIGY of the EARL of SALISBURY, in Salisbury Cathedral.
EFFIGY of the EARL of PEMBROKE, in the Temple Church, London,
KING JOHN's SILVER CUP, in the possession of the Corporation of King's Lynn, Norfolk.
ILLUMINATED MSS., in the *British Museum*, *Bodleian* and *Bennet College* Libraries, and the Works of *Camden*, *Montfaucon*, *Sandford*, *Strutt*, *Gough*, *Stothard*, *Meyrick*, *&c*.

N.B. The Costumes are published, and may be had of J. MILLER, 69, *Fleet-street*, and all other Booksellers.

☞ The Proprietors of this Theatre request leave respectfully to inform the Publick that should their present exertions to do honour to the productions of *Shakspeare* be rewarded by its approbation and patronage, it is their intention to revive, in succession, the rest of his acting Plays, Cast in the most effective manner, and Dressed in the same splendid, novel, and interesting style.

After which (with, if possible, more than its original Magnificence,) the Grand Melo-Drama of

TIMOUR,

THE TARTAR.

(For the Characters and Scenery of Timour the Tartar *see the next Page.)*

Printed by W. Reynolds, 9, Denmark-court, Strand.

Covent Garden Theatre playbill of November 24, 1823, announcing the first performance of *King John* with historically accurate costumes. *Courtesy of the Folger Shakespeare Library.*

—with a sudden self-upbraiding, as if he asked why he had let senseless feuds come between him and the exulting joy of life."[158] But his good humor is not subdued for long:

> Ay, ay, a scratch, a scratch. Marry, 'tis enough.

This line, Marston declared, Kemble spoke with "a quaint comic touch of expression, that said the jade, Fate, *will* play men such tricks." Then he recalled: "How fine was it, next, to note the *bonhomie*, the old love of jest struggling with, and for a moment subduing, the pains of death, in the answer to Romeo's encouragement:

> No, 'tis not so deep as a well, nor so wide as a church door; but it is enough. . . . Ask for me to-morrow, and you shall find me a grave man.

Kemble's Mercutio, after uttering the quip, gave a "bright, though quickly fading smile," which suggested again the "Mercutio of old—the gay, rash, loyal, boon-companion: it was a smile to call up tears, it conjured up so much of youth and the merry past, while it was well-contrasted and kept within reality by the brief techiness, still not unmixed with the humour, that succeeded." Mercutio's reproof of Romeo for his interference—

> Why the devil came you between us? I was hurt under your arm—

was accompanied by a striking piece of business in the Kemble productions. The reproof was "nobly and pathetically redeemed by the loving courtesy with which he held out his hand to him, a moment after, in token of full forgiveness—a point," Marston noted, "I believe original

158. Marston, *Our Recent Actors*, p. 124.

with Charles Kemble, and which has since become an acting tradition of the character." Kemble's admirer concluded:

> Then there came a deep, wistful expression into his face, reminding you of Romeo's strange avowal to the Nurse— . . . that he was 'one whom God had made himself to mar' —and that there were higher possibilities in the Mercutio of this brief, bright, tragic story, than had ever come to light; but it is too late, said the look; let us wind up with a jest, though it be a grim one—"A plague o' both your houses!"[159]

Such was the final glimpse of Charles Kemble's Mercutio, a humorist from beginning to end, but a heroic and courtly humorist whose death was not without pathos.

Faulconbridge

From his first appearance as Philip Faulconbridge in the 1800–1801 season, Charles Kemble captivated London audiences in the role of the spirited heir of Richard Coeur de Lion. With most spectators Kemble's Faulconbridge competed with his Mercutio for the distinction of being his greatest second part. Unlike the role of Mercutio, however, which Kemble did not undertake until he was an experienced actor at the peak of his career, Faulconbridge was one of the characters undertaken by him in his apprentice years when he was still pretty well confined to second-, third-, or even fourth-rate parts; and it was a role which helped him to establish his reputation. A notice in the *Monthly Mirror* of his first performance in the part at Drury Lane, November 20, 1800, in which he supported his brother's King John, suggests his initial reception in the role:

159. *Ibid.*, pp. 124, 125, 126.

> C. Kemble appears to considerable advantage in this character, which he has studied with attention, and executes with spirit. His powers occasionally sunk under the weight of the part; but, if some of the points fell with diminished effect from his lips, there were others in which he came up to the pitch of the character. Upon the whole, his performance was such as will greatly enhance his abilities in the opinion of the public.[160]

In subsequent years the prediction of the *Monthly Mirror* proved true. Not only did the public raise its opinion of the younger Kemble, but such eminent critics as Leigh Hunt and William Hazlitt joined the ranks of those praising his Faulconbridge. Hazlitt declared: "Faulconbridge, the bastard, is one of Charles Kemble's happiest hits"; and Hunt judged: "Charles Kemble, always elegant, with a chivalrous air, and possessing a strong taste for contemptuous irony, is as complete a Faulconbridge as one can desire."[161] For some, Kemble's personation of the Bastard in *King John* appeared as his greatest achievement. The actor James Hackett felt that this portrayal was, "of all the characters of the Bard of Avon," Kemble's "greatest, most perfect, and admirable."[162] Even those who did not usually like Kemble's acting admired his Faulconbridge. Charles Leslie, for example, who bluntly remarked, "The only character I ever liked him in was Faulconbridge," judged

160. *Monthly Mirror*, December 1800.

161. William Hazlitt, in *The Times*, December 18, 1817; see *Complete Works*, ed. P. P. Howe (London: J. M. Dent and Sons, 1930), XVIII, 270. Leigh Hunt, in the *Theatrical Examiner*, June 3, 1810; see *Dramatic Criticism: 1808–1813*, ed. L. H. Houtchens and C. W. Houtchens (New York: Columbia University Press, 1949), p. 39.

162. Hackett, *Shakespeare's Plays and Actors*, p. 175.

his portrayal of the Bastard to be "as perfect as the Coriolanus of his brother John."[163] Begrudging Kemble too much praise for his art, Leslie concluded that "the spirit he threw into the reputed son of Coeur de Lion . . . was too natural not to be his own." One observer suggested that whenever Kemble played the part, he stole the show. "He threw it out upon the canvas, he gave it all the heedless daring, and sarcastic humour that belong to it, and constitute its charm," William Robson proclaimed. "In his hands, it became . . . the favourite character of the piece."[164]

Season after season Charles Kemble continued to play Faulconbridge with success, and as he did so, he was constantly perfecting the part. By reviewing the comments of spectators who, over the years, left a record of their impressions of Kemble in the role, by examining the text and stage directions in the various acting editions based on performances in which Charles Kemble appeared as the Bastard, by noting R. J. Lane's record of Kemble's word emphasis in his public readings, and by studying John Philip Kemble's promptbook used in productions in which Charles played Faulconbridge to his brother's John and Thomas Barry's promptbook used in the October 1, 1832, production at the Park Theatre in New York in which Kemble played the Bastard to Barry's John, it is possible to recapture many of the highlights of the actor's popular characterization.[165]

163. Charles Leslie, *Autobiographical Recollections*, ed. Tom Taylor (Boston, 1860), p. 198.

164. William Robson, *The Old Play-Goer* (London, 1846), p. 49.

165. The acting editions of *King John* which indicate that they publish the text of the play and the stage business for Covent Garden

From his first entrance the general impression which Charles Kemble's Faulconbridge conveyed to the audience was that of a chivalrous and gallant nobleman. Even before the spectacularly costumed 1823 production of *King John,* the tall and handsome performer invariably presented a striking figure, which was especially impressive in the later scenes in which he appeared in a glittering suit of mail armor.[166] Hazlitt was struck by his manly figure and martial appearance; and Donne noted that "his Faulconbridge bore us back to Runnymede and the group of barons bold who wrested the great charter from the craven John."[167] He was indeed the express image of a medieval

---

productions in which Charles Kemble appeared as Faulconbridge include John Kemble's edition (1804), John Cumberland's edition (c. 1826), and W. Oxberry's edition (1819). For Lane's notations of Kemble's emphasis in his public readings, see *Kemble's Shakespere Readings,* II, 317 ff. One of the two promptbooks which provide information about Charles Kemble's performances is Folger Shakespeare Library promptbook *King John* 10, which is a promptbook used in performances at Covent Garden Theatre in which Charles Kemble played Faulconbridge to his brother's King John. Professor Charles Shattuck describes it as a "much used promptbook marked in [J.P.] Kemble's hand," and associates it particularly with a performance at Covent Garden on May 1, 1810. It is a Kemble edition (1804) with interleaves watermarked 1807, and contains calls, stage business, maps, cues for effects, and timings. Hereafter I shall cite it as Folger 10. The second promptbook of *King John,* in the Walter Hampden Memorial Library of the Players Club, belonged to Thomas Barry and was used for the performance at the Park Theatre in New York, October 1, 1832, in which Barry played King John, Charles Kemble played Faulconbridge, and Fanny Kemble played Constance. It is a Cumberland edition and includes notes by Barry on the playing of King John, calls, some stage business, and cues for effects. Hereafter I shall cite it as Barry's *King John,* The Players.

166. Oxberry edition; Cumberland edition.

167. Hazlitt, in *The Times,* December 18, 1817; see *Complete Works,* XVIII, 270. Donne, *Essays on the Drama,* p. 168.

warrior, and moved always with an air of "grace and gallantry."[168]

Elinor, it will be remembered, says significantly of Faulconbridge:

> He hath a trick of Coeur-de-lion's face;
> The accent of his tongue affecteth him.
> Do you not read some tokens of my son
> In the large composition of this man?

Kemble evidently took these lines as the key to the character of the spirited Philip and "modelled his conception of the part upon the fact that Faulconbridge was the son of Richard the 'Lion-hearted.'" Indeed, as he "portrayed him, he might have well stood for Richard himself, with the addition, perhaps, of a dashing carelessness and license springing from the consciousness that his illegitimacy had at once given him an illustrious father, and yet left him free from all bonds of kindred, save those he imposed upon himself." Among the traits of Richard which Kemble's Faulconbridge inherited were "intrepidity, the love of danger and frolic," and an "occasional penetration and sagacity"; and to these qualities were added "the untaught grace and freedom of a barbarian chief."[169]

Charles Kemble's Faulconbridge, moreover, never failed to convey to the audience a certain overflow of life, which underlay his wit. William Oxberry perceptively remarked that Shakespeare's character differs significantly from the comic figures of Congreve or the French comedies, who are "wits by profession," and whose aim is "ever to say smart pointed things." Faulconbridge, in contrast to these

168. W. P. Frith, *My Autobiography and Reminiscences* (New York, 1888), p. 21.

169. Marston, *Our Recent Actors*, p. 127.

characters "for whom wit is an assumption, a thing of education," is "humorous from the overflowing abundance of his fancy, and from animal spirits that are incapable of restraint; with him wit is a part of his nature, a quality which he can no more change than the height of his stature."[170] It was exactly this sense of a natural wit emerging from a zest for life which Charles Kemble so skillfully portrayed. Marston recalled:

> It is hard to convey an impression to those who have not seen him, of his delivery of the dialogue—hard to express the wide difference between his Faulconbridge and the renderings of other actors, who have delivered the text with spirit and just appreciation, and yet fallen so far short of Charles Kemble as to put comparison out of the question. The secret of his superiority lay, perhaps, in the fulness of life which seemed to radiate from him—to make war a gay pastime, diplomacy a play of wit, and to clothe worldliness itself with a glow of bright, genial satire.

His humorous lines, it seems, were given with a "zest and ardour that were resistlessly contagious," and "his impersonation . . . seemed to blend the spirit of Mercutio with those of the warrior and statesman."[171]

In Act I the audience typically caught its first glimpse of Kemble's spirited bastard as he entered from the left upon a stage that was moderately crowded and impressively regal.[172] Upstage center on a throne that was graced by a

170. Preface, Oxberry edition.

171. Marston, *Our Recent Actors*, pp. 127–28.

172. Unless otherwise noted, the staging described in the discussion of the play is based on the various diagrams, notations, and directions in John Kemble's promptbook, Folger 10, which was used in performances in which Charles Kemble played Faulconbridge to his

state canopy King John was seated. The King was flanked on his right by three guards, two English gentlemen, and Pembroke and on his left by three guards, two English gentlemen and Essex. Queen Elinor was seated on a stool at the foot of the throne just to the right. An added dignity was afforded the first appearance of the gallant Faulconbridge. Instead of the customary Sheriff, an English Herald served to usher in young Philip and his brother Robert. The Herald entered from the left, alone, just as Elinor was concluding her lines blaming the "ambitious Constance" for the new difficulty with France and before the King declared:

> Our strong possession and our right for us!

The Herald then "whispers Essex" as the King and Elinor continued to converse. Subsequently, after telling the King:

> My liege, here is the strangest controversy,

the Herald departed at the King's "Let them approach" and returned escorting the two Faulconbridges, with Charles Kemble looking very handsome in a "brown old English tunic with buff satin trimming and buff kerseymere pantaloons."[173]

---

brother's John. The notations in Barry's *King John,* The Players, and the printed stage directions in the Cumberland and Oxberry editions, although less detailed, are generally complementary. Where any differences exist between the staging suggested by Folger 10 and Barry's promptbook or the printed stage directions in the Oxberry or Cumberland editions, they will be pointed out; and when the notations in Barry's promptbook or the directions in the Oxberry or Cumberland edition indicate additional business not included in Folger 10, they will, of course, be cited.

173. Oxberry edition. A similar costume is indicated in the Cumberland edition.

As the two brothers argued their case before the King, Charles Kemble's refined delivery of the Bastard's witty defense of his inheritance must have been impressive to the Covent Garden crowd. At least R. J. Lane's notations of Kemble's accented words suggest a sprightly delivery of the lines in his public readings:

> Now, whether I be TRUE begot, or no,
> That still I lay upon my mother's head;
> But, that I am as WELL begot, my liege,
> Compare our faces, and be judge yourself.
> If old Sir Robert did beget us BOTH,
> And were our father, and this son like him;—
> O! old Sir Robert, father, on my knee
> I give heaven thanks, I was not like to thee.

With careful emphasis he brought out the word play in Philip's reply to Robert's query:

> *Rob.* Shall then my father's will be of no force,
> To dispossess the child which is not his?
> *Faul.* Of no more force to DISPOSSESS me, sir,
> Than was his will to GET me, as I think.[174]

The spirited Faulconbridge decides it is better to be a "landless knight" than a "landed squire," however, and kneels before the King to "arise more great" as "Sir Richard and Plantagenet." Here Charles Kemble's Bastard subtly registered his changed status. Hazlitt observed that "he is no sooner knighted, than he seems made for his rank."[175] Omitting the rather coarse and unknightly exchange with Elinor in reply to her invitation to call her grandam,

174. *Kemble's Shakespere Readings,* II, 321, 322.
175. *The Times,* December 18, 1817; see *Complete Works,* XVIII, 270.

Kemble's Sir Richard simply bid a gentlemanly farewell to his brother Robert; and then to the accompaniment of a flourish of drums and trumpets he momentarily joined the grand procession following the King in his exit and with great dignity and grace led out Queen Elinor "like a 'lordly gallant.'"[176]

Faulconbridge's long soliloquy following the exit of the court and preceding the entrance of his mother was invariably cut sharply;[177] the others had scarcely left the stage when Kemble's Faulconbridge declared:

> But who comes in such haste!
> What woman post is this?

This was but the first of many substantial cuts in Faulconbridge's longer speeches; and as in almost all the cases in which his lines were deleted, it involves a passage which displays the lively imagination of the knight, who so loves to let his mind rove unchecked from image to image and to give full play to his exuberant wit. The omissions were no doubt made in order to reduce the time required for the play. Oxberry recorded that the total "time this piece takes in representation is two hours and thirty minutes."[178] In an early-nineteenth-century production this meant that considerable cutting was necessarily involved, and Charles

176. *Ibid.* In his earliest performances Kemble evidently did not employ this business of leading out Elinor which Hazlitt comments on. Folger 10 has Elinor exit "led by Pembroke."

177. The Oxberry, Cumberland, and Kemble editions all cut the speech similarly.

178. Folger 10 indicates a somewhat longer time for the performance. John Kemble has marked "3H-10" at the end of his promptbook. Other timings in Folger 10 are; Act I, "24m"; Act II, "35m"; Act III, "50m"; Act IV, "40m."

Kemble could hardly have expected the verbal excursions of Faulconbridge to escape untouched. Still, he must have sorely missed the opportunities afforded by several of the Bastard's more fanciful speeches.

In the rather rough and lively encounter between Faulconbridge and his mother which concludes Act I no omissions were made, despite some persistent complaints against the "indecencies" of the scene.[179] Kemble, however, chose to soften the rudeness and indelicacy of the dialogue and to temper the coarser side of his character by his manner and business. Kemble's Bastard was evidently careful not to let his humor descend into impudence, and to preserve a certain "manly tenderness" toward his mother which heightened the comedy of the situation. Mrs. Cowden Clarke remarked that "his manly tenderness, his filial coaxing way of speaking and putting his arm round her as he thanks her for having made Richard Coeur de Lion his father, was something to be grateful for having witnessed."[180] Hazlitt, too, praised Kemble in this part of the scene and was especially impressed by his reading of

> Sir Robert never holp to make this leg,

where "suiting the action to the word, as well he might, it had a great effect upon the house."[181]

The long scene comprising Act II, with the raillery of

179. The Kemble, Oxberry, and Cumberland acting editions print the full dialogue between Faulconbridge and his mother, with the exception of one line ("Subjected tribute to commanding Love") in the midst of Faulconbridge's last speech.

180. Mary Cowden Clarke, *My Long Life* (New York, 1896), p. 100.

181. *The Examiner*, December 8, 1816; see *Complete Works*, V, 347.

Austria, the advice to England and France to unite in order to crush Angiers, and the famous speech on commodity, was, of course, a favorite among admirers of Kemble's Faulconbridge. With Charles Kemble exits and entrances always received careful study. His Faulconbridge is said to have entered here before the gates of Angiers in the middle of a long and colorful procession with the "'indolent grace' of a tawny lion emerging from an African jungle, as if the imagination of his mother had been imbued with his royal father's hand to paw encounter with the king of the forest."[182] Sound effects, of course, heightened the impressiveness of his heroic entry. As Chatillon advised King Philip to turn his attention from "this paltry siege" of Angiers to the "mightier task" of confronting the "dauntless spirits" of the approaching English forces, "wind instruments with drums and fifes" began "a distant march."[183] This march steadily increased in volume as Chatillon concluded his speech, King Philip replied, and finally the French all retired, right. The English then entered from the left and formed a matching and balanced line along the left side of the stage opposite the French forces. When the entrance was completed King John stood opposite King Philip, downstage center, and Faulconbridge was still farther downstage left, across from his antagonist, Austria. All the while the march "continues louder and louder till King John is ready to speak."

182. Lacy, *The Green Room,* p. 52. The reference to Faulconbridge's position in the middle of a long and colorful procession is based on notations in Folger 10.

183. Folger 10 indicates that this march was played by four trumpets, two drums, and two fifes. A notation in Barry's *King John,* The Players, calls for wind instruments and a piano to supply the march.

Faulconbridge's first chaff of Austria was skillfully executed and "kept well within the bounds of high comedy."[184] Kemble did not depend on any bravado of gesture to create his effect. Leigh Hunt noted that it was "with much skill that he suddenly bursts into a proud ridicule of the Duke of Austria, without indulging in the flourish of fist which common actors mistake for indignation: he does not, like a South-sea warrior, waste half his strength on the enemy by a preliminary bravado of gesture. All great effects are produced by contrast. Anger is never so noble as when it breaks out of comparative continence of aspect: it is the earthquake bursting from the repose of nature."[185] Kemble's Faulconbridge, it seems, always maintained a "very bold spirit of raillery, a gay insolence," in his banter with the blustering Austria, which Hunt felt appeared "justified by the contemptibility of its object." Evidently, however, he was careful not to let his relations with Austria establish the character of Faulconbridge as that of a bully. The old actor Walter Lacy recalled that in his "pastoral days" when he was "ambitious of playing the Bastard," Kemble had given him an "invaluable hint: 'Take care, Lacy, Faulconbridge is very near being a bully!'"[186]

The staging of this scene before Angiers tended to heighten and emphasize the feud between Faulconbridge and Austria, which apparently always proved to be a popular feature with Kemble's audiences. For example, after the Citizens refused to acknowledge either the French or English king and Philip shouted, "Mount, chevaliers! to

184. Lacy, *The Green Room,* p. 52.
185. Hunt, *Dramatic Essays,* p. 109.
186. Lacy, *The Green Room,* p. 52.

arms!" a flourish of drums and trumpets followed and both forces completely left the stage "at the entrances they stand on," leaving Austria and Faulconbridge alone to command the full attention of the audience in the ensuing taunts:

Faul. Saint George, that swinged the dragon, and e'er since
Sits on his horseback, at mine hostess' door,
Teach us some fence!—Sirrah, were I at home,
At your den, sirrah, with your lioness,
I'd set an ox-head to your lion's hide,
And make a monster of you.
Aust. Peace! no more.
Faul. O tremble! for you hear the lion roar.

Austria then departed, right, and Faulconbridge, left, after which alarms were heard, right and left, and eventually a French Herald entered to sound a parley. It should be noted, too, that Faulconbridge in his antagonism toward Austria had no competition from a battling Elinor and Constance. The rough exchanges between the two women were apparently considered offensive to the sensibilities of an early-nineteenth-century audience and were largely omitted.[187]

After a parley was sounded, the French and English Heralds again ordered Angiers to open wide its gates; charges were heard, right and left; and finally the kings with their powers returned to hurl challenges at each other, much to the delight of the gay warrior Faulconbridge. Subsequently Faulconbridge's speech, following the chal-

187. The Oxberry, Cumberland, and Kemble acting editions all omit most of the Constance-Elinor feud.

lenges of the two kings, was concluded by Kemble's boldly marching up to Angiers's gates:

> Ha, majesty! how high thy glory towers,
> When the rich blood of kings is set on fire!
> Why stand these royal fronts amazed thus?
> Cry, havock, kings! back to the stained field,
> You equal potents, fiery kindled spirits!
> Then let confusion by one part confirm
> The other's peace. Till then, blows, blood, and death!
> (Goes up to the gates.)

The extremely rhetorical lines,

> O, now doth Death line his dead chaps with steel;
> The swords of soldiers are his teeth, his fangs;
> And now he feasts, mousing the flesh of men,
> In undetermin'd differences of kings,

were, it will be noticed, omitted from the passage.[188] Later, when the Citizen declares he will not open the gates, Kemble's Faulconbridge came "down between the kings" as he cried out:

> By heaven, these scroyles of Angiers flout you, kings,

and proceeded to give his plan for a joint attack against the stubborn town. Kemble's Bastard, although repeatedly termed a gentlemanly and chivalrous hero, apparently retained a sufficient amount of bluster here. For some spectators's tastes, indeed, he was apparently a bit too loud-mouthed. One critic reviewing the English actor's first appearance in the role of Faulconbridge at the Park Theatre in New York in 1832 generally praised his portrayal highly,

188. The Oxberry, Cumberland, and Kemble acting editions all print this speech similarly with the four lines cut.

but he felt obliged to complain about his bombast: "His speech to the kings, in which he exhorts them to unite their force against the town, was a piece of absolute rant, and if they could understand the words even which swayed their counsels, they had better ears than we who sat further from the noise."[189]

Faulconbridge's plan is rejected; the English and French "all sheathe their swords" and bow before "that sly devil, . . . tickling Commodity." Here the citizens opened the gates "with noise of heavy bolts and chains," entered, and knelt to the left of the gates, "the first citizen holding the keys of the town." To the sounds of a "march with drums and trumpets" the stage emptied, leaving Faulconbridge alone to cry out:

> Mad world! mad kings! mad composition!

But even Faulconbridge's famed speech on commodity did not get by uncut in Kemble's performances, as thirteen lines were invariably omitted from the middle of the passage.[190] The subsequent exit of Faulconbridge as he disappeared through the gates into the town was one point in Charles Kemble's personation which drew praise from nearly all who saw him. His excellence here is characteristic of his great attention to the most minor points in a performance. The painter W. P. Frith recalled Kemble's "swagger into Angiers" in his *Reminiscences:* "I can see him now, as with the elegant saunter appropriate to the character, he disappears under the portcullis, and, the place being

189. Newspaper clipping in Barry's *King John,* The Players. I have not been able to identify the paper or to establish the precise date.

190. The Kemble, Oxberry, and Cumberland editions all cut the speech similarly.

new to him, he looks to the right and left with the insolence of a conqueror."[191] The departure so impressed Fanny Kemble's friend and correspondent Edward FitzGerald that years later, in a letter, he remembered the incident: "I was reminded . . . of your Father—his look up at Angiers's Walls as he went out in Act II."[192]

In the opening scene of Act III (set in "the French King's Tent") Kemble's Faulconbridge entered regally to a flourish of drums and trumpets among the large parties accompanying King John and King Philip, just after Constance had cried out,

> Here is my throne, bid kings come bow to it,

and had dramatically thrown herself to the ground. In the process of the entrance two English gentlemen placed a state chair for John, left, and two French gentlemen placed a state chair for Philip, right. John took his seat "immediately the chair [was] placed for him"; the French took positions on the right of the stage, the English on the left, and Kemble's knight paused just to the rear and left of John's chair. Inevitably this is Constance's scene; but Faulconbridge gets further opportunity to pursue his raillery of Austria, and Charles Kemble again won the applause of his audiences in his delightful delivery of the Bastard's taunts. Frith observed: "Of the tone in which he repeated again and again to Austria, 'And hand a calf-skin on those recreant limbs,' no description can give an idea."[193] The stage directions followed by Kemble prove

191. Frith, *Autobiography and Reminiscences*, p. 21.
192. Edward FitzGerald, *Letters to Fanny Kemble, 1871–1883*, ed. William Aldis Wright (New York, 1895), p. 176.
193. Frith, *Autobiography and Reminiscences*, p. 21.

interesting here. Constance, downstage left with Arthur by her side, in her disappointment over the news of the marriage of the Dauphin and Blanch lashes out at Austria, downstage right, "advancing toward her":

> Thou wear a lion's hide? Doff it for shame,
> And hang a calf's-skin on those recreant limbs.

Constance crosses right with Arthur following her, and after Austria replies,

> O, that a man should speak those words to me!

Faulconbridge picks up her ridicule:

> And hang a calf's-skin on those recreant limbs.

This first taunt Kemble spoke from behind King John's chair. But after Austria's retort,

> Thou dar'st not say so, villain, for thy life,

Kemble repeated his line in a threatening manner, rushing down to the front of the stage. Then with the king's

> We like not this; thou dost forget thyself,

Faulconbridge returned to his original position and Austria crossed behind to Arthur's right, as a trumpet sounded to announce the arrival of Cardinal Pandulph. Subsequent taunts from the Bastard were apparently without further physical bluster and were all made from behind King John's chair. The climax of this hostility had to await the next scene.

In Charles Kemble's performances the spectacle of Faulconbridge's appearance at the beginning of Act III, scene ii, displaying Austria's head, was somewhat tempered and hence the callousness of the character played down. At the same time the opportunity was seized for presenting a finel encounter between these two antagonists. The scene opened with alarms sounding right and left as Faulconbridge entered the battlefield alone from the left, exclaiming:

> Now, by my life, this day grows wondrous hot!
> Some airy devil hovers in the sky
> And pours down mischief.

At this point a charge was heard from the right as Austria appeared; Austria and Faulconbridge engaged in a vigorous duel and Faulconbridge drove Austria off the stage, right. Presently the victorious warrior reentered, not with Austria's head, but with a substitute trophy, the lion's skin, in his hand. Curiously, Faulconbridge's line still remained:

> Austria's head lie there,
> While Philip breathes,

although it must have seemed somewhat inappropriate in the new version of the scene. Another charge from the left punctuated Faulconbridge's line, as King John, Arthur, and four English gentlemen arrived, left, "meeting Hubert," right. Faulconbridge watched as King John flung Arthur over to Hubert, who caught him up and carried him off.[194] The scene ended as it began, to the sound of a charge, after a heroic Faulconbridge had assured the King that he had rescued Queen Elinor.

In Act IV, Kemble's Faulconbridge found less chance to display his particular brand of boundless energy, natural

194. In contrast to Folger 10, Barry's *King John,* The Players, indicates that Arthur "runs over to Hubert" at this entrance. Apparently in the New York performances the business of King John flinging Arthur over to Hubert was omitted.

wit, and chivalric spirit and fewer opportunities to attract the specific attention of the audience. Still several points concerning his performance here seem noteworthy. As King John becomes debased by his actions toward Arthur, Faulconbridge, in contrast, grows in stature and alone maintains the audience's respect and admiration. With Kemble this contrast between the chivalrous knight and the much less heroic King apparently was emphasized. In scene ii his Faulconbridge evidently cast an especially challenging, penetrating, and accusing eye toward the guilty King as he reported his encounter with Essex, Salisbury, and the others who have said that Arthur was "kill'd to-night" at the King's "suggestion."[195] When Thomas Barry acted John to Charles Kemble's Faulconbridge at the Park Theatre in New York in 1832, he noted in his promptbook how the King must, in his subsequent reply, acknowledge the effect of Faulconbridge's piercing and overpowering glance: "Either meet the eye of Faulconbridge and shrink from it—or—speak this speech without looking at him." Previously in this scene, it should be remarked, the Bastard alone had the responsibility of warning King John that the people were "possess'd with rumors, full of idle dreams," for the part of the prophet Pomfret was regularly omitted

195. Actually this conversation was generally a part of the third scene in Act IV in productions at Covent Garden. In the productions in which Charles Kemble played with his brother, and in later productions in England, there was regularly a scene break after John concludes his conversation with Salisbury, Pembroke, and Essex and just before he says to the messenger (Herald), "A fearful eye thou hast!" The Kemble and Cumberland editions indicate this break. This division was not made in the New York productions at the Park Theatre in 1832, however, according to Thomas Barry's promptbook.

in the productions in which Kemble played.[196] Without Pomfret the attention of the audience, of course, was more directly focused on Faulconbridge here; but the Bastard, while he indicated something of the bad omens, did not refer to the prediction that "ere the next Ascension Day" the King shall deliver up his crown. Thus later the significance of the scene between King John and Pandulph at the beginning of Act V must have been somewhat diminished.

In the final scene of Act IV, Kemble's heroic Faulconbridge found further opportunity to demonstrate his strength and leadership as he confronted the situation of a threatened skirmish between Hubert and the rebellious lords, Salisbury, Pembroke, and Essex, following the discovery of Arthur's body. The powerful knight, who had earlier caused a weakened King to shrink from his glance, once more proved his dominance. As Kemble's warrior commanded the sword-drawn rebels and Hubert to "keep the peace," he drew his own sword to put a prompt end to the threatened outbreak. Salisbury, Essex, and Pembroke departed, and Kemble had to forgo Faulconbridge's first vehement outburst to Hubert in which he assures him he is "more deep damned than Prince Lucifer" if he has killed "this child." Still more, however, he must have lamented the fact that Faulconbridge's final speech to Hubert, in which he commands him to carry away the body of Arthur, was sharply cut. The lines which show the imaginative quality of his mind were again the ones excluded. His speculation upon seeing Hubert lift the lifeless boy,

196. The Cumberland, Kemble, and Oxberry editions all omit Pomfret.

How easy dost thou take all England up!
From forth this morsel of dead royalty
The life, the right and truth of all this realm
Is fled to heaven; and England now is left
To tug and scramble, and to part by the teeth
The unowed interest of proud-swelling state.
Now for the bare-pick'd bone of majesty
Doth dogged war bristle his angry crest
And snarleth in the gentle eyes of peace,

was all regularly omitted.[197] Concluding with the order to Hubert to "bear away that child" and the expression of the fear that "Heaven itself doth frown upon the land," Kemble's Faulconbridge exited with Hubert, who bore Arthur in his arms. At least this was the procedure in his early performances when he acted with his brother John. Later apparently he sometimes departed alone, while Hubert remained "bending over the dead body of Arthur" as the curtain slowly descended.[198]

In the presentation of the first scene of Act V, the contrast between the vacillating, weak, and incompetent King and his courageous and indomitable knight was considerably heightened. The scene opened with a tableau that underscored King John's ignominious submission to Rome; it closed with a particularly patriotic outburst from Faulconbridge as he set out to "sweep off" all "base invaders from the land." The curtain rose with a flourish of drums and trumpets to discover King John kneeling before Cardinal Pandulph, who was seated in a state chair with "his hands

197. The Cumberland, Kemble, and Oxberry editions are similar in their omission of Faulconbridge's lines here.

198. The Cumberland edition suggests this later staging. Barry's promptbook (which is a Cumberland edition) notes no changes in the printed directions in Cumberland.

on cushion on which the crown is placed," while two of the Cardinal's attendants, an English Herald, and four English gentlemen looked on. After the King spoke his first line, the Cardinal gave back the cushion and crown to King John, who rose and delivered them to the Herald, who placed them on a table. Then Cardinal Pandulph left his chair as John rather pathetically remarked, "Now keep your holy word"; he soon departed with his attendants, right, as an energetic Faulconbridge entered, left, and proceeded to implore the King to "be stirring as the time" and "glister like the god of war." When Faulconbridge learns of the new alliance between King John and the Pope, he is, of course, greatly upset by the pact. Normally the Bastard's speech here concludes by simply imploring King John to keep armed in the hope that

> Perchance the Cardinal cannot make your peace;
> Or if he do, let it at least be said
> They saw we had a purpose of defense.

Charles Kemble's Faulconbridge, however, concluded with lines more indicative of the lion-hearted temper of the gallant warrior. He ended this passage with a spirited and chauvanistic declaration which John Kemble had added to his acting edition:

> Let us, my liege to arms.
> Sweep off these base invaders from the land:
> And, above all, exterminate those slaves,
> Those British slaves, whose prostituted souls,
> Under French banners, move in vile rebellion,
> Against their king, their country, and their God.[199]

199. The Cumberland and Oxberry editions, as well as the Kemble edition, print this added speech. It apparently continued to be used

A tone of arrogance pervaded Kemble's discourse with Pandulph and the Dauphin in the next scene; at least such a tone seems indicated by the words which he emphasized in his public readings which R. J. Lane witnessed. In speaking Faulconbridge's lines in Act V, scene ii, following his interruption of Pandulph's unsuccessful attempt to get the Dauphin to submit to a truce, Kemble indicated the Bastard's bluster by a repeated stress on the word *me:*

> *Faul.* According to the fair play of the world,
> Let ME have audience; I am sent to speak; . . .
> *Pand.* The Dauphin is too wilful-opposite,
> He flatly says, he'll not lay down his arms.
> *Faul.* By all the blood that ever fury breath'd,
> The youth says well:—Now hear our English king,
> For thus his royalty doth speak in ME.[200]

His blustering delivery, however, had to compensate for the loss of some of his more picturesque lines. Several of Faulconbridge's more colorful passages, as for example when he describes how the English previously have made the French cower in fright, "dive like buckets in concealed wells," "couch in litter of your stable planks," or when he tells the rebels, the "bloody Neroes," how their own ladies "like Amazons come tripping after drums," were omitted.[201]

A brief and foreboding meeting of Faulconbridge and Hubert at the shadowy ("lamps down") entrance to

---

until Macready banished it. See *William Charles Macready's King John,* ed. Charles H. Shattuck (Urbana: University of Illinois Press, 1962), p. 10.

200. *Kemble's Shakespere Readings,* II, 360.

201. The Cumberland, Kemble, and Oxberry editions show these omissions.

Swinstead Abbey in scene vi prepared for the final scene in the orchard of Swinstead Abbey. The last scene regularly opened with the entrance of six English guards with torches, Essex, and Prince Henry. After the Prince spoke his first few lines, Salisbury arrived with two English gentlemen bearing a couch. Salisbury told of the King's desire for the open air, and shortly afterward the dying monarch appeared, attended by Pembroke and two English gentlemen. Thus when Kemble's Faulconbridge entered, accompanied by Hubert, Essex was at stage right; the King was on the couch at the center of the stage; the Prince, Salisbury, and Pembroke were to his left; and the guards and gentlemen stood at the rear of the stage behind the King. Upon entering, Hubert immediately went behind the couch, but Kemble's loyal and spirited warrior ran to the front of the couch and knelt before the dying King:

> Oh, I am scalded with my violent motion,
> And spleen of speed to see your majesty.

Subsequently as Faulconbridge concluded his news and the King died, Prince Henry fell upon his father's body. Here the young Prince remained, silent, only rising when Faulconbridge referred to his putting on "the lineal state and glory of the land." The focus of attention in Kemble's performances apparently rested primarily on Faulconbridge, not the Prince, in this last scene. Prince Henry's lines in reaction to the King's death ("Even so must I run on . . .") were deleted; the Bastard's response alone was heard:

> Art thou gone so? I do but stay behind
> To do the office for thee of revenge,
> And then my soul shall wait on thee to heaven,
> As it on earth hath been thy servant still.

The announcement that the King's body shall be interred a Worcester likewise was denied the Prince; it came instea from Essex, to be followed, of course, by Faulconbridge' approval, "Thither shall it then." Prince Henry rose a Faulconbridge referred to his coronation, and the Bastar and all the others kneeled before the Prince.[202] But afte young Henry had thanked them for their love "with tears," he again threw himself "on his knees by his father's body" as the barons rose. Here, it seems, the weeping Princ remained while Kemble's indomitable Faulconbridge de livered his final patriotic prophecy:

> O, let us pay the time but NEEDFUL WOE.
> This England never did (nor never SHALL)
> Lie at the proud foot of a conqueror,
> But when it first did help to WOUND ITSELF.
> Now these her princes are come home again,
> Come the three corners of the world in arms,
> And we shall shock them: Nought shall make us rue,
> If England to itself do rest but true.[203]

The curtain descended "to a grand symphony in th orchestra." The final glimpse of Charles Kemble's gallan warrior must have been impressive indeed, for many year later in a letter to Fanny Kemble dated November 17, 1874 Edward FitzGerald still recalled the scene and mentione how the actor effectively "looked sideways and upwar before the curtain fell on his speech."[204]

202. Barry's *King John*, The Players, indicates a flourish as a kneel.

203. *Kemble's Shakespere Readings*, II, 365.

204. FitzGerald, *Letters to Fanny Kemble*, p. 55.

III

Manager Charles Kemble

The Climax of a Dream

Charles Kemble's career might have been considerably happier—and undoubtedly less hectic—if the events which culminated in his assumption of the management of Covent Garden Theatre on March 11, 1822, had never happened. At the time, however, to this younger member of the famous theatrical family, the chance at last to become an owner and manager of London's renowned patent house appeared as the climax of a magnificent dream.

On June 23, 1817, John Kemble, after the usual fanfare of a farewell season, had formally retired from the stage. At that point neither his health nor his finances were in the most prosperous condition, and consequently he and his wife left England to pass their final years in Switzerland and southern France.[1] In October, 1820, however, news reached the tragedian which brought him hastily home to London. His old partner Thomas Harris, who owned one-half of the shares of Covent Garden, had died; and following his death, affairs at the Theatre were reported to be going from bad to worse. While old Harris lived, the absolute

1. Herschel Baker, *John Philip Kemble: The Actor in His Theatre* (Cambridge: Harvard University Press, 1942), p. 342.

control and management of the Theatre was vested in him and could be delegated to whomever he chose; but at his death this right did not automatically descend to Henry Harris, his son.[2] Soon "the remaining proprietors were bickering sadly," and understandably nervous creditors began threatening to foreclose.[3]

To John Kemble, a one-sixth shareholder, the situation at Covent Garden Theatre looked grim indeed. In addition to daily deficits, "the building-debt was enormous, and each of the patentees was personally responsible for discharging it." The elder Kemble concluded that although his share was estimated by some to be worth forty-five thousand pounds, there was slight hope of his ever realizing a profit on his investment. Meanwhile he was running the constant risk of unpleasant litigation with the creditors.[4] John Kemble shrewdly made up his mind—he must divest himself of all personal interest in the Theatre.

In November, 1820, an event took place which would shape the rest of Charles Kemble's life. John Kemble transferred by deed of gift his entire holdings in Covent Garden Theatre to his youngest and favorite brother.[5] To John Kemble this transaction marked a welcome release, his biographer Herschel Baker suggests; "and to Charles, who had no funds to tempt a creditor with, it was the chance of a lifetime."[6] Fanny Kemble, however, looking back on the occasion half a century later, recorded the event in a somewhat different light:

2. James Boaden, *Memoirs of the Life of John Philip Kemble* (London, 1825), II, 568.

3. Baker, *Kemble,* p. 345.

4. *Ibid.*

5. *Ibid.,* p. 346; also, Boaden, *Kemble,* II, 569.

6. Baker, *Kemble,* p. 346.

> My father received the property my uncle transferred to him with cheerful courage, and not without sanguine hopes of retrieving its fortunes; instead of which, it destroyed his and those of his family; who had he and they been untrammelled by the fatal obligation of working for a hopelessly ruined concern, might have turned their labours to far better personal account.[7]

For Charles Kemble the step from proprietor to manager f Covent Garden took nearly two years, since it required rst the resignation of Henry Harris, principal stockolder, from the post. The younger Harris and Kemble had ever been friends. Alfred Bunn alleged that during a uarrel in 1817 Henry Harris publicly struck Charles emble on the stage;[8] in 1819 another dispute between the wo led to Kemble's temporarily withdrawing from the ompany.[9] Moreover, besides disliking the man personally, emble, professionally, could not help but be annoyed by hat he considered Harris's managerial faults. Financially, ffairs at Covent Garden were such that in 1820 the actors ad to agree to a moratorium on their salaries;[10] and the heatre was plainly staggering under the weight of accuulated debt. Artistically, Harris depended heavily on the upposed appeal of gaudy spectacles and gilded melorama.[11] Even Shakespeare had to bow to the scene painters

7. Fanny Kemble, *Records of a Girlhood* (London, 1879), I, 59.

8. Alfred Bunn, *The Stage: Both Before and Behind the Curtain* London, 1840), I, 13.

9. William Macready, *Reminiscences, and Selections from his iaries and Letters*, ed. Frederick Pollock (New York, 1875), p. 139; so, *Theatrical Inquisitor*, November 1819.

10. Baker, *Kemble*, p. 345.

11. This is a common complaint in theatrical reviews of programs Covent Garden from 1819 to 1822.

and musicians, as the operatic revival of *The Two Gentlemen of Verona* in November, 1821, which was offered almost uninterruptedly for twenty-nine nights, attests.

Kemble was not unique in his dissatisfaction. By 1821 Henry Harris, among the shareholders, pretty well stood alone. At that time the ownership of Covent Garden was as follows: Henry Harris held fourteen twenty-fourths of the stock of the Theatre; Kemble, four twenty-fourths; John S. Willett and Captain John Forbes together three twenty-fourths; and F. Const the remaining three twenty-fourths as executor of the estate of A. Martindale. Willett and Forbes had become Charles Kemble's staunch allies, and together they worked out a plan by which they could release Covent Garden from Harris's control, as well as save the thousand pounds that was annually paid to him as manager. The three proposed to Harris that they would form a "Committee of Management" and as such lease Covent Garden from the proprietors, thus assuring Harris as principal stockholder of a reasonable rent, which he, in turn, might apply to his very troublesome debt. They explained to Harris that their purpose was solely to obtain the management of the Theatre to themselves and not to obtain any other profit from the bargain.[12]

After some negotiation Harris agreed in principle, but he held out for an exceedingly high rent. The final agreement stated that Kemble, Willett, and Forbes would become the lessees of Covent Garden Theatre for a term of ten years, computed retroactively from August 1, 1821, at a yearly rent of twelve thousand pounds, of which seven thousand pounds represented stockholder Harris's share. It was

12. "Harris vs. Kemble," *The Vice-Chancellor's Judgment*, London, April 12, 1827.

agreed, however, that no part of the rent should be paid to Harris until the current debt of the Theatre was discharged, and that the whole profits of the Theatre in the meantime should be applied to the reduction of the debt.[13] On March 11, 1822, the lease was signed; and Henry Harris officially withdrew from the management of Covent Garden Theatre, while Charles Kemble as "viceroy" of the new committee took over.[14]

The change of management was handled very quietly. Charles Kemble, returning from a dinner meeting of the Theatre's stockholders on March 11, excitedly recorded in his journal: "This day I signed the Deed of arrangement, by which I become manager of Covent Garden";[15] but the

13. "Articles of Agreement between Henry Harris . . . and John Saltren Willett of Park Street, West, John Forbes of Winkfield Place, and Charles Kemble of Gerrard Street, West," March 11, 1822. A copy of this agreement is preserved in the Archives of the London County Council. The terms are also made clear in *Harris* v. *Kemble, The Vice-Chancellor's Judgment*, April 12, 1827.

14. Macready (*Reminiscences*, p. 170) refers to Kemble as "viceroy" of the committee. It was generally understood that Charles Kemble was the principal figure among the three lessees and would act as general manager. Henry Harris, however, in "A Letter to John White, Esq, August 14, 1829" (a statement to one of his creditors which he eventually had printed), declared that he would not have agreed to the lease by Kemble without the "collateral security" afforded by Willett and Forbes, who were "men of property and entitled to large incomes under their marriage settlements from the property of the late Mr. White." Little is known about Kemble's two partners. Both were sons-in-law of George White, who bequeathed them his three twenty-fourths share of Covent Garden. J. R. Planché (*Recollections and Reflections* [London, 1872], p. 100) remarks that Willett "was a quiet person who seldom spoke," and that Forbes was a "rude and boisterous captain of the sea," who was "utterly destitute of literary taste and ignorant of theatrical usage."

15. "Professional Memoranda of Charles Kemble," British Museum Ad. MS 31976.

general public was still quite unaware of the move. On Wednesday the thirteenth the new manager introduced his partners, Willett and Forbes, to the Theatre's company in the Green Room,[16] and by the sixteenth and seventeenth the newspapers were just beginning to get word of the change.

The production of *The School for Scandal* on March 19, however, was the event which clearly signaled to the public the inauguration of a new regime. Cast with Macready as Joseph Surface and Kemble as the spirited Charles, it marked the latter's first appearance of the season on the Covent Garden stage.[17] The *Theatrical Observer* reported that the new actor-manager

> was greeted from every Box, the Pit, and the Galleries with that hearty expression of welcome which is the just recognition of his public and private claims on the respect and admiration of everyone. He appeared in good health and spirits and advanced with a celerity of warm and gentlemanly feeling to make his bow.

Of the performance that followed, the *Observer* continued: "There are few but who are acquainted with his easy and elegant representation of 'Charles' and we can only say that last night he even exceeded himself."[18] Coming amidst the run of an elaborate spectacle called *Montrose,* the mere selection of an old favorite like *The School for Scandal* was hailed by many discriminating playgoers "as a happy omen

16. *Ibid.*
17. During the period of negotiations on the management of Covent Garden Theatre, Charles Kemble did not perform at the Theatre. His absence was noted with regret and surprise in several letters to the editor columns in London newspapers. In January he appeared at Bath for a three-week engagement.
18. *Theatrical Observer,* March 20, 1822.

of the new manager's regard for the legitimate drama."[19] One theatrical reviewer in his account of the proceedings of March 19 began:

> Last night was a night of distinction for this Theatre. Forgetting for a moment the power of Spectacle and Music, it relied on the genuine Drama for attraction.... The result was a crowded and brilliant audience, who were delighted with a most admirable display of talent in every part of the performance.... We trust we may safely congratulate the public on the new arrangement at this House, which constitutes Mr. Charles Kemble chief manager.[20]

The audience in general appeared to agree: the assumption of the management by a man who was a "scholar, gentleman, and perfect master of his art" and who possessed the advantages of long experience, strong connections, and "superior taste" seemed to offer proprietors and patrons of Covent Garden Theatre alike new prospects for a prosperous future.[21]

The next few months confirmed the hopes of critics and playgoers who looked to Charles Kemble for a display of better taste. By the end of March both *Montrose* and *The Exile*—two gaudy productions which drew their applause from the antics of neighing horses—had finally been withdrawn, while frequent performances of more classic dramas ensued. On April 15, Charles Young acted Macbeth with some acclaim and on May 21 he selected for his benefit to perform King John. In the latter appearance the highly respected tragedian had not only the support of Charles

19. *Theatrical Inquisitor*, March 16, 1822.
20. *Theatrical Observer*, March 20, 1822.
21. London *Mirror*, March 17, 1822.

Kemble as the bastard Faulconbridge, but William Mac ready, who surprisingly humbled himself to play Huber For his own benefit Kemble chose the *Second Part of Henr IV*, which had proved especially popular at the end of th previous season when it was revived in anticipation of th coronation of George IV. The play was "got up with grea splendour,"[22] and Macready as King Henry and Kemble a the Prince of Wales won enthusiastic applause. Othe programs which appealed to discerning theatregoers tha spring included Macready in his popular roles of Othello an Virginius, and Young in his first London performance o Lear.

The hit of Charles Kemble's first managerial seaso however, was a production which proved a theatrica connoisseur's delight. *Julius Caesar* was brought out a Covent Garden on April 22, and the *Theatrical Pocke Magazine* unqualifyingly declared: "It was the most perfec representation that has been seen on the stage in man years." Charles Kemble had long shared with his brothe John a great respect for the attraction of the plays o Shakespeare, and he determined during his management t give the works of the master the noblest treatment of whic the company was capable. *Julius Caesar* in April marked a early fulfillment of this aim. Seldom had Londoners en countered "such a rare combination of dramatic power i one piece."[23] Young represented to perfection the nobl Brutus, Macready was superb as the wily Cassius, an Charles Kemble in Mark Antony found one of his fines parts. The critics bowed before "this triumverate of talent who worked together in a display in which "there was n one meteor whose beams eclipsed the surrounding lumi

22. *Theatrical Observer*, May 10, 1822.
23. *The Drama; or, Theatrical Pocket Magazine*, May 1822.

ıaries"; while night after night overflowing crowds com-›eted for seats in Covent Garden and congratulated them-elves on "redeeming the honour of our metropolitan aste."[24]

The Troubles Begin

On June 29 the theatrical year came to a close, and Charles Kemble looked forward to a peaceful summer levoted to making plans for his first full season. Scarcely ıad the spring engagements ceased, however, when the ıew manager was faced with a serious problem. Three of is leading performers—Young, John Liston, and Miss Kitty Stephens—grew discontented over a question of alary, with the result that next season Londoners were pplauding them at the rival theatre Drury Lane.

Kemble's actions in this matter led to considerable riticism. William Macready immediately charged him with he greatest impolicy,[25] while a recent scholar has harshly ıdged: "As manager Kemble alienated most of the actors who were box-office attractions by refusing to pay them alaries commensurate with their drawing power."[26] There s little doubt that the new manager, awed by the burden-ome debt and shaky finances of the Theatre, exercised an nwise economy. The precise details of the situation, owever, remain somewhat obscure. Macready asserted that Covent Garden's three popular performers were all lost

24. *Theatrical Observer*, April 23, 1822; *Theatrical Pocket Magazine*, May 1822.

25. Macready, *Reminiscences*, p. 203.

26. Dewey Ganzel, "Patent Wrongs and Patent Theatres," *PMLA*, XXVI (September 1961), 389.

"for an inconsiderable weekly sum." According to him, fo Kemble to have agreed to the demands of Young, Listor and Miss Stephens (which would have required a five pound-per-week advance in Macready's salary, too) woul have meant a total weekly addition to the Theatre's expenses of only twenty pounds—an addition which Kembl abruptly refused to allow.[27] Julian Young, the famou tragedian's son, wrote that the management, under pressur of the budget, "felt constrained to reduce the salaries of th principal actors on their staff," and that his father le Covent Garden to avoid a reduction from twenty-five t twenty pounds a week, and from three months vacation fo provincial tours to two.[28] A third account of the "secessions" suggests that—at least in the case of Young—ther was more than money involved. The *Theatrical Observe* reported:

> His [Young's] demands . . . were not merely an increase o salary, but to be placed in identically the same circum stances that Mr. John Kemble enjoyed when here—that —to select his own parts—to play when he pleased—an to be at liberty to absent himself from the Theatre for given time at his own option.[29]

One wonders, too, just what part manager Elliston o Drury Lane played in the Covent Garden contract dispute Alfred Bunn is among those with harsh words for the Drur Lane official. Bunn charged Elliston with breaking a important code of the theatre, as well as inaugurating a

27. Macready, *Reminiscences*, pp. 201, 203.
28. Julian Young, *A Memoir of Charles Mayne Young, Tragedia* (London, 1871), p. 81.
29. *Theatrical Observer*, October 14, 1822.

unfortunate era of inflated salaries.[30] Up to this point there was a convention between the two patent theatres which stipulated that "no performer engaged at one house should be qualified to engage at the other without undergoing a year's absence from the metropolis."[31] Disregarding this agreement, Elliston offered to hire the Covent Garden stars with an increase of salary that constituted no inconsiderable amount. Liston in 1822–23 reportedly jumped from seventeen to fifty pounds a week,[32] and Young, instead of receiving twenty pounds a week, earned that amount for a single performance![33] Whether Charles Kemble opposed it or not, the trend toward enormous salaries could not be stopped—and the following season Charles Young was back at Covent Garden earning his Drury Lane wage of twenty pounds a night.[34]

When Young, Liston, and Miss Stephens left Covent

30. Bunn, *The Stage,* I, 21 ff. Although Bunn's statements must always be considered with some skepticism, his remarks here with respect to Elliston's actions would appear to be especially free from bias. Elliston gave Bunn his "first appointment" as stage manager of Drury Lane in 1823, and Bunn offers great praise of Elliston as a person and as a manager. His criticism of Elliston's behavior in this instance comes amidst a warm tribute and is offered almost apologetically and as "a duty" to set the record straight.

31. *Ibid.*, p. 21.

32. *Ibid.*

33. Macready, *Reminiscences,* p. 203. According to Macready each of the three performers got twenty pounds a night at Drury Lane.

34. The "Covent Garden Paybook," British Museum Ad. MSS 23163–23166, shows that Charles Kemble continued to draw twenty pounds a week himself, when Young was getting twenty pounds a night. As late as 1826–27 Kemble was still only drawing twenty pounds a week in salary when he was acting six nights a week. In 1827–28 Kemble's salary advanced to twenty pounds a night and was equal to Young's; but this same season Kean, who was then acting at Covent Garden, was paid fifty pounds a night.

Garden, one personnel problem remained—the temperamental William Macready. Charles Kemble had always had the highest respect for the talents of this remarkable actor. James Planché recalled that Kemble had been among the first to recognize the dawning genius of Macready and had remarked to his skeptical brother John: "That young man will be a great actor one of these days." [35] But from the time that Charles Kemble became manager of the Theatre, it was evident to most that "he and Macready could by no means pull in the same boat." [36] A letter from Macready to Willett and Forbes dated May 1, 1822, in which he complained bitterly that Kemble, invoking an old regulation that prevented a Drury Lane performer from appearing at Covent Garden, refused to let Kean come to Covent Garden for his benefit, foretold the stormy relations ahead: "My fortunes," the actor angrily complained to Kemble's partners, "are surrendered to the single sway of an actor, whose aspirations to supremacy in his profession must render my reputation but of secondary moment to him, while he who has the motive, is also armed with the power to molest and distress me." [37] With such feelings on Macready's part, only perpetual misunderstandings could follow. "There were, no doubt, faults on both sides," Macready's biographer William Archer declared, "but it is clear that Macready worked himself into a state of unreasonable irritation which often warped his saner judgment." [38]

35. Planché, *Recollections and Reflections,* p. 254.

36. William Archer, *William Charles Macready* (London, 1890), p. 58.

37. Macready's letter is quoted by Alan S. Downer, *The Eminent Tragedian William Charles Macready* (Cambridge: Harvard University Press, 1966), pp. 89–90; and also by Archer, *Macready,* p. 58.

38. Archer, *Macready,* p. 58.

And Macready himself was later to admit that much of the "perplexity, disquiet, and irritation" which he experienced in his association with the new management "was attributable to the excitability of my own undisciplined temperament."[39]

During the 1822–23 season Macready's antagonism toward Charles Kemble grew more and more bitter and his expression of it more perverse. At one moment he was angrily demanding to examine the Theatre's books,[40] at the next he was objecting to playing his parts.[41] An incident which occurred early in March suggests the actor's recalcitrant spirit. Kemble was scheduled to play at a benefit in behalf of the Western Philanthropic Institution when news of his brother John's death (February 26, 1823) forced him to withdraw. Subsequently "a deputation was sent to Macready. As soon as their spokesman broached the business to him, he interrupted him, saying, 'So, sir, because the CORPORAL refuses to do his duty, you apply to the COMMANDER-IN-CHIEF!'"[42] The final and inevitable breach between the two came by the end of the season. Macready had signed a five-year contract with Harris placing his salary at twenty pounds a week, but it was supplemented by a verbal promise that he should have the highest salary in the Theatre. As might have been predicted, a dispute arose over the verbal pledge. According to Macready,

39. Macready, *Reminiscences*, p. 202.

40. "Letterbook of Henry Robertson," British Museum Ad. MS 29643, contains a copy of a letter, dated May 27, 1823, sent to Macready denying him permission to "inspect the Books of the Theatre." Robertson was secretary to the Committee of Management during Kemble's term as manager.

41. Archer, *Macready*, p. 62.

42. *Ibid.* Archer asserts that this "extravagant piece of arrogance is vouched for by an ear-witness."

"the committee sought to nullify the verbal part of my agreement."[43] The actor, in turn, ultimately declared that he considered his whole contract void; and in 1823–24 Macready joined the ranks of the former Covent Garden actors performing at Drury Lane.

Meanwhile on-stage Charles Kemble's first full managerial season was marked by a continually varied program in which new pieces were occasionally interspersed among old favorites. Kemble himself led off the year in a round of his favorite parts while awaiting Macready's late return from an extensive Italian tour. Hamlet on October 7 was followed quickly by Oakly (*Jealous Wife*) and Jaffeir (*Venice Preserved*). In the latter role Kemble must have been especially pleased by a compliment he received in a comparison with his Drury Lane competitor Edmund Kean: "Mr. Kean's Jaffeir is a fine performance, marked by many bursts of genius, but it has not the uniform stamp of *natural feeling* on it which we see in Mr. C. Kemble's representation," the *Theatrical Observer* wrote.[44] In leading roles in *Wonder*, *The Stranger*, *Isabella*, and *Jane Shore*, Kemble continued to win applause. Many of these plays were selected for the opportunities they provided for a series of new actresses who were busy making their London debuts. Miss Chester, Miss Patton, Miss Lacy, Miss Kelly, and Mrs. Ogilvie were among new faces successfully introduced at Covent Garden that fall; and Kemble, as manager, was praised for his determination "to bring forward new and talented performers wherever they are to be obtained."[45]

43. Macready, *Reminiscences*, p. 202; Archer, *Macready*, p. 63; Downer, *Macready*, pp. 88 ff.

44. *Theatrical Observer*, December 17, 1822.

45. *Ibid.*, November 12, 1822.

Macready finally reappeared to take his turn in November; and, in the words of one of the theatrical journals, on the thirteenth at Covent Garden "one of the most brilliant exhibitions of histrionic skill took place." Macready, supported by Charles Kemble in Cassio, reportedly performed Othello "in a style that, taking it altogether, never was surpassed."[46] After that, the talented actor—despite his difficulties with the management—was given the chance to undertake three new Shakespearean roles. In January he gave a "powerful delineation of the lofty, daring, aspiring mind" of Wolsey,[47] and was again ably seconded by Kemble in Cromwell, in a well-received revival of *Henry VIII*. Later in the spring he appeared very successfully for the first time as Shylock and won "qualified praise" in his initial portrayal of a "violent, yet weak-minded" King John.[48]

Among the new pieces that season *Maid Marian*, a legendary opera founded on the story of Robin Hood, proved exceptionally popular and provided Kemble with one of his liveliest parts. The "old play-goer" William Robson long remembered seeing the actor perform the character of the merry Friar "with such an extraordinary abandonment and gusto, that you were forced back to the 'jolly green wood, and bonny forest bramble.'" Robson recalled that Kemble "absolutely rollicked through the part, as if he had lived all his life with Robin and his men, quaffing fat ale, and devouring venison pasteries."[49] Another new play called *Julian*, however, did not fare

46. *Ibid.*, November 14, 1822.
47. *Theatrical Pocket Magazine*, January 1823.
48. *Theatrical Observer*, March 4, 1823.
49. William Robson, *The Old Play-Goer* (London, 1846), p. 48.

nearly so well. Written by Mary Mitford and purchased by Covent Garden for two hundred pounds,[50] it was a tragedy that was designed for and dedicated to Miss Mitford's favorite actor, William Macready. The author noted that Charles Kemble behaved most "fairly and honorably" toward the temperamental star on this occasion and indeed gave Macready "full power in getting up the play."[51] Nevertheless, despite Macready's efforts as hero and director, the new piece survived for only eight nights.

Off-stage that year Kemble spent a good deal of time attempting to untangle the Theatre's books. Macready, and more recently Professor Dewey Ganzel, have suggested that as manager Kemble—in contrast to Harris—was inept in financial affairs.[52] But a review of the early letters sent out by the Committee of Management seems to indicate quite the reverse. The correspondence of the new management suggests that not only did Harris leave Covent Garden encumbered by a heavy debt, he also failed to keep records by which his successor could determine to whom was owed what.[53] Henry Robertson, who served as the Theatre's

50. "Letterbook of Henry Robertson," British Museum Ad. MS 29643, contains a copy of a letter sent by the Committee of Management dated May 20, 1823, in which the payment of two hundred pounds for Miss Mitford's *Julian* is discussed.

51. Mary Mitford, letter to Sir William Elford, dated February 28, 1823, quoted in *Life of Mary Russell Mitford,* ed. A. G. L'Estrange (New York, 1870), II, 2.

52. Macready, *Reminiscences,* p. 201 ff.; Ganzel, "Patent Wrongs and Patent Theatres," pp. 389–90.

53. The "Letterbook of Henry Robertson, Secretary to the Committee of Management of Covent Garden Theatre," British Museum Ad. MS 29643, contains copies of many of the business letters sent out by Robertson either on behalf of the committee or by Charles Kemble himself for the years of Kemble's management. This

secretary during the Kemble regime, summed up the dreadful situation in which the new management found the establishment's books in a note of May 27, 1823, addressed to the Theatre's solicitor, W. H. Surman: "In reply to your letter of yesterday's date," the secretary began, "I beg to state that there are no documents in the Theatre of any description by which any account of the debt of the concern could possibly be made up." Robertson continued: "There are two books called Ledgers which have been kept here, each contradicting the other, and from neither of which could any account be extracted to show the state of any tradesman's account at any period."[54]

As a result of this state of affairs, Kemble was kept busy during his early seasons sending notes of request to Harris to furnish "particulars of sums outstanding" as well as letters of explanation to creditors such as the following: "No accounts have been rendered . . . from Mr. Harris of any such claim, but if it is acknowledged by him to be correct, it will be immediately paid by the present lessees."[55] As late as 1825, Kemble was still being troubled for money owed during Harris's reign, as a curious note of March 3 concerning bills for bricklaying in the years 1817–19

"Letterbook" is filled with letters indicating that Kemble was unaware of debts contracted by Harris, showing Kemble's persistent efforts to determine what was legitimately owed by the Theatre, and illustrating Kemble's readiness to pay substantiated claims. The failure of Harris to present Kemble with accurate financial records is further attested to in the case of *Harris* v. *Kemble*. See *The Lord Chancellor's Judgment*, May 19, 1829.

54. Copy of letter to W. H. Surman, May 27, 1823, in "Letterbook of Robertson," British Museum Ad. MS 29643.

55. Copy of letter to J. W. Robinson, September 12, 1823, from Robertson on behalf of C. Kemble and the committee, "Letterbook of Robertson," British Museum Ad. MS 29643.

attests.[56] Meanwhile the conscientious new manager was trying to eliminate as quickly as possible the Theatre's burdensome debt, and records indicate that in the first six months alone payments of £22,388 were made for that purpose.[57]

The dismissal at the end of the 1822–23 season of an old Covent Garden employee and favorite of Henry Harris provided Charles Kemble with another managerial headache which lasted until the following fall. On June 30, 1823, secretary Robertson wrote to James Brandon, the Theatre's boxkeeper, the following note:

> I am desired by the Committee of Management to acquaint you that they propose next season to make a new arrangement for the management of the Box Office of this Theatre, and they regret they cannot avail themselves of your future services.[58]

Brandon, however—who was "three score and ten" and the Theatre's "oldest servant"[59]—did not agree with his employers that the time had come to retire quietly. Despite the fact that he was offered a very generous pension of two hundred pounds per annum, he proceeded to fight the unwelcome dismissal tooth and nail.[60] He refused to vacate

56. Copy of letter to Harris, March 3, 1825, "Letterbook of Robertson," British Museum Ad. MS 29643.

57. "Covent Garden Theatre General Ledger: 1822–1829," British Museum Ad. MS 23167.

58. Copy of letter from Robertson to James Brandon, June 30, 1823, "Letterbook of Robertson," British Museum Ad. MS 29643.

59. *John Bull*, August 22, 1823.

60. Two hundred pounds is the sum offered in Robertson's letter of June 30, 1823, dismissing Brandon. Later when the dispute arose, Harris refused to pay any part of the expense of the allowance to Brandon in protest to the firing; and Const, another proprietor, also

his house, which was part of the Theatre's property, until the management was moved to employ force as a means of getting him out; and finally, much to Charles Kemble's dismay, the disgruntled boxkeeper took his case to the public press. A series of letters to the editor of the *John Bull* and *Morning Herald* newspapers ensued in which employer and employee offered charge and countercharge in a battle for public opinion.[61] Brandon demanded that the specific causes for his removal be proclaimed; and the management, after expressing reluctance "in consideration of his age and length of time he had been with the Theatre"[62] to make its charges public, was called on to publish a detailed bill of complaint. The boxkeeper's misconduct, the Theatre's lessees declared, included withholding the salaries of various servants, clandestinely selling "free admissions" to the Theatre's boxes, and failing to sell tickets to theatregoers who refused to pay him an "annual fee."[63] Brandon, in turn, of course promptly published a complete denial of all the charges.[64] Finally, by mid-September the whole matter had quieted down, but not before much wringing of hands had taken place on the part of Covent Garden's publicity-conscious proprietors.

---

declined to contribute to the pension, feeling Brandon unworthy of any consideration. Consequently on August 16, 1823, another letter was sent to Brandon from the committee offering a pension of £150 per annum during the period of the committee's lease, which sum was to be paid solely by Kemble, Willett, and Forbes.

61. See *John Bull* and *Morning Herald* newspapers for the period August 22, 1823–September 10, 1823.

62. London *Morning Herald,* August 23, 1823. See letter to the editor from Henry Robertson.

63. *John Bull* and *Morning Herald* newspapers, August 31, 1823.

64. *Ibid.,* September 4, 1823.

A Historically Accurate *King John*

When the Theatre opened its doors for the 1823–24 season, it proudly displayed a magnificently remodeled interior. In addition to an entirely new stage, proscenium and drop curtain, Covent Garden now boasted such elegant features as new cut-glass chandeliers, cushions for the boxes covered with the richest silk tabaret, and mahogany backs to the seats.[65] The splendor of the house betokened the season ahead. This year London theatregoers witnessed the most memorable event in Charles Kemble's managerial career. His November revival of *King John*, with its unprecedented attention to costume, received well-merited acclaim and marked a significant new departure in the art of theatrical production.

In the past the costuming in Shakespearean performances had regularly been one of the weakest features. James Robinson Planché, the dramatist and antiquary who worked with Kemble on *King John*, observed:

> It had long been a subject of special regret to the lovers and patrons of the theatre that the greatest number of the plays of Shakespeare, the grandest dramatic constructions which this . . . nation can boast, should be decidedly the worst dressed and most incorrectly decorated of any productions . . . exhibited upon our metropolitan boards.[66]

In the eighteenth century, for the most part, Garrick and his colleagues had performed the tragic heroes in contemporary dress no matter what the time or setting of the

65. *Theatrical Observer*, September 27, 1823.
66. James Robinson Planché, *Dramatic Costume: Costume of Shakespeare's Historical Tragedy of King John* (London, 1823), p. 3.

play.[67] Garrick, indeed, on several occasions had expressed some interest in the use of historic dresses in Shakespeare;[68] and one of his final performances of *Lear* (May 21, 1776) was reported to have been graced by characters "habited in Old English Dresses."[69] But, as Miss M. St. Clare Byrne points out, what generally passed at that time for Old English stage habits was simply "a picturesque mixture of Tudor, Elizabethan and Caroline costume."[70] On October 22, 1773, Macklin had introduced "old Scots dresses" to the English stage in a production of *Macbeth* in which, Miss Byrne suggests, Macbeth's costume in Act I consisted of "something in the nature of a tunic, with a plaid, a Balmoral bonnet, the calf-length tartan stockings of the Highlander, the eighteenth century basket hilted 'claymore' and shoes approximating to the simplest forms of brogues." In Act II, however, he evidently changed into a

67. Kalman A. Burnim, *David Garrick Director* (Pittsburgh: University of Pittsburgh Press, 1961), p. 76.

68. See letters from Garrick to Sir Grey Cooper, December 1772, and Sir William Young, January 10, 1773, quoted by M. St. Clare Byrne, "The Costuming of 'Macbeth' in the Eighteenth Century," in *Studies in English Theatre History in Memory of Gabrielle Enthoven* (London: Society for Theatre Research, 1952), p. 59.

69. London *Chronicle,* May 21–23, 1776, quoted by Burnim, *Garrick,* p. 151. For a discussion of costuming in Garrick's productions, see Burnim, pp. 75–78. Robert G. Noyes, *Ben Jonson on the English Stage: 1660–1776* (Cambridge: Harvard University Press, 1935), mentions Garrick's productions of Jonson's *The Alchemist* and *Every Man in His Humour* with "the characters dress'd in the Habits of the Time."

70. Byrne, *Studies in English Theatre History in Memory of Gabrielle Enthoven,* p. 54. Donald T. Mackintosh, "New Dress'd in the Habits of the Times," *The Times Literary Supplement,* August 25, 1927, similarly defines "old English habits" as Tudor and Elizabethan. He suggests there were a number of productions so costumed at both Drury Lane and Covent Garden between 1762 and 1776.

"more dignified gentleman's costume, with Scottish touches," and Lady Macbeth wore throughout "fashionable contemporary costume."[71] John Kemble, during his years at Drury Lane and Covent Garden, had initiated several reforms in dramatic dress. Among other things, Charles's brother had rescued Othello from his traditional footman's garb and had finally abolished the ridiculous bagwig of Brutus.[72] But at the time when Charles Kemble assumed the management of Covent Garden, dramatic costuming remained in a rather crude state. Planché, while acknowledging John Kemble's efforts, remarked:

> The alterations made in the costume of the plays founded upon English history in particular, while they rendered them more picturesque, added but little to their propriety; the whole series, *King Lear* included, being dressed in the habits of the Elizabethan era, . . . and, strictly speaking, very inaccurately representing the costume even of that period.[73]

The credit for originating the idea of the revival of *King John* with historically accurate costumes is not easily assigned. An article in the *New European Magazine* the previous spring possibly provided a significant hint. After reviewing Macready's first performance as John, a sharp-eyed critic had written:

> We cannot close our remarks upon this play without noticing the impropriety of dressing the English Herald in a tabard charged with the arms of France and England quarterly, when it is so well known that it was not until the

71. Bryne, *Studies in English Theatre History in Memory of Gabriëlle Enthoven*, pp. 59, 55, 58, 53.

72. Planché, *Recollections and Reflections*, p. 36; *Fraser's Magazine*, December 1854.

73. Planché, *Recollections and Reflections*, p. 36.

> time of Edward the Third, some four reigns later, that the British Monarchs assumed the French Fleurs de Lis. . . . It is full as easy to be correct as erroneous and whatever misleads the ignorant, while it offends those who know better, is at least worth improving.[74]

J. R. Planché in his *Recollections and Reflections* implied that it was he who deserved honors for first suggesting the plan for the production in a casual conversation with Charles Kemble.[75] On another occasion, however, Planché stated that a revision of costuming in the Shakespearean plays was a reformation which Kemble had long been anxious to introduce;[76] and the press at the time generally attributed the original idea to the manager himself.

In any case, Charles Kemble became excited by the possibilities of the project and assigned his friend Planché to work out the details. At this time Planché, who was regularly employed at Covent Garden as a writer, knew little about the subject of costume, which, he declared, "afterwards became my most absorbing study."[77] In order to carry on the necessary research for the production the dramatist sought the help of two noted antiquaries, Sir Samuel Meyrick, who had just published an elaborate work entitled *A Critical Inquiry into Ancient Arms and Armour*, and Francis Douce, who offered the resources of a valuable library. Planché also hastened to examine personally all the early-thirteenth-century shields, seals, monuments, arras, and stained-glass windows that he could discover.[78]

74. *New European Magazine*, March 1823.
75. Planché, *Recollections and Reflections*, pp. 35, 36, 39.
76. Planché, *Dramatic Costume: Costume of King John*, p. 4.
77. Planché, *Recollections and Reflections*, p. 36.
78. Planché, *Dramatic Costume: Costume of King John*, p. 7; *Recollections and Reflections*, pp. 36–37.

The results of Planché's energetic efforts were finally displayed in the magnificent costumes he designed. King John was to appear first in a splendid court dress copied from his effigy in the choir of Worcester Cathedral, and secondly, armed for battle in the precise habit depicted on his Great Seal. Faulconbridge was to make his entrance in a rather plain brown cloak, trimmed in blue, and in pink tights, a costume authenticated by *Strutt's Dress and Habits* as well as by enameled figures on King John's silver cup. Later the spirited warrior would dazzle the audience dressed after the effigy of a knight of the thirteenth century in Malvern Church, Worcestershire, with the added attraction of a spear suggested by an illuminated Cotton Manuscript.[79] Queen Elinor, Blanch, Prince Henry—even the least prominent soldier in the field was similarly provided by Planché with a costume designed from "indisputable authorities."

Although Charles Kemble immediately voiced his enthusiastic approval, Planché's innovations were reportedly "regarded with distrust and jealousy" by other members of the company. Fawcett, the stage manager, was offended by the play being put so greatly under Planché's direction; and according to Planché, Fawcett hardly spoke to him again for nearly three years. Farley, the "recognized purveyor and director of spectacle," was upset at "expenditures of a few hundred pounds on any drama, except an Easter piece or a Christmas pantomime." "If Shakespeare is to be produced with such splendour and attention to costume, what am I to do for the holidays?" he exclaimed. The actors, too, viewed their new wardrobe with considerable skepticism.

79. Planché, *Dramatic Costume: Costume of King John*, pp. 13–14, 21–22.

"Never shall I forget the dismay of some of the performers when they looked upon the flat-topped *chapeaux de fer* (*fer blanc*, I confess) of the twelfth century, which they irreverently stigmatized as *stewpans*," Planché recalled. "Nothing but the fact that the classical features of a Kemble were to be surmounted by a precisely similar abomination would, I think, have induced one of the rebellious barons to have appeared in it."[80]

Just in case the audience might have its own reservations about the new project, Kemble had Planché prepare a booklet entitled *Dramatic Costume* to be circulated a few days before the first performance. Explaining the management's new program for rendering "the dresses and decorations of Shakespeare's plays, if possible, worthy of them," it was designed to stimulate interest and put the spectators in the right frame of mind.[81] Such extra precautions, however, proved quite unnecessary. On November 24, *King John*—with Young in the lead and Charles Kemble as Faulconbridge—was an unqualified success. Planché wrote:

> When the curtain rose, and discovered King John dressed as his effigy appears in Worcester Cathedral, surrounded by his barons sheathed in mail, with cylindrical helmets and correct armorial shields, and his courtiers in the long tunics and mantles of the thirteenth century, there was a roar of approbation, accompanied by four distinct rounds of applause, so general and so hearty, that the actors were astonished; and I felt amply rewarded for all . . . my labours.[82]

80. Planché, *Recollections and Reflections*, pp. 37–38.
81. Planché, *Dramatic Costume: Costume of King John*, p. 4.
82. Planché, *Recollections and Reflections*, p. 38. Evelyn Richmond, in "Historical Costuming; a Footnote," *Shakespeare Quarterly*, XI, No. 2 (Spring 1960), 233–34, points out that the date of the first

The theatrical reviewers next day were lavish with praises for the "liberality and taste"[83] of the Covent Garden manager and assured their readers that the *King John* production would "form a memorable epoch in the history of the British stage."[84] Many critics called for Kemble to "devote an equal share of pains and talent to the other plays of the immortal bard"—a request which the manager was quick to heed.[85] Before the end of the season Londoners were seeing Henry IV "dressed after his effigy in the Chapel of St. Thomas a Beckett"; and in subsequent years *As You Like It*, *Hamlet*, *The Merchant of Venice*, *Othello*, *Cymbeline*, and *Henry VIII* were produced by Kemble with similar attention to costume. In the later revivals special efforts were also made to use only entirely accurate scenery. Thus in *Henry VIII* theatregoers were presented not only with Henry wearing an authentic crown, but with views of "St. Paul's and London Bridge, as they were in 1533."[86] Charles Kemble had indeed initiated a new fashion—though it was one which would find its ultimate fulfillment in the remarkable productions of Macready, Phelps, and Charles Kean. Still, as one admirer would say: To these managers belongs "the full credit of having followed a good example; to Charles Kemble appertains the honour of having led the way."[87]

---

performance of Kemble's *King John* has been vaguely and erroneously recorded in several stage histories.

83. *Theatrical Pocket Magazine*, December 1823.

84. *Theatrical Observer*, November 25, 1823.

85. *John Bull*, December 1, 1823.

86. Playbill for Covent Garden Theatre production of *King Henry VIII*, November 2, 1831, in the Harvard Theatre Collection.

87. *Fraser's Magazine*, December 1854. For Macready's use of the costumes originally designed for the Kemble production in his

Legal Problems

While Charles Kemble was enjoying his greatest public success following the production of *King John*, privately he was already beginning to encounter the legal difficulties which would cloud the remainder of his managerial career. The agreement of March 11, 1822, it seems, had been entered into by Kemble with an eagerness and enthusiasm that precluded the proper investigations and negotiations. Now that ill-considered lease had come home to haunt him and to give rise to endless litigation.

Somehow during the negotiations that led up to the lease, the proprietors had failed to consult with one of the Theatre's stockholders, F. Const, who held a one-eighth share as executor for the Estate of A. Martindale. Everyone simply assumed that Const—who had previously taken no active interest in the affairs of the Theatre—would concur in the intended lease, but at the last minute this expectation was disappointed. Consequently the agreement was executed by Harris, Kemble, Willett, and Forbes without Const—the only other shareholder—being a party.[88]

It was not long before the abstaining stockholder, Const, was causing trouble. He began by demanding his right to review Covent Garden's accounts.[89] Next he was delving

famous revival of *King John* at Drury Lane on October 24, 1842, see Charles Shattuck's Introduction, *William Charles Macready's King John*, ed. Shattuck (Urbana: University of Illinois Press, 1962), pp. 7 ff.

88. *Harris* v. *Kemble, The Vice-Chancellor's Judgment*, April 12, 1827.

89. "Letterbook of Henry Robertson," British Museum Ad. MS 9643, contains a copy of a letter to Const from Robertson on behalf of the committee, March 18, 1823, discussing Const's "wishes regarding the accounts" and advising that "the Books of every description are always ready for your inspection at the Theatre."

into the archives of the Theatre, examining any old con tracts and agreements that he could find. Finally on th fifteenth of April, 1823, Const filed a bill in the Court c Chancery against the lessees Kemble, Willett, and Forbes.[9 Const, it appears, had discovered a long disregarded dee dated March 9, 1812, by which the proprietors of Coven Garden at that time had contracted with each other that th funds of the Theatre should be applied in payments o certain specified debts until the whole thereof were satisfied Stating that some of these debts remained undischarged an that the funds of the Theatre were now applied contrary t the provisions of the deed of 1812, Const requested in hi suit that effect be given to the old deed and that for tha purpose a receiver of the profits of the Theatre be ap pointed. Much to the dismay of the lessees, the plaintiff ha his way; and on February 19, 1824, the receivership a Covent Garden began.[91]

Charles Kemble, meanwhile, had grown most unhapp about the arrangements under the 1822 lease for the pay ment of a fixed rent. He had originally requested that th rent be determined annually on the basis of the Theatre' profits, but this idea Harris had firmly opposed. By the tim of the Const suit it had become obvious to the manager tha the rent of twelve thousand pounds was exorbitant. Face with an impossible rent and now a receivership that took th financial control of the Theatre out of his hands, Kembl wrote to Harris expressing the intention of the lessees t repudiate the agreement of March 11.[92]

90. *Harris* v. *Kemble, The Vice-Chancellor's Judgment,* April 12 1827.
91. *Ibid.*
92. *Ibid.*

Henry Harris, however, knew an advantageous situation hen he saw one; and from his point of view the arrange- ent of March 11, 1822, couldn't have been better. While uaranteed a handsome rent, he was free from any worries bout the Theatre—and above all, the problems that might rise from its heavy debt. Harris did not need to pause long consider Charles Kemble's letter, and he served his reply y summoning poor Kemble and his fellow lessees once ore to court. On April 24, 1824, Harris filed suit for the urpose of compelling Kemble, Willett, and Forbes to dhere to the terms of their lease.[93]

The litigation which followed dragged on for seven long ears, during which time, Fanny Kemble remarked, "that iserable subject became literally the sauce to our daily read; embittering my father's life with incessant care and arassing vexation." She recalled with feeling:

> For years that dreary Chancery suit seemed to envelop us in an atmosphere of palpitating suspense or stagnant uncertainty, and to enter as an inevitable element into every hope, fear, expectation, resolution, or action of our lives. How unutterably heartsick I became of the very sound of its name, and how well I remember the expression of my father's careworn face one day, as he turned back from the door, out of which he was going to his daily drudgery at the theatre, to say to my aunt, who had reproached him with the loss of a button from his rather shabby coat, "Ah, Dall, my dear, you see it is my Chancery suit!"[94]

n April 12, 1827, the lessees heard the harsh news that the ice-chancellor's judgment had gone against them; but the ase was appealed, and Kemble, Willett, and Forbes had

93. *Ibid.*
94. Kemble, *Records of a Girlhood,* I, 143–44.

occasion to cheer when the lord chancellor proclaimed hi decision. The defense, in insisting that the 1822 agreemen ought to be laid aside, based its case on three main points First, the lessees claimed that since their lease was enacte for the sole purpose of acquiring complete control over th Theatre's management and funds, and by the appointmen of a receiver under the deed of 1812 that very control wa denied them, the lease should be no longer binding. Seconc they pointed out that at the time of the lease they were nc informed of the deed of 1812 and that it was the plaintiff' duty to have apprised them of its existence. Third, th defendants were ready to show that they were obliged t agree to an exorbitant rent in consequence of financia misrepresentations on the part of Harris.[95] With thes contentions Lord Chancellor Lyndhurst in his judgment c May 19, 1829, was moved to agree, and he exercised hi authority to reverse the vice-chancellor's opinion.[96] Thi time it was Harris's turn to appeal, and he took the case t the House of Lords, England's highest tribunal. It was th autumn of 1831 before the warring proprietors learned th ultimate decision. By that time the troublesome lease ha expired; but in view of the accumulated rent, Kemble anc his partners were anxiously awaiting the word. No man i England was happier than Charles Kemble the night o October 13 when he finally heard the news: His lega troubles were over at last—the House of Lords had uphelc the lord chancellor's verdict.[97]

95. *Harris* v. *Kemble, The Vice-Chancellor's Judgment,* April 12 1827; *Harris* v. *Kemble, The Lord Chancellor's Judgment,* May 19 1829.

96. *Harris* v. *Kemble, The Lord Chancellor's Judgment,* May 19, 1829

97. *Harris* v. *Kemble, Journals of the House of Lords,* LXII (1831), 1085.

A Manager's Routine

The middle years of Charles Kemble's reign at Covent Garden were ones in which the major problems of the chancery suit and the Theatre's tottering finances were sometimes mercifully submerged beneath the daily pressures of a manager's routine—at least a glance at Kemble's voluminous business correspondence so suggests.[98] For one thing, there were constantly new plays to be read and their purchases negotiated. In this task Kemble was especially conscientious. He tried always to make the purchase price of a play contingent upon its success by agreeing to pay the author so many pounds for each night that his play would run.[99] In rejecting a manuscript submitted by a hopeful playwright Charles Kemble invariably displayed the utmost courtesy. Occasionally he even received a would-be author's thanks for taking time to pencil in constructive criticism.[100]

98. See the "Letterbook of Henry Robertson," British Museum Ad. MS 29643 for Kemble's business correspondence.

99. A typical arrangement for purchasing a play is indicated in the terms for Mary Mitford's tragedy *Foscari*. Miss Mitford was offered one hundred pounds for the third night; one hundred pounds for the ninth night; one hundred pounds for the fifteenth night, and one hundred pounds for the twentieth night that *Foscari* played. See "Letterbook of Robertson," British Museum Ad. MS 29643. This method of paying dramatists was fairly standard. See E. B. Watson, *Sheridan to Robertson: A Study in the Nineteenth Century Stage* (Cambridge: Harvard University Press, 1926), p. 435. Obviously this arrangement protected the manager by insuring him against paying a sizable amount for a play which might be hooted down the first night. Sometimes writers objected to this method of payment, and occasionally payment was actually made before a piece was written. Robertson's "Letterbook" includes a copy of a letter to Theodore Hook, March 24, 1830, enclosing a check "for £100 for an afterpiece in two acts to be written and delivered . . . by 15 September next."

100. One such thank-you note was sent by Edward Gandy,

There were, of course, always new members of the company to be hired, old members to be fired, and a great many contracts to renew. Oxberry recalled that it was a peculiarity of Kemble's that he was actually very fond of auditioning young aspirants—"a circumstance sufficiently astonishing, when we consider the tedium attending these exercises." He added, however, that Kemble's great urbanity frequently prevented him from telling these eager young performers disagreeable truths.[101] Quite often there were recalcitrant and temperamental actresses to be dealt with: Miss Gifford fails to attend rehearsals; Mrs. Chatterly objects to playing certain parts; and Miss Tree wants time off for a provincial tour.[102] Each such offender had to be cautiously but firmly reprimanded, and some made to pay a stipulated fine.[103] Occasionally there were extra arrangements for a performance to be made, as when the king paid the house a visit. Then manager Kemble might have to dash off a hurried note to the police requesting that "carriages may not be permitted to enter Hart Street from the west, until His Majesty is in the Theatre this evening."[104]

December 17, 1824, for Kemble's criticism of his rejected play *Caswallan*. Kemble's letter to Gandy rejecting his play and Gandy's reply are in the Harvard Theatre Collection.

101. W. Oxberry, *Dramatic Biography and Histrionic Anecdotes*, III (London, 1825), 10.

102. See letters to Miss Gifford, November 16, 1825; Mrs. Chatterly, November 17, 1824; and Miss Tree, January 22, 1824, "Letterbook of Robertson," British Museum Ad. MS 29643.

103. Fines were sometimes extremely high. A letter of March 10 1827, to James Bradshaw levies a penalty of one thousand pounds for the nonfulfillment of an engagement by Mrs. Bradshaw ("Letterbook of Robertson," British Museum Ad. MS 29643).

104. Letter of December 3, 1823, "Letterbook of Robertson," British Museum Ad. MS 29643.

In the course of fulfilling all these managerial duties, Charles Kemble never failed to maintain his company's admiration and respect. Edward Fitzball remembered him as "the most gracious manager that ever breathed," and recalled "how agreeable and intellectual all rehearsals invariably were at Covent Garden in those days";[105] while B. E. Hill testified that Kemble, though a perfectionist in his own acting, "was to all about him very lenient of defects and imperfections."[106] It was not that he would let "imperfections" pass unnoticed. With respect to his inaugural production of *School for Scandal* the *Theatrical Observer* had been quick to remark: "Even the servants who removed the chairs or handled the tea and coffee were done to life."[107] Like his brother, Charles Kemble was convinced that a good manager should not neglect detail. But his manner, whether he was correcting a careless or less skillful actor at rehearsal or telling an unhappy playwright that his piece had to be withdrawn, was consistently gentle and kind. Fitzball indeed could never forget the manager's remarkable kindness to him on one occasion. As a hopeful dramatist he had experienced a painful evening when his first piece for Covent Garden (*Father and Son*) proved quite obviously to be a failure. Heartsick, the author hurried away from the Theatre, but he soon discovered that he had been followed:

> When I heard a voice calling after me in a *very* friendly tone, I was almost afraid to turn my head; when I did so, however, what could equal my astonishment at seeing the

105. Edward Fitzball, *Thirty-five Years of a Dramatic Author's Life* (London, 1859), I, 108, 177.
106. Benson Earle Hill, *Playing About* (London, n.d.), I, 143.
107. *Theatrical Observer,* June 6, 1822.

> manager Mr. Charles Kemble at my elbow. He had inquired the way I had taken, and followed me from the Theatre to *console* me. Was he not a manager! And taking me by the hand, he conjured me in a most amiable way to keep my spirits. . . . Was he not a manager![108]

During these middle years of Kemble's management there were, of course, various on-stage pleasures which helped to ease the back-stage pain. The Shakespearean revivals which followed *King John* continued to bring acclaim, though one critic, after seeing a "historically accurate" presentation of *Cymbeline,* somewhat caustically declared: "We expect next to see legitimate authority produced for the dressing of Puck, and authenticated wings allotted to Mustardseed."[109] On one occasion, at least, these revivals provided Charles Kemble with a widely talked-about new role. Much to everyone's surprise, bills for the performance of *Henry IV* on May 3, 1824, announced Charles Kemble as Falstaff. "Who could suppose the ardent and enthusiastic Romeo ready to leap up to Juliet in the balcony as a person likely to 'lard the lean earth as he walk'd along?'" the *Theatrical Pocket Magazine* exclaimed.[110] The rest of London felt the same way, and curiosity brought them to the Theatre in great droves. Apparently the handsome actor sustained the character of the humorous knight "better than could have been supposed."[111] He was reportedly "eminently successful" in the Gad's Hill episode,[112] and later "made a palpable hit by his swaggering manner of pointing out the fallen

108. Fitzball, *Thirty-five Years of a Dramatic Author's Life,* I, 115
109. *Theatrical Observer,* May 17, 1827.
110. *Theatrical Pocket Magazine,* May 1824.
111. *Theatrical Observer,* May 4, 1824.
112. *Ibid.*

Percy as a trophy of his own powers."[113] One viewer suggested that Kemble rescued the part from some of the "coarseness with which it had usually been represented," and that "in the presence of the King, and in the conversation with Westmoreland, he invested it with a gentility and courtly bearing."[114] The novelty of his personation, however, soon wore off; and in later years whenever he played the part, critics were quick to suggest that Charles Kemble would be wise to return to the more fitting role of Prince Hal.

In 1824–25 Covent Garden experienced a phenomenal success in the presentation of Carl von Weber's opera *Der Freischütz*, which drew packed houses for fifty-two performances and greatly replenished the Theatre's depleted funds. Fanny Kemble wrote fifty years later: "Few operas, I believe, have had a wider or more prolonged popularity; none certainly within my recollection ever had anything approaching it."[115] Weber's music alone proved a great attraction, but the elaborate production given the German piece at Covent Garden made it a spectacle that was long remembered. A theatrical journal described the atmospheric appeal of the famous incantation scene:

> It represented the gloom of midnight hanging over the Wolf's Glen—the moon eclipsed—the magic circle formed—the wind's hollow sound breathing through the forest—the spirit, invoked, appearing in the opening rock enveloped in flames—the casting of each bullet, attended by the chorus-howling of daemons and noises resembling the discharge of artillery and firearms—the skeleton chase in

113. *Theatrical Observer*, May 11, 1824.

114. John Genest, *Some Account of the English Stage: From the Restoration in 1660 to 1830* (Bath, 1832), IX, 257.

115. Kemble, *Records of a Girlhood*, I, 153.

> the sky—the assemblage of frightful monsters creeping—and in the air—a chariot of fire bearing death, a skeleton of flame . . . . This scene closed amidst the cheers of the audience.[116]

Fanny Kemble, who was then at the impressionable age of fifteen, used to witness the performance regularly from her father's box at the Theatre and soon knew it all by heart. Her enthusiasm became so great, she later confessed, that she wore the rather homely composer's picture "like an amulet round my neck, until I completely wore it out." Indeed the remarkable success of *Der Freischütz* induced Charles Kemble to write to Weber proposing that he compose an opera expressly for Covent Garden Theatre. The aging German musician readily accepted, and the chivalric fairy tale of Wieland's "Oberon" was selected for the subject. Fanny recalled that "it was very gracefully and poetically treated by Mr. Planché, to whom the literary part of the work—the libretto—was confided"; and the following season Weber himself came to England to superintend the final rehearsals. On April 12, 1826, *Oberon* was brought out, but it failed to match *Der Freischütz*'s acclaim. Fanny wrote that it "succeeded, but in a degree so far below the sanguine expectations of all concerned, that failure itself, though more surprising, would hardly have been a greater disappointment than the result achieved at such a vast expenditure of money, time, and labour."[117]

In the 1825–26 season Covent Garden proudly announced the acquisition of the colorful singer and actress Mme Vestris, as well as the tragedian Warde. Concerning the former, the *Theatrical Observer* suggested: "The addi-

116. *Theatrical Observer,* October 15, 1824.
117. Kemble, *Records of a Girlhood,* I, 154, 155, 162.

tion of Madame Vestris to this establishment is perhaps one of the most fortunate steps the management could have taken. Whatever may be the nature of her private amusements . . . she certainly possesses the power of attraction still."[118] Mme Vestris did in fact prove to be a box-office favorite; she won great applause in all musical productions, especially *The Beggar's Opera.* The most striking addition to the Theatre's personnel, however, came in the fall of 1827 with the engagement of the famous Drury Lane star and long-standing rival to the Kemble acting tradition Edmund Kean. With Kean, Young, Vestris, and Kemble in its ranks Covent Garden could indeed afford this season to boast of its superior talent. Kean first appeared at Covent Garden on October 15 in the character of Shylock, which he reportedly performed "with all his consummate mastery of style and unrivalled execution."[119] His reception was a triumphant one; and he followed it up with a round of his favorite roles, including Richard III, Sir Giles Overreach, Othello, Sir Edward Mortimer (*Iron Chest*), and Lear. Charles Kemble considerately offered the remarkable actor his support in second parts and played opposite him as Bassanio, Richmond, Wellborn, and Cassio. The production of *Othello* on December 21 turned out to be an especially gala event, with a cast of Kean, Kemble, and Young. Apparently there was such a terrific crush in the house that some young men climbed from the pit into the lower boxes to escape suffocation, while others, in a fainting condition, were passed by friendly hands toward the door for air.[120] According to all reports, the performance proved worth the squeeze: "We

118. *Theatrical Observer,* November 16, 1825.
119. *Ibid.,* October 16, 1827.
120. [John] Doran, *Their Majesties Servants* (London, 1888), III, 411.

can scarcely imagine a higher intellectual gratification," the critic for the *Theatrical Observer* exclaimed.[121]

Just before introducing his Covent Garden patrons to the talents of Edmund Kean, Kemble had enjoyed a great acting success of his own in an early autumn appearance at a newly opened English theatre in Paris. In September, Fanny Kemble wrote anxiously to her closest friend:

> My father is in Paris, where he was to arrive yesterday, and where to-morrow he will act in the first regularly and decently organized English theatre that the French ever saw. He is very nervous and we, as you may easily conceive, very anxious about it; when next I write to you I will let you know all that we hear of the result.

The result was a far happier one than Charles Kemble or his family could have predicted. Fanny, in her next letter, dated October 11, 1827, proudly reported: "My father has obtained a most unequivocal success in Paris, the more flattering as it was rather doubtful; and the excellent Parisians have not only received him very well, but forthwith threw themselves into a headlong *furor* for Shakespeare and Charles Kemble."[122] Kemble and the Covent Garden performers who accompanied him that autumn indeed won a tremendously enthusiastic appraisal from the French (in sharp contrast to the harsh treatment of an earlier English company that had attempted to give Shakespeare in France in 1822.)[123] And subsequent appearances by Macready and

121. *Theatrical Observer,* December 22, 1827.

122. Kemble, *Records of a Girlhood,* I, 185, 191.

123. Robert Eddison, "Souvenirs du Théâtre anglais à Paris, 1827," *Theatre Notebook,* IX (July–September 1955), 100 ff. For a further discussion of Kemble's reception in Paris, see J. L. Borgerhoff, *Le Théâtre anglais à Paris sous la Restauration* (Paris: Hachette, 1912), pp. 75 ff., 132–33.

Kean in Paris in the spring likewise met with great success. France had long been "in the rigid clutches of classical tragedy performed in a cold and formal style."[124] But the time was right, it seems, for a revolution; and the new realism of the English actors, the display of flesh-and-blood passions on the stage, made a great impact on the French theatre. As Professor Alan Downer has recently observed, "the effects of this season of English acting were far-reaching" and led ultimately to "the complete reversal of the French technique of playwriting and acting."[125]

Kemble's performances that first stirred Paris were in *Romeo and Juliet*, *Othello*, and *Hamlet*. In the latter play the warm praise given by a French reviewer to his portrayal of "simulated madness" has already been noted;[126] and with the actor's sensitive performance of Romeo, Parisian critics were equally impressed. "How these adieux are touching," one French writer reported, adding: "It is impossible to project further . . . the semblance of agony and, as it were, convulsion, that precedes the death scene." Taken altogether, Kemble's acting seemed to "approximate more closely to Gallic desiderata than Kean's." As one Parisian playgoer expressed it, compared to Kean's "altogether British verve," Kemble's "truth is less impetuous, but more persuasive."[127]

A Financial Crisis

No matter how diverting the routine duties of his job might be, or how cheering the effect of a successful appear-

124. Downer, *Macready*, p. 112.
125. *Ibid.*, p. 116.
126. See p. 80 above.
127. "Souvenirs dû Théâtre anglais à Paris," p. 101.

ance or new production, Charles Kemble was unable t dispel for long the worry occasioned by Covent Garden' tottering finances. The problem of "insufficient funds" wa called to mind every time he received a bill or viewed a rov of empty seats. From the 1825–26 season on, he could no help but feel that his Theatre was headed for a financia crisis.

The cause of Covent Garden's fiscal distress—which wa indeed shared at this time by Drury Lane—is not easil explained. A multiplicity of contributing factors wer obviously involved. The Theatre, of course, inherited heavy deficit from past administrations, including a sizabl building debt remaining from the construction of th elaborate house in 1809. Then, too, the trouble with Cons and the resulting receivership and the chancery suit wit Harris provided endless financial complications. Poo attendance, resulting from public apathy and the increase competition of the minor theatres and the Opera House, o course, cannot be denied. Although Covent Garden ha enjoyed an Indian summer of prosperity during several earl seasons under Charles Kemble's control, from 1826 to 182 receipts were extremely low;[128] and in the opening weeks o

128. Receipts at Covent Garden Theatre from 1821–22 to 1831–3 as published in the "Report of the Select Committee on Dramati Literature of the House of Commons," *Great Britain Parliamentar Reports*, VII (1831–1832), Appendix, are as follows:

1821–22	£58,171
1822–23	52,318
1823–24	60,496
1824–25	72,160
1825–26	58,017
1826–27	53,032
1827–28	55,212
1828–29	41,029

he 1828–29 season they barely averaged two hundred pounds a night.[129] At the same time inflated salaries and high production costs became, more and more, an unavoidable expense. Alfred Bunn contended that part of the distress could be charged to an indiscriminate distribution of orders, or free admissions. He claimed that 11,003 such passes were issued from May 17 to July 12, 1824, alone—which, calculated at the rate of 7s. each, amounts to the considerable sum of £3,851. Bunn suggested that had these orders not been given, "at least one half of the amount might have found its way into the treasury of the Theatre."[130] Professor Dewey Ganzel has cited overstaffing at the patent houses as another important cause of monetary troubles. In addition to the regular tragedies and comedies, "the general public demanded farce, ballet, and pantomime as well, and these necessitated additional actors." Moreover, the rage for opera made it imperative that the theatres also have an orchestra and a company of soloists and chorus. "Only if they maintained all three of these companies could the patent theatres hope to attract all the audience they claimed as their exclusive right," yet scarcely one-third of the performers "would be used in a single evening."[131] Finally, an unfortunate accident at Covent Garden in the late fall of 1828 dealt the Theatre's rapidly failing treasury a deadly blow. A gas explosion in the basement of the Theatre resulted in

---

1829–30	57,431
1830–31	42,248
1831–32	43,318

129. "Covent Garden Theatre Diary, 1828–1829," British Museum Ad. MS 23159.

130. Bunn, *The Stage*, I, 82, 85.

131. Ganzel, "Patent Wrongs and Patent Theatres," p. 390.

the death of several workmen and the closing of Covent Garden, at the height of the season, for several weeks.

Whatever the causes of the Theatre's troubled finances, some effects could easily be perceived by the middle of Charles Kemble's reign. At Covent Garden each season, beginning with 1825–26, witnessed a further reduction in personnel and a greater inability to pay outstanding debts.[132] At home, Fanny Kemble declared, "The constantly darkening prospects of that unlucky theatre threw a gloom over us all" and necessitated the most rigid sort of domestic economy. At one point poor Kemble had to move his family in order to keep his son Henry in school; and at another Fanny, in a letter to a close friend, pathetically confessed:

> It seems that my father, as proprietor of Covent Garden Theatre . . . is liable at any time to be called upon for twenty-seven thousand pounds; which, for a man who cannot raise five thousand, is not a pleasant predicament.

As affairs at the Theatre grew worse and worse, Fanny Kemble in later years revealed, "My father used to speak of selling his shares in it for anything he could get . . . and going to live abroad; or sending my mother, with us, to live cheaply in the South of France, while he continued to work in London."[133]

In the summer of 1829 the financial crisis at Covent Garden reached its peak. By the end of July the Theatre faced demands for the immediate payment of rates and taxes, and it simply did not possess the necessary funds.

132. This situation is clearly indicated by the correspondence in the "Letterbook of Robertson," British Museum Ad. MS 29643.

133. Kemble, *Records of a Girlhood,* I, 274, 177, 175.

Kemble was away on a provincial tour when Henry Robertson was forced to write to stockholders Const and Harris the following note apprising them of the disastrous situation:

> I have to acquaint you that a notice has been served at the Theatre relative to the arrears of Poor and Parochial Rates to midsummer last amounting to £1126-8-8 and that it has been intimated to me that unless some portion thereof is immediately paid, a warrant will be taken out on Monday next for their recovery.
>
> A similar notice has been given to me today by M. Richardson of King Street, Covent Garden, that he shall put in a distress on Monday morning for between £500 and £600 due for land and assessed taxes to midsummer last.
>
> I have further to inform you that I have no funds in hand . . . to enable me to pay any part of the claim.[134]

Within a few days of Robertson's letter of July 25, the dire intimations had come to pass. The distress warrants for rates and taxes had been issued, and the Theatre was in the possession of bailiffs. Newspapers sadly announced that Covent Garden would be closed the next season and that the famous theatre and all its properties would eventually be sold.

Charles Kemble determined, however, to make a final effort to save Covent Garden if he could. In a letter from Dublin dated August 13, he promised that although his wealthy partners Willett and Forbes "desert the vessel in the storm," he would do everything in his power "to carry on the concern" if "the obstacle to re-opening can by any means be removed."[135] The manager hurried back to

134. Copy of a letter from Robertson to Const and Harris, July 25, 1829, "Letterbook of Robertson," British Museum Ad. MS 29643.

135. Letter from Charles Kemble to Messrs. Londham Parke and Company, August 13, 1829, in Harvard Theatre Collection.

London and by the first week in September had various projects for rescuing Covent Garden underway. A subscription was arranged whereby "friends of the Theatre" were requested to contribute, through gifts or loans, to a six thousand pound fund-raising goal; principal creditors were asked to waive their claims for the present; Covent Garden shareholders agreed to make a complete sacrifice of profit for the ensuing season and to suspend payment of dividends for three years; various actors offered to play gratuitously for from three to ten nights; and finally, a benefit performance for Covent Garden Theatre, to take place at the King's Theatre, was announced. As a result of Kemble's tireless efforts, on September 11 the *Theatrical Observer* carried welcome news to London playgoers: "Doubts as to the opening of Covent Garden . . . are at an end."

Kemble's rescue mission was only half completed when the obstacle to reopening had finally been removed. The serious problem of how to keep Covent Garden open—beyond the first few nights—remained. For this difficulty Charles Kemble's nineteen-year-old daughter provided the solution. To the amazingly successful debut of Fanny Kemble belongs the ultimate credit for retrieving the position of the Theatre.

For Fanny Kemble the idea of a career on the stage was not an entirely new one in the fall of 1829. Charles Kemble's daughter had as early as February, 1828, written to Harriet St. Leger expressing an interest in becoming an actress:

> The stage is a profession that people who have a talent for it make lucrative, and which honourable conduct may make respectable; one which would place me at once

> beyond the fear of want, and that is closely allied in its nature to my beloved literary pursuits.[136]

But not long after this note was sent, Fanny was off to spend a year in Edinburgh with Mrs. Henry Siddons, and her reasons for a career in the theatre were soon forgotten.

When the financial disaster struck in the late summer of 1829, the question of a career was necessarily revived. After hearing from her mother the dreadful words, "Our property is to be sold," Fanny wrote a "most urgent entreaty" to her father asking him to let her seek employment as a governess. But Mrs. Kemble had a different plan. The next day, Fanny recalled, "she asked me whether I seriously thought I had any real talent for the stage . . . . She begged me to learn some part and say it to her, that she might form some opinion of my power." The young girl chose Portia, her "ideal of a perfect woman," and eagerly recited Shakespeare's famous lines; her mother's only comment was: "There is hardly passion enough in this part to test any tragic power. I wish you would study Juliet for me."[137]

Charles Kemble returned from his engagement in Ireland at this point, and Fanny was soon displaying her histrionic abilities for her father to judge. After a drawing-room audition the manager took his daughter to the vacant Theatre to try whether her voice "was of sufficient strength to fill the building." Fanny Kemble vividly described the scene:

> That strange-looking place, the stage, with its racks of pasteboard and canvas—streets, forests, banqueting-halls, and dungeons—drawn apart on either side, was empty and

136. Kemble, *Records of a Girlhood,* I, 221.
137. Kemble, *Records of a Girlhood,* II, 5, 6.

> silent; not a soul was stirring in the indistinct recesses of its mysterious depths, which seemed to stretch indefinitely behind me. . . . Set down in the midst of twilight space as it were, with only my father's voice coming to me from where he stood hardly distinguishable in the gloom, in those poetical utterances of pathetic passion I was seized with the spirit of the thing; my voice resounded through the great vault above and before me, and completely carried away by the inspiration of the wonderful play, I acted Juliet as I do not believe I ever acted it again.

Unperceived by Fanny, a close friend of Charles Kemble's, Major Dawkins, viewed the remarkable solo performance from the back of one of the private boxes. He was "a man of the world," a "passionate lover of the stage, an amateur actor of no mean merit," and "a first-rate critic," whom Kemble had asked to attend the unusual audition to guard against any mistakes from a father's bias. Joining Kemble at the end of the recital, Major Dawkins emphatically offered his advice: "Bring her out at once!" he declared; "it will be a great success."[138]

Charles Kemble agreed, and the next thing Fanny knew, bills were proclaiming the program for Covent Garden's opening night: "Miss Fanny Kemble—Juliet; Mr. Abbot—Romeo; Mr. Charles Kemble—Mercutio; Mrs. Charles Kemble—Lady Capulet." Mrs. Kemble, it seems, although she had been retired from the stage for many years, was determined to return to it on the night of her daughter's first appearance—"that I might have the comfort and support of her being with me in my trial," Fanny Kemble explained.[139] The selection of Abbot as Romeo was

138. *Ibid.*, pp. 7–8.
139. *Ibid.*, p. 59.

occasioned by Charles Kemble's distaste for playing a romantic lead opposite his daughter. Indeed there had been some thought, during the emergency of finding a substitute, of Fanny's brother Henry trying the part. But Henry's audition not only convinced everyone that he was far too young, it ended in an outburst of laughter that the family found impossible to repress.[140]

The prospect of the debut of Charles Kemble's daughter plus a sympathetic desire to support the nearly defeated house led throngs of playgoers to Covent Garden for the opening on October 5. The Theatre literally overflowed in every part soon after the doors were open, and hundreds of eager spectators were turned away from the pit for want of room.[141] Backstage Fanny Kemble, with only three weeks' coaching from her father to support her, waited with the palms of her hands "pressed convulsively together" and the tears welling up in her eyes. She recalled: "Once and again my father came to the door, and I heard his anxious 'How is she?' to which my aunt answered, sending him away with words of comforting cheer." Then the curtain rose and the terrified debutante was led to the spot from which she would make her entrance on the stage. At last she heard her cue: "Juliet," the Nurse cried out. Fanny Kemble would never forget that moment:

> My aunt gave me an impulse forward, and I ran straight across the stage, stunned with the tremendous shout that greeted me, my eyes covered with mist, and the green baize flooring of the stage feeling as if it rose up against my feet; and got hold of my mother, and stood like a

140. *Ibid.*, pp. 21–22.
141. *Theatrical Observer*, October 6, 1829.

> terrified creature at bay, confronting the huge theatre full of gazing human beings.

Fortunately the ovation lasted long enough for poor Fanny partly to regain her composure, and by the next scene she was already forgetting herself. In "the balcony scene, I had done so," the debutante later confessed, "and for aught I knew, I was Juliet. . . . After this, I did not return into myself till all was over."[142]

When the curtain fell there could be no doubt that Fanny Kemble's debut was an unprecedented triumph—for the young actress, for her father, and for Covent Garden. Bravos and wild shouting ascended from the pit. In the galleries and boxes theatregoers stamped their feet and threw flowers toward the stage. In vain Charles Kemble and his wife tried to conceal the tears of joy as they took their many bows, while Fanny Kemble finally left the stage still too entranced to comprehend fully the signs of her impending fame.[143]

During the last three years of Charles Kemble's management at Covent Garden, Fanny Kemble was the mainstay of the Theatre. The actor-manager spent the remainder of the 1829–30 season, as well as the following two, supporting his talented daughter, as the enthusiastic reception of October 5 was repeated night after night. The applause for *Romeo and Juliet* continued unabated until December 9, when the young actress appeared in her second role, Belvidera, in an old favorite, *Venice Preserved.* In Pierre,

142. Kemble, *Records of a Girlhood,* II, 59, 60.

143. *Dramatic Magazine,* November 1829; *Theatrical Observer,* October 6, 1829; Kemble, *Records of a Girlhood,* II, 60 ff; *Monthly Theatrical Review,* October 1829.

Charles Kemble unfortunately did not find one of his better parts, but Fanny's performance was pronounced to be "as beautiful as it was affecting."[144] In January the recent debutante was successfully brought forward as Euphrasia–Charles Kemble played Evander—in *The Grecian Daughter*, a play which had scarcely been acted since Mrs. Siddons had left the stage; and in coming months the youngest Kemble followed in her aunt's footsteps as Mrs. Beverley and Isabella. In supporting his daughter in *The Gamester* and later in *The Merchant of Venice*, Charles Kemble was forced to undertake two unfamiliar parts: Beverley was an entirely new role for the veteran actor, and Shylock a character he had performed in London only once before.[145] In the former personation he won considerable acclaim, but in the latter most critics agreed that Kemble failed to convey "sufficient expression of malignity and revenge."[146] Still there were aspects of his performance of the Jew which proved worthy of respect. One reviewer noted with pleasure his "suddenly falling on his knees when the intelligence is brought to him of Antonio's losses,"[147] and another singled out for praise "the artfully jocose manner" in which the terms of the bond were first proposed.[148] On May 28, Fanny Kemble made her final appearance of the season in a new character, Lady Townly (*The Provoked Husband*); and amidst great applause and shouting Charles Kemble

144. *Dramatic Magazine*, December 1829.

145. Although several newspaper articles declared that Kemble's performance of March 25, 1829, was his first appearance as Shylock, he had played the character of the Jew at the Haymarket once many years before, on August 29, 1798.

146. *Dramatic Magazine*, April 1830.

147. *Ibid.*

148. *Theatrical Observer*, March 29, 1830.

graciously thanked the audience for the reception they had accorded his daughter.[149]

The furor caused by Fanny Kemble this season had been really quite astounding—certainly it extended far beyond what either the Covent Garden manager or his daughter could have expected. Fanny claimed that at first she remained skeptical of her power to continue long as an attraction, but she confessed:

> When I saw the shop-windows full of Lawrence's sketch of me, and knew myself the subject of almost daily newspaper notices; when plates and saucers were brought to me with small figures of me as Juliet and Belvidera on them; and finally, when gentlemen showed me lovely buff-coloured neck-handkerchiefs which they had bought, and which had, as I thought, pretty lilac-coloured flowers all over them, which proved on nearer inspection to be minute copies of Lawrence's head of me, I not unnaturally . . . believed in my own success.[150]

In financial terms that success amounted to £350, £400, or sometimes £500 in the box-office coffers each night that Fanny played;[151] and by the end of the year the Theatre's fiscal crisis had—at least momentarily—subsided. Fanny and her father had postponed collecting their salaries during the season in consideration of the treasury's distress; but at the beginning of the summer both were able to draw their wages, calculated at the modest rate of five pounds per night.[152] In the traditional speech of thanks at the last per-

149. *Ibid.*, May 29, 1830.

150. Kemble, *Records of a Girlhood*, II, 67.

151. "Covent Garden Theatre Diary, 1829–1830," British Museum Ad. MS 23160.

152. Receipt for £910, "amount of my salary from 5th October 1829 to 28 May 1830. 182 Nights at £5 per Night," signed by Frances

formance the stage manager, Bartley, offered welcome news: the Theatre was now able to repay the loans that friends had recently subscribed, and shareholders could entertain a reasonable hope of seeing the commencement of the liquidation of their claims next year.[153]

The great popularity of his daughter kept Charles Kemble nearly as busy supporting her off-stage as on. For several years Fanny was undeniably the belle of London society, and her father regularly served as her escort and chaperon. No matter how hard the young actress worked at the Theatre, it seems that she was never too tired to dance—and never willingly refused an invitation to a ball. Consequently, after an evening's performance the handsome actor-manager customarily dressed in his finest formal attire in order to escort his daughter to an elegant party—where, according to Fanny, he enthusiastically entered into the festivities by talking and flirting with all the prettiest ladies and casting a blind eye to the clock.[154] In the summer, when playing in the provinces, the famous father and daughter were frequently asked to stay at the homes of nearby nobility, or to visit local families of prominence and fame. Thus one weekend Charles Kemble would be dining with his daughter at Heaton, the country seat of the Earl of Wilton, and the next, breakfasting in Edinburgh with Sir Walter Scott.[155] At home in the large house on Great

---

Ann Kemble, May 29, 1830, in private collection of Roy Plomley, London; Receipt for £930, "amount of my salary from 5 October 1829 to 3 June 1830. 186 Nights at £5 per Night," signed by Charles Kemble, June 3, 1830, in Harvard Theatre Collection.

153. *Dramatic Magazine,* July 1830.

154. Kemble, *Records of a Girlhood,* III, 42.

155. *Ibid.,* II, 192 ff., 126.

Russell Street next door to the British Museum—which was formerly the residence of John Philip Kemble—a constant stream of visitors were entertained. Old family friends such as the painter Sir Thomas Lawrence and Washington Irving now seemed especially eager to call and to talk with the famous Fanny. Young Thackeray, who confessed to being in love with Charles Kemble's fascinating daughter and to keeping her portrait proudly displayed in his room, was a frequent guest these days at the Kemble home;[156] while John Mitchell Kemble's college friends Tennyson and Arthur Hallam were among the notable figures who were constantly besieging the Kemble household and paying Fanny court.[157]

The summer of 1830 saw Charles Kemble and Fanny set off for provincial theatres, where they received a hearty welcome at Bath, Birmingham, Dublin, Glasgow, and Edinburgh; and the winter of 1830–31 witnessed the young actress, supported by her father, make her initial appearance in seven additional roles. That season the pair performed together as the Stranger and Mrs. Haller (*The Stranger*), Calista and Horatio (*The Fair Penitent*), Benedick and Beatrice (*Much Ado*), Constance and Faulconbridge (*King John*), Camiola and Bertoldo (*Maid of Honour*), and Lady Teazle and Charles Surface (*School for Scandal*); while Fanny performed once without her father as Bianca in *Fazio*. Her houses were still reasonably good; but in contrast to the almost unanimous acclaim of her debut season, this

156. William Thackeray, *Letters and Private Papers*, ed. Gordon N. Ray (Cambridge: Harvard University Press, 1945), I, cxliv; Gordon Ray, *Thackeray: The Uses of Adversity* (New York: McGraw Hill [1955]), pp. 150 ff.; Kemble, *Records of a Girlhood*, III, 170; Kemble, *Records of Later Life* (New York, 1882), p. 627.

157. Kemble, *Records of a Girlhood*, III, 191, 207.

year she was beginning to receive a few dissenting opinions. The season started out on a sour note when the popular young lady was scurrilously libeled in a poem attributed to Charles Westmacott, editor of the *Age*. Charles Kemble quickly played the part of an irate father. Encountering Westmacott one night at the Theatre, he inflicted upon the offending poet a severe drubbing. The public wholeheartedly sympathized with the avenging parent; and according to one report, "there was some danger of the audience assisting in the beating." But the Covent Garden manager was taken in hand by the police nonetheless, and the newspapers had the great pleasure of publishing detailed accounts of the fight.[158] Later in the season more conventional theatrical reviews indicated that the young star's performances were not to remain impervious to criticism. Concerning her portrayal in *Fazio*, for example, the *Dramatic Magazine* ventured to suggest that "Miss Kemble has not sufficient sensibility for the heroine."[159] Indeed, Fanny herself, despite the adulation of society and a good portion of the press, had come to see in her acting numerous flaws and to recognize that her performances were decidedly uneven. After portraying Lady Teazle for the first time she candidly had to admit: "I was as flat as a lady amateur."[160]

A Lucky Escape

The 1831–32 season was Charles Kemble's last one as manager of Covent Garden, and in retrospect his departure

158. *Theatrical Observer*, October 17, 1830; *British Traveller*, October 18, 1830; clipping from unidentified newspaper in Enthoven Collection, Victoria and Albert Museum.
159. *Dramatic Magazine*, February 1831.
160. Kemble, *Records of a Girlhood*, III, 10.

for America at the end of the year must be viewed as a lucky escape. Both Fanny's fame and her father's health had begun to wane, and with them, once again, the finances of the famous Theatre. At the same time the minor houses so long opposed by Drury Lane and Covent Garden suddenly seemed on the brink of victory in their war against the 172-year-old patent rights.

The season started out well enough. Young returned after a three-year absence and announced his intention of taking his farewell in favorite roles. The prospect of the popular tragedian's final performances led to crowded houses on the nights he played. Then *Henry VIII*, Charles Kemble's last historically accurate Shakespearean revival, proved to be a moderate success. As Katharine, Fanny lacked "dignity and natural power," the *Tatler* complained; but Charles Kemble, it declared, played Henry "excellently well."[161] The *Theatrical Observer* exclaimed: "Charles Kemble is so well dressed and so well stuffed that if Holbein's picture of the bluff King Hal could walk out of its frame and speak, we question if it would present us with a more perfect portrait of that gross sensualist."[162]

In November, however, the manager's luck began to change. For the first time since his school days at Douay, he was confined to his bed by a serious illness. It seemed that the years of constant anxiety and strain had at last taken their toll. In an entry in her diary for November 30, 1831, Fanny Kemble wrote:

> On my return home, I heard that Dr. Watson had seen my father, and requested that Dr. Wilson might be sent for.

161. *Tatler,* October 25, 1831.
162. *Theatrical Observer,* October 27, 1831.

> They fear inflamation of the lungs; he has gone to the very limit of his tether, for had he continued fagging a night or two longer, the effects might have been fatal. Poor, poor father![163]

The doctors' worst fears were realized. In a letter a few weeks later Thackeray informed his correspondent: "C Kemble has been very ill, nearly given up."[164] In mid-December hopeful signs of recovery appeared; but they were followed by a sudden relapse, and the actor's wife and children grew more and more concerned. During the first weeks of her father's confinement Fanny Kemble simply did not act, since, as she explained to a friend, "all my plays require him"; but gradually Warde and Young offered their services to fill Charles Kemble's place. Still the young star much preferred to remain at home. In a letter to Miss St. Leger she confessed:

> The exertion I have been obliged to make when leaving him to go and act, was so full of misery and dread lest I should find him worse, perhaps dead, on my return, that no words can describe what I suffered at that dreadful theatre.[165]

By the first of January the tide had turned. Charles Kemble slowly regained his strength, and for the first time in nearly three months appeared at Covent Garden on January 9. He no longer wore his usual robust look, but he performed Mercutio with his customary spirit: "It is infinitely the best

163. Kemble, *Records of a Girlhood,* III, 117–18.
164. William Thackeray to Mrs. Carmichael-Smyth, December 15–16, 1831, in *Letters and Private Papers,* ed. Gordon Ray, I, 177.
165. Kemble, *Records of a Girlhood,* III, 123, 132. The letter is dated December 18, 1831.

picture of this character which modern times has witnessed," *The Times* observed the next day.[166]

To add to the ailing manager's worries, the long-standing problem of competition from the minor theatres now reached a climax. For years attempts had been made to end, or at least to circumvent, the theatrical monopoly established in 1660, whereby the two patent companies were given exclusive right to present the legitimate drama in London. One by one minor houses had requested and received temporary licenses from magistrates to give various stage entertainments; and by the 1820s and early 1830s these entertainments had grown to approximate the fare at the two patent theatres. Singing, dancing, and dumb shows had given way to *Hamlet*, *Macbeth*, and *Lear*, with only the disguise of an added dance or chorus.

To counteract this trend the proprietors of Drury Lane and Covent Garden initiated a series of prosecutions against the minor theatres for infringement of their patent rights. Indeed they went so far as to send spies into the competing houses to take notes on productions, so that later they might give testimony in court as to the illegal nature of the programs presented there.[167] But the efforts of the patent theatres to protect their rights were to no avail. Frequently through a technical slip the patentees were unable to prove what everyone knew to be a fact;[168] and even when they did obtain a favorable verdict, the minor

166. *The Times*, January 10, 1832.

167. The Harvard Theatre Collection possesses several interesting examples of the statements made by men who attended the Surrey, Tottenham, and Strand theatres for the purpose of offering testimony concerning the illegal performances there.

168. Watson Nicholson, *The Struggle for a Free Stage in London* (Boston: Houghton Mifflin, 1906), p. 309.

houses would simply take the benefit of the Insolvent Act and pay no damages.[169]

The only effect the lawsuits had was to excite public opinion—which in the full tide of the reform movement of 1831–32 was not a desirable circumstance for Drury Lane or Covent Garden. Public meetings, newspaper articles, petitions for the repeal of all existing restrictions relating to the drama, and finally a Parliamentary investigation of the whole question of patent rights were the result. The Select Committee on Dramatic Literature of the House of Commons, with Edward Bulwer as chairman, was formed early in 1832; and it called thirty-nine witnesses, including Charles Kemble, in an inquiry into the current state of the drama, and more specifically, into the issue of theatrical monopoly.

Charles Kemble, in testifying before Bulwer's committee, expressed his concern over the injustice of suddenly abolishing the long-standing rights of the two patent theatres without some sort of indemnification, and he elaborated on the evils which seemed likely to arise from unrestricted competition. He predicted that the two great companies, comprising England's finest performers, would be broken up and dispersed, that new companies would form which would be weak and inferior, and that productions at all houses would soon be second-rate. Ultimately, he suggested, financial failures would cause most of the new theatres to close.[170] Chairman Bulwer and the committee, however, were of another mind; and their report, when

169. Such was Charles Kemble's testimony before the Select Committee on Dramatic Literature of the House of Commons, *Great Britain Parliamentary Reports*, VII (1831–32), 1 ff.

170. *Ibid.*

issued, represented a severe blow to Covent Garden and Drury Lane. It declared:

> The Committee believe that the interests of the drama will be considerably advanced by the natural consequences of a fair competition in its representation. They recommend that the Lord Chamberlain should continue a license to all the theatres licensed at present . . . and that the proprietors and managers of the said theatres should be allowed to exhibit, at their option, the legitimate drama, and all such plays as have received or shall receive the sanction of the censor.[171]

Faced with such a statement, Charles Kemble was pretty well forced to admit that the battle with the minor theatres was lost. Official repeal of the patent rights did not come until 1843; but as Professor Dewey Ganzel suggests, after the events of 1832 and the report of Bulwer's committee, the issue of theatrical monopoly essentially was dead.[172]

Harassed by the prospect of a worthless patent and weakened by the months of severe illness, Charles Kemble, in the spring of 1832, viewed a financial situation at Covent Garden which was sadly reminiscent of that of the summer of 1829. The actors were again drawing only a small fraction of their salaries, while the monstrous debt once more threatened to engulf the house. The only difference was that the aging manager no longer possessed the spirit to put up another fight. There were times when he would exclaim, "Oh, if I but had ten thousand pounds, I could set it all right again, even now";[173] but mostly he grimly faced the fact that his beloved Theatre was doomed. In an entry in her

171. *Ibid.*
172. Ganzel, "Patent Wrongs and Patent Theatres," p. 396.
173. Kemble, *Records of a Girlhood*, III, 194.

diary for March 10, Fanny recorded with great concern the signs of her father's severe depression:

> My father continued to walk up and down the room for nearly half an hour, without uttering a syllable; and at last flung himself into a chair, and leaned his head and arms on the table. I was horribly frightened, and turned as cold as stone, and for some minutes could not muster up courage enough to speak to him. At last I got up and went to him, and, on my touching his arm, he started up and exclaimed. "Good God! what will become of us all?"[174]

In an attempt to counteract the dreadfully thin houses and to enable the Theatre to keep its doors open until June, two new productions were hastily prepared. The first was *Francis I*, an original play by Fanny Kemble written a few years before. Charles Kemble's daughter was unhappy at the prospect of her maiden literary effort being subjected to such a test; but considering the desperate circumstances, she felt that she could not oppose her father's wishes. *Francis I* did attract an enthusiastic audience—at least for a few performances; but as Fanny herself declared,

> The success of "Francis I" was one of entirely indulgent forbearance on the part of the public. An historical play, written by a girl of seventeen, and acted by the authoress at one and twenty, was not unnaturally, the subject of some curiosity; and, as such, it filled the house for a few nights. Its entire want of real merit, of course, made it impossible that it should do anything more.[175]

The second spring production, *The Hunchback*, by Sheridan

174. *Ibid.*, p. 203.
175. *Ibid.*, pp. 181, 205.

Knowles, enjoyed far greater acclaim. *The Times* probably exaggerated slightly in its notice of June 13:

> *The Hunchback* was performed last night, we think, for the 31st time, and the House was crowded as usual. Since the first representation it has never drawn less than £300, and sometimes considerably more;

but the production did serve to "extricate Covent Garden from the jaws of bankruptcy" and enable the actors, once again, to draw their full pay.[176]

By the end of the season, however, Charles Kemble had had enough; he would not risk extending his lease at Covent Garden another year.[177] For some time the actor-manager had been receiving generous offers to make a tour in America; and now, at last, he willingly accepted. Kemble arranged with Stephen Price, a former lessee of Drury Lane and the manager of the Park Theatre in New York, to perform with his daughter for two years in the principal theatres of the United States.[178] On June 22 the Kembles gave their final performance of the season at Covent Garden; and when the curtain fell, the spectators clamored for them until they were obliged to reappear. Fanny recalled: "They rose to receive us, and waved their hats and handkerchiefs, and shouted farewell to us." The young

176. *The Times,* June 13, 1832.

177. In the autumn of 1831 when the lease of March 11, 1822, both expired and was declared void by the ruling of the House of Lords in *Harris* v. *Kemble,* Charles Kemble had come to an agreement with Harris to continue as manager for 1831–32.

178. Kemble, *Records of a Girlhood,* III, 205; clipping from an unidentified newspaper, June 20, 1832, in the Enthoven Collection, Victoria and Albert Museum. As early as May, 1827, Price had been attempting to get Kemble to make the American tour. See the *Theatrical Observer,* May 10, 1827.

actress appeared dismayed at the prospect of leaving her "good, indulgent audience," her "friends and countrymen";[179] and her father, too, seemed deeply affected. Nevertheless, after performing a few weeks in Edinburgh, it was with great relief that the pair left behind the cares and worries of Covent Garden and set sail, on August 1, for the United States.

179. Kemble, *Records of a Girlhood*, III, 209.

IV

The Curtain Falls

Success in America

Charles Kemble's career following his resignation from Covent Garden in 1832 was not carefree; but it did possess a welcome variety, coming after nearly thirty-eight seasons of uninterrupted performances on the London stage. The trip to America especially, although it was by no means a vacation, provided a pleasant relief from the familiar routine.

On September 3, 1832, after five weeks at sea, Charles Kemble, his daughter Fanny, and Aunt Dall—Mrs. Kemble's sister Adelaide De Camp, who had lived with the family for many years—first sighted the shoreline of New York. The crossing in the handsome sailing vessel the *Pacific* had been both long and rough. Indeed, it had served to convince Fanny that she had left all traces of civilization far behind and to instill in her a most fervent patriotism and nostalgia for England. But for the weary actor-manager the voyage had provided a much needed rest and a final cure from the severe illness of the previous winter.[1] Upon arrival the travelers went directly to their lodgings at the American House, where, according to Fanny, they found the wine and champagne dear, the rooms, "a mixture of French

1. Fanny Kemble Butler, *Journal* (Philadelphia, 1835), I, 1 ff.

finery and Irish disorder and dirt," and the servants, barely "a quarter as many as the house required."[2] They remained, nevertheless; and just thirteen days later Charles Kemble experienced his first American opening night.

The reception accorded to Kemble at the Park Theatre in New York on September 17, 1832, has already been noted;[3] it need only be added that the cheers, bravos, and hat waving, as well as the comments of theatrical reviewers, grew more enthusiastic with each subsequent performance. In *Romeo and Juliet*, *School for Scandal*, *Venice Preserved*, *Much Ado*, *King John*, and *The Hunchback* the English actor won unbridled applause: "So gentlemanly and finished a piece of acting is really delightful," the New York *Mirror* exclaimed after witnessing Kemble's Charles Surface; and without qualification it declared his Pierre to be "magnificent, the best by far ever seen here."[4] Fanny, too, quickly captured the hearts of the New York theatregoers, and her popularity soon rivaled the fame she had earned in London during the season following her debut. "Her playing in the fifth act of *Fazio* last night was never approached on the American boards," the New York *American* announced after her first appearance on September 18 as Bianca; and after attending her opening performance the prominent New Yorker Philip Hone recorded in his *Diary:* "I have never witnessed an audience so moved, astonished, and delighted. . . . I am quite satisfied that we have never seen her equal on the American stage."[5] Henceforth, like her father, the young

2. *Ibid.*, pp. 127–28.
3. See above, pp. 61 ff.
4. New York *Mirror*, September 29, 1832.
5. New York *American*, September 19, 1832; Philip Hone, *Diary*, ed. Allan Nevins (New York: Dodd, Mead and Company, 1936), pp. 77–78.

actress received an ovation each time that she appeared. Indeed the enthusiasm among New Yorkers for the Kembles continued unabated, not only during their initial visit, but throughout four additional engagements in the 1832–33 season as well as numerous performances the following year.[6] According to the early historian of the New York stage Joseph Ireland, "the sensation created by the appearance of Mr. and Miss Kemble had been equaled in kind only in the days of Cooke and Kean, and in duration and intensity was altogether unparalleled. The intellectual, the educated, and the refined crowded the theatre when they performed, and during their entire stay their popularity never waned."[7]

In October the pair made their way, partly by steamboat, partly by stagecoach, partly by train, to Philadelphia, where they found the city just emerging from a terrible epidemic of cholera and, like the rest of the nation, in the midst of great excitement over the Jackson-Clay presidential election campaign.[8] There at the Chestnut Street Theatre they discovered that they would have to compete against the

6. The Kembles' first engagement in New York was September 17–October 5, 1832. They returned for a second engagement on November 8, a third on February 7, 1833, a fourth on March 25, and a fifth on May 20. In the 1833–34 season they played, in all, forty-nine performances in New York.

7. Joseph Ireland, *Records of the New York Stage* (New York, 1867), II, 38. Ireland's figures for the receipts at the Park Theatre during the 1832–33 season suggest, too, the great financial success of the Kembles. "The aggregate receipts for sixty nights of their performances" amounted "to more than $56,000." For twelve nights in September their performances "averaged $1,235." For further financial records, see Ireland, p. 52, and George C. D. Odell, *Annals of the New York Stage*, III (New York: Columbia University Press, 1928), 673–74.

8. Butler, *Journal*, I, 139 ff.

popular American tragedian Edwin Forrest, who had been engaged by the rival Arch Street Theatre and was scheduled to appear for the first time in Bird's *Oralloossa* on October 10, the night of Charles Kemble's opening in *Hamlet*.[9] Neither the excitement of politics, fear of the cholera, nor competition from Forrest, however, served to divert the crowds from the Kembles' performances. In her *Journal* on October 17, 1832, Fanny Kemble noted: "It seems there has been much fighting, rushing, and tearing of coats at the box-office, and one man has made forty dollars, by purchasing and reselling tickets at an increased price."[10]

Subsequently in Baltimore, Washington, and Boston, wherever they appeared, Charles Kemble and his daughter achieved a similar success.[11] Stampeded box offices, full houses, cheering spectators, and glowing reviews greeted them at every stop. Of course, in Boston the critics were somewhat more sedate in their expressions of approbation: "Mr. Kemble is always respectable, and often great," was

9. Francis Courtney Wemyss, *Twenty-Six Years of the Life of an Actor and Manager* (New York, 1847), I, 209.

10. Butler, *Journal*, I, 160. The Kembles' first engagement in Philadelphia was October 10–November 3, 1832. They returned on December 5 and stayed until December 29. In the remainder of the 1832–33 season they played in Philadelphia January 25–February 4; March 15–March 22; and June 12–June 14. In the 1833–34 season their engagements here were October 28–November 9; December 23–January 10; March 10–March 19; and May 26–June 6. The reception accorded the Kembles in Philadelphia is suggested by Wemyss, *Life of an Actor and Manager*, I, 208 ff., as well as by Fanny's *Journal* and various newspaper accounts of their performances.

11. The Kembles' first engagement in Baltimore began on January 4, 1833. They went on to Washington on January 13. Their first visit to Boston was in April, 1833. Charles Kemble opened at the Tremont Theatre on April 18, 1833.

the *Weekly Messenger*'s conservative praise.[12] And naturally neither father nor daughter could escape occasional criticism by playgoers and reviewers. Charles Kemble in his initial appearance as Hamlet in Philadelphia was judged by some to be correct but stiff and lifeless, and in New York, Philip Hone found him too formal in the part.[13] In Boston the *Evening Gazette* complained: "Clifford might have fitted him thirty years ago; it is too late now for him to think of the character."[14] When he saw Fanny Kemble as Lady Teazle, her admirer Hone had to admit that comedy was not her forte; and when the New York *Post* reviewed her Constance it declared that she lacked the "requisite physical powers" for the role.[15]

Fanny's most difficult moment came in Philadelphia, where one night she faced a decidedly hostile crowd. It seems that a rumor had been spread that the English actress had "spoken disrespectfully of the Americans in their own capital," and handbills were distributed among the audience claiming that while in Washington she had remarked to a young man whom she supposed to be English that "she had not seen a lady or gentleman fit for her to

12. Boston *Weekly Messenger and Massachusetts Journal*, April 25, 1833. In Boston, it might be added, the ticket-scalpers were particularly clever. Fanny tells how "these worthies" would "smear their clothes with molasses, and sugar, etc., in order to prevent any person of more decent appearance, or whose clothes are worth a cent, from coming near the box office" (*Journal*, II, 133).

13. *American Sentinel and Mercantile Advertiser*, October 16, 1832; Leota Driver, *Fanny Kemble* (Chapel Hill: University of North Carolina Press, 1933), p. 62; Wemyss, *Life of an Actor and Manager*, I, 211; Hone, *Diary*, p. 77.

14. Boston *Evening Gazette*, September 14, 1833.

15. Hone, *Diary*, 78; New York *Post*, October 2, 1832.

associate with since she came to America."[16] Fortunately, after a hasty but persuasive speech by Charles Kemble in which he explained that the charges against his daughter were wholly false, all jeers turned to "unanimous applause."[17] Hostile audiences, harsh reviews, and unfavorable comments, however, were the exception. Basically the tremendous interest and enthusiasm aroused by the Kembles was everywhere pretty much the same. The actor Francis Courtney Wemyss, who was at that time associated with the Arch Street Theatre in Philadelphia, credited their extreme popularity—especially Fanny's—with making the theatres "once more a fashionable place of amusement" and reviving "the prostrate fortunes of the drama in the United States."[18]

The fashionable audiences attracted by Charles and Fanny Kemble indeed included some of America's most distinguished and to-be-distinguished citizens. Young Oliver Wendell Holmes, who was in New York awaiting the sailing of the packet *Philadelphia,* was among those vigorously applauding the Kembles at the Park Theatre in March, 1833.[19] The next month Charles Sumner was one of many Harvard students who developed a particularly strong devotion to Fanny Kemble and walked "again and again" from Cambridge to the Tremont Theatre in Boston to see

16. Wemyss, *Life of an Actor and Manager,* I, 216; newspaper clipping, Harvard Theatre Collection (I have been unable to identify the paper or to determine the exact date). For Fanny's account of this incident, see *Journal,* II, 102 ff.

17. Newspaper clipping, Harvard Theatre Collection. I have been unable to identify the paper or to determine the exact date.

18. Wemyss, *Life of an Actor and Manager,* I, 210.

19. John T. Morse, *Life and Letters of Oliver Wendell Holmes* (London, 1896), I, 83, quotes a letter in which Holmes writes of seeing the Kembles and remarks of Fanny: "She is a very fine affair, I assure you."

her perform.[20] According to one report, Sumner, who finally met Charles Kemble's attractive daughter some years later, was "almost beside himself then over Fanny Kemble's acting."[21] In Washington the Kembles played to perhaps their most inspiring audiences, which included Supreme Court Justices John Marshall and Joseph Story. Here it seems the elder statesmen, too, were especially captivated by Fanny Kemble's art and charm.[22] When she played Mrs. Haller in *The Stranger*, the audience was moved to tears; and according to his colleague Justice Story, Chief Justice Marshall "shed them in common with the younger eyes." The learned Justice Story was himself so inspired by the actress's art that he paid tribute to her in verse.[23]

The enthusiasm of American audiences helped to atone for some of the technical difficulties which the touring actors encountered at nearly every turn, for barnstorming in the United States in the early 1830s proved a far cry

20. Edward L. Pierce, *Memoirs and Letters of Charles Sumner* (Boston, 1877), I, 102.

21. Young Sumner's attraction to Fanny Kemble is thus described by a Miss Peters, whose remarks are quoted by Pierce, *Memoirs and Letters of Charles Sumner*, I, 127.

22. Claude G. Bowers, *The Party Battles of the Jackson Period* (Boston: Houghton Mifflin Company, 1928), p. 16.

23. Joseph Story, *Life and Letters*, ed. William Story (Boston, 1851), II, p. 117. Story wrote the following lines to Fanny Kemble:

Genius and taste and feeling all combine
To make each province of the drama thine.
She first to Fancy's bright creation gives
The very form and soul; it breathes—it lives.
She next with grace inimitable plays
In every gesture, action, tone and gaze.
The last to nature lends its subtlest art
And warms and wins and thrills and melts the heart.
Go, lovely woman, go. Enjoy thy fame.
A second Kemble with a deathless name.

from playing at Covent Garden, supported by the finest company available, magnificent scenery, elaborate costumes, and an expert stage crew. Fanny's *Journal* abounds in accounts of various mishaps. After a Baltimore performance of *Romeo and Juliet* on January 7, 1833, Charles Kemble's daughter recorded: "The play went off pretty smoothly, except that they broke one man's collar-bone, and nearly dislocated a woman's shoulder by flinging the scenery about" (II, 82). Despite such vigorous efforts, Fanny noted: "My [Juliet's] bed was not made in time, and when the scene drew, half a dozen carpenters in patched trowsers and tattered shirt sleeves, were discovered smoothing down my pillows, and adjusting my draperies." Actually the Baltimore engagement had already got off to a bad start the week before. When the travelers arrived, the theatre they had originally booked proved upon inspection to be "dirty, dilapidated, and looking as if there had been eleven executions in it that morning" (II, 75); so they spent their first days arranging for a suitable place in which to perform. In Philadelphia a somewhat different variety of misfortune occurred. Fanny's excitement in playing, for the first time, Violante in *Wonder* was considerably increased when she discovered that her costume could not be delivered until the very last minute. It arrived just as the curtain was due to rise; but when the actress tried to get into it, the bodice proved to be several inches too small. After every scene the unlucky gown had to be pinned together; and finally, "in the laughing scene," Fanny observed, "it took the hint from my admirable performance, and facetiously grinned in an ecstasy of amusement till it was fairly open behind, displaying, I suppose, the lacing of my stays, like so many teeth, to the admiring gaze of the audience" (II, 33).

Almost always, except in Boston, the Kembles encountered an inferior supporting cast. On Fanny's opening night in New York a dreadful actor named Keppel appeared as Fazio and "nearly ruined the performance."[24] This same young man soon proved that he could be equally bad as Jaffeir.[25] After their first New York performance of *King John* both the *American* and the *Post* expressed shock and dismay over the quality of the company which had been selected to support the stars.[26] The latter paper remarked that it seemed "hardly fair to pronounce critical comment on the Constance of Miss Kemble and the Faulconbridge of her father, annoyed as both of them must have been by the stammerers and the stutterers with whom they had to deal!" Judging from Fanny's account this production must have been one of the worst:

> What a cast! . . . what botchers! what butchers! In his very first scene, the most christian King stuck fast; and there he stood, shifting his truncheon from hand to hand, rolling his eyes, gasping for breath, and struggling for words, like a man in a nightmare. . . . In the scene before Angiers, when the French and English heralds summon the citizens to the walls, the Frenchman applied his instrument to his mouth, uplifted his chest, distended his cheeks, and appeared to blow furiously; not a sound! he dropped his arm and looked off the stage in discomfiture and indignation, when the perverse trumpet set up a blast fit to waken the dead,—the audience roared. . . . When Cardinal Pandulph came on, the people set up a shout, as usual; he was dreadfully terrified, poor thing, and all the time kept giving little

24. Odell, *Annals of the New York Stage,* III, 605.
25. Ireland, *Records of the New York Stage,* II, 44.
26. New York *Post,* October 2, 1832; New York *American,* October 5, 1832.

> nervous twitches to his sacred petticoat, in a fashion that was enough to make one die of laughter. He was as obstinate, too, in his bewilderment as a stuttering man in his incoherency; for once, when he stuck fast, having twitched his skirts, and thumped his breast in vain for some time, I thought it best, having to speak next, to go on; when lo and behold! in the middle of my speech the "scarlet sin" recovers his memory, and shouts forth the end of his own, to the utter confusion of my august self, and the audience. I thought they never would have got through my last scene; king gazed at cardinal, and cardinal gazed at king; king nodded and winked at the prompter, spread out his hands, and remained with his mouth open; cardinal nodded and winked at the prompter, crossed his hands on his breast, and remained with his mouth open; neither of them uttering a syllable! what a scene, O, what a glorious scene![27]

When they were not performing, however, Charles Kemble and his daughter found many opportunities to enjoy the pleasures of this "brave new world." Soon after arriving in New York the actor, equipped with a letter of introduction from the British minister, called on the wealthy and prominent New York politician Philip Hone, who promptly arranged a party for the Kembles at his home on September 15. Hone's dinner—at which Charles Kemble impressed his host as "a gentleman of fine manners and dignified deportment, somewhat stiff, for he is a Kemble, but evidently well bred and accustomed to good society"—marked the beginning of an exhaustive social life.[28] Wher-

27. Butler, *Journal,* I, 112–13.

28. Hone, *Diary,* pp. 75, 77. Hone, after this party, noted that Fanny's manners were "somewhat singular" and thought that she displayed "an air of indifference and nonchalance not at all calculated to make her a favorite with the beaux" (p. 76). He soon changed his

ever they traveled the two were feted at teas, parties, and balls, and were, as Fanny expressed it, "introduced to all the world and his wife!"[29] In Philadelphia they "made quite a sensation in the fashionable circles of society"; and in the nation's capital their friend Washington Irving observed that "Charles Kemble and his talented daughter" turned "the heads of young and old" alike.[30]

In addition to the endless parties, each city, of course, offered its own special attractions to the English visitors. In New York the young actress delighted in shopping with Aunt Dall and in strolling leisurely along Broadway with her father, while Charles Kemble experienced the interesting privilege of attending "a grand democratic dinner" at Tammany Hall in honor of the election triumph of President Jackson.[31] In Washington—which Fanny described as "a rambling red-brick image of futurity, where nothing *is*, but all things *are to be*"—the Kembles toured the Capitol, where they heard speeches by the eloquent Daniel Webster and Henry Clay, and noted with curiosity "a man sitting with his feet upon the table, reading, which is an American fashion." Here the pair also called on President Jackson, who "talked about South Carolina, and entered his protest against scribbling ladies, assuring us that the whole of the

mind, however. He wrote in his *Diary* on September 29: "The more I see of this wonderful girl the more I am pleased with her" (p. 79). Several years later Hone became rather upset with Fanny Kemble for publishing her *Journal*, in which she had recorded her impressions of Hone's party (p. 145).

29. Butler, *Journal*, II, 14.

30. Wemyss, *Life of an Actor and Manager*, I, 215; Washington Irving, *Life and Letters*, ed. Pierre M. Irving (New York, 1883), II, p. 173.

31. Butler, *Journal*, I, 238.

present southern disturbances had their origin in no larger a source than the nib of the pen of a lady."[32] In Boston father and daughter climbed to the cupola of the State House to enjoy a favorite view, rode to Cambridge, Concord, and Mount Auburn, and visited historic Bunker Hill. And in this "most *belles-letterish* and blue town" they came to know some of the country's more "learned men."[33] Charles Kemble grew especially fond of "Dr. Channing," whom he described as "a mild, engaging person in discourse, an eloquent and impressive preacher in the pulpit."[34] A steamboat ride up the Hudson to West Point and a trip to Niagara Falls (on which they enjoyed the company of their fellow countryman Edward Trelawny) gave the travelers a taste of the natural beauty of the land.[35] The prospect of the former spot indeed inspired the younger Kemble to compose a passage in her *Journal* which Emerson, and later Walt Whitman, might have admired:

> Where are the poets of this land? Why such a world should bring forth men with minds and souls larger and stronger than any that ever dwelt in mortal flesh. Where are the poets of this land? They should be giants too; Homers and Miltons, and Goethes and Dantes, and Shakespeares. . . . Oh, surely, surely, there will come a time when this lovely

32. *Ibid.*, II, 101, 89, 96. I have not been able to identify the lady or the work referred to by Jackson.

33. Fanny Kemble, letter to William Harness, May 5, 1833, quoted in *The Literary Life of the Reverend William Harness*, ed. A. G. L'Estrange (London, 1871), p. 67.

34. Charles Kemble, letter to William Harness, April 24, 1834, quoted in *The Literary Life of Harness*, p. 72.

35. See R. Glynn Grylls, *Trelawny* (London: Constable, 1950), pp. 179 ff. On this trip to Niagara the carriage in which they were riding overturned, and Aunt Dall apparently sustained an injury which led ultimately to her death. She died in Boston on April 20, 1834.

> land will be vocal with the sound of song, when every close-locked valley, and waving wood, rifted rock and flowing stream shall have their praise (I, 212).

Finally, in Philadelphia—where in imitation of the beautiful English actress the ladies were "all getting up upon horses and wearing the 'Kemble cap' "—Charles Kemble's daughter made the most important of her many new acquaintances in the United States.

Among the scores of young gentlemen who each night flocked to see Fanny Kemble at the Chestnut Street Theatre in the fall of 1832 and who each day begged her to accompany them for a brisk ride along the scenic banks of the Schuylkill was a wealthy Philadelphia lawyer and heir to a vast Georgia plantation, Pierce Butler. Before long, in Fanny's eyes, Mr. Butler had begun to stand out from the rest. Within a few months, in fact, everyone had started to whisper that the young actress had fallen in love. When the Kembles left Philadelphia to play again in New York and Boston, Pierce Butler followed; and as early as October, 1833, there were repeated rumors in England that Charles Kemble's daughter had married. Actually the wedding awaited the end of the two-year tour in the summer of 1834. Original plans called for Fanny to return to England with her father before her marriage and with him to "take leave of the British stage in a manner worthy of the house of Kemble."[36] Eventually, however, this program was given over. On June 6, 1834, the Kembles played for the last time in Philadelphia, and the next day at Christ Church, Charles Kemble gave his daughter away. Then after a brief but

36. Charles Kemble, letter to William Harness, April 24, 1834, quoted in *The Literary Life of Harness*, p. 72.

triumphant farewell engagement in New York, the fifty-eight-year-old actor sailed home to England alone.[37]

Farewell to the Stage

Following summer appearances at the Haymarket and in the provinces in 1835 and at Covent Garden in 1835–36, Charles Kemble announced that his performances in the 1836–37 season would be his last. After forty-four years on the stage the veteran actor deemed that the time had come to retire. As was the custom, Covent Garden Theatre circulated notices early in September announcing that the famous performer would soon be seen for the last time in his favorite parts. On September 12, Kemble led off the season as Macbeth, closely followed by Hamlet on the fourteenth. Soon his Beverley, Shylock, and Charles Surface were attracting large crowds eager for a final glimpse of the well-known star. William Macready was back at Covent Garden this year after a falling-out with Drury Lane manager Alfred Bunn and offered support to his one-time rival by playing King John to Kemble's Faulconbridge, Othello to his Cassio, and Brutus to his Antony.

At the end of October an event occurred which somewhat hastened Charles Kemble's final withdrawal from the stage. The actor had intended to return to Covent Garden in the spring for his ultimate farewell;[38] but now he found that his plans needed to be rearranged. The death of George Colman left vacant the office of Examiner of Plays; and on October

37. The last appearance of the Kembles in New York was on June 20, 1834. *Peabody's Parlour Journal,* June 28, 1834, carries an interesting account of their final performance.

38. London *Observer,* November 6, 1836.

28, 1836, it was announced that Kemble had been chosen to fill the post. The Examiner was, by tradition, an appointee of the Lord Chamberlain whose duties entailed the examination, for the purpose of licensing, of all new plays, "tragedies, comedies, operas, farces, and interludes, or any other entertainment of the stage"[39]—for which he was awarded a nominal salary of four hundred pounds per annum plus a fee of two guineas, given more or less by custom, for each item submitted to be licensed.[40] Nearly everyone connected with the theatre greeted the news of the new appointment with the greatest pleasure and agreed that no one better qualified for the position could possibly have been selected.[41] Certainly the appointment seemed a suitable and proper reward for Kemble's long years of service to England's playgoing public. One note of protest was sounded, however. Alfred Bunn, the manager of Drury Lane—who, it was rumored, had attempted to obtain the Examiner's post for himself[42]—took exception to the selection because of Kemble's active interest in the affairs of Covent Garden. He complained that "the selection of a performer in any one theatre . . . to sit in judgment upon the forthcoming novelties of the other . . . was an alarming arrangement."[43] Faced with Bunn's protest as well as the

39. Oath of Office for Examiner of Plays, quoted by Frank Fowell, *Censorship in England* (London: Frank Palmer, 1913), p. 354.

40. "Report of the Select Committee on Dramatic Literature of the House of Commons," *Great Britain Parliamentary Reports*, VII (1831–32), Appendix.

41. London *Observer*, October 30, 1836.

42. *Ibid.*, October 30 and November 6, 1836.

43. Alfred Bunn, *The Stage: Both Before and Behind the Curtain* (London, 1840), II, 149. Bunn, on October 29, after being informed that Kemble was the new Examiner of Plays to whom he should send the manuscripts of all new plays, decided to by-pass Kemble in

immediate prospect of the duties of his new job, Kemble determined to cut short his farewell season. Announcement was made at Covent Garden on December 1 that the renowned actor would perform only twelve more times.

December 23 was *the* great night, when Charles Kemble would make his final bow. He chose for the occasion a part perhaps never before selected for a farewell—but one in which, as the *Examiner* declared, he had no equal.[44] He

---

protest, and sent a new piece, *The Yankee Pedlar,* directly to the Lord Chamberlain with a note expressing his dismay that Kemble, "a performer and proprietor of the rival house" should "sit in judgment upon the productions of this." On November 1, 1836, Kemble wrote to Bunn a courteous letter in which he noted the "irregularity" of Bunn's procedure: "I have this day, only, received a manuscript entitled '*The Yankee Pedlar,*' which I perceive by the play-bills is advertised for performance this evening. To prove my desire to do everything in my power, consistently with my duty, to forward the interests of the theatre over which you preside, I have read it, and forwarded my application to the Lord Chamberlain for his license. I beg, however, to direct your attention to the irregularity of the proceeding, and to request that, in future, any manuscripts which you may desire to have licensed, may be forwarded to me in proper time. My messenger is this moment returned from Dudley-house; the Lord Chamberlain is unfortunately not at home; but I am convinced that he would not be displeased if, under the present circumstances, the piece were to be acted. The license shall be forwarded as soon as ever I receive it" (Bunn, *The Stage*, p. 152). It should be noted that Bunn freely admitted that Kemble's personal qualifications for the post were high ("A gentleman more fitted for the situation could not possibly have been selected—a fine scholar, an experienced artist, and one bearing the high and honoured dramatic name of Kemble" [p. 148]). The objections which Bunn expressed were entirely based on Kemble's connections with Covent Garden Theatre.

44. *Examiner,* December 25, 1836. The unique excellence of Kemble's Benedick is remarked upon in reviews of his performances from the time of his first appearance in the role at Drury Lane, May 30, 1803. The reviewer for the *Examiner,* in commenting upon the unusual selection of Benedick for a farewell, remarked that he thought

would play Benedick in *Much Ado About Nothing*, supported by the brilliant Helen Faucit, who in contrast to her aging partner was acting her role, Beatrice, for the first time. All London turned out for the event. On the afternoon of the performance crowds began to gather outside the Theatre as early as three o'clock; and when the hour for opening the doors arrived, there was a multitude assembled which could have filled the Theatre several times.[45] The orchestra was converted into stalls for the occasion, and the musicians performed behind the stage; but police, nevertheless, had to be called in to turn away the excess crowd. The boxes, of course, had all been taken weeks in advance. The Duchess of Kent and Princess Victoria and their suite were to be seen in one, and in another nearby, the illustrious performer's family—including Mrs. Pierce Butler, who had come from America for the event.

On his entrance Charles Kemble was hailed "with shouts of applause which seemed to shake the Theatre."[46] The entire audience rose, and the cheering continued for a considerable time as the still handsome actor stood waiting, obviously greatly affected. What memories must have rushed into his mind as he faced that crowd for the last time!—memories of the now distant past when he had stood in the same spot alongside Mrs. Siddons and John Philip Kemble, desperately hoping someday to reach the top of his profession, memories of the more recent past when he had

that it was "with great good taste" that Kemble "played one of his own characters on this occasion; one of those characters in which he has no rival and of which he leaves no copy."

45. Clipping from London newspaper of December 24, 1836, in Harvard Theatre Collection. I have not been able to identify the paper.

46. *Ibid.*

stood there beside his talented daughter Fanny with the audience prostrate at their feet. Finally the tumult subsided, and the actor began to lose himself in his part. He had told his old friend Fitzball in the morning that his one wish was to be able to play that night better than ever.[47] According to reports of the performance his "last request" was granted.

In the first act those qualities which Londoners had so long admired in the "inimitable Benedick" quickly became apparent:[48] "the delicate shades of coloring, . . . the richness, depth and force with which he combined 'the wit, the humorist, the gentleman, and the soldier' "; the amazing "buoyancy of spirits"; the "elegance and finish"; the perfectly natural, unforced gaiety; the spontaneity and lack of "effort, parade, or pretense."[49] The high points of the scene before Leonato's house were of course Benedick's initial match of wits with Beatrice and his subsequent teasing of Claudio. After a quick exchange of greetings, all the characters retired up the stage except Benedick and Beatrice, who this night more than ever held the audience's undivided

47. Edward Fitzball, *Thirty-five Years of a Dramatic Author's Life* (London, 1859), II, 52.

48. Clipping from a London newspaper account of Kemble's farewell performance in Enthoven Collection, Victoria and Albert Museum. I have not been able to identify the paper or to establish the precise date.

49. Introduction, *Much Ado About Nothing*, in *French's Standard Drama* (New York: H. L. Hinton, n.d.); William Robson, *The Old Play-Goer* (London, 1846), p. 47; *Theatrical Inquisitor*, December 1817; Henry Crabb Robinson, *The London Theatre, 1811–1866*, ed. Eluned Brown (London: Society for Theatre Research, 1966), p. 101; clipping from London newspaper, April 12, 1840, in Theatre Collection of New York Public Library, Lincoln Center (I have not been able to identify the paper).

attention as they advanced toward each other to begin their "merry war":[50]

> *Bea.* I wonder that you will still be talking, Signior Benedick! nobody marks you.
>
> *Ben.* What, my Lady Disdain! are you yet living?

In the reading of the sparkling lines between Benedick and Beatrice the audience savored for the "last time"[51] the "*grand vin* of comedy": "In sally and repartee there was the nicest precision and point, which yet seemed spontaneous, and a vein of light but ceremonious courtesy in the strife which suggested the grace of accomplished fencers as well as the glitter of the foils."[52] When the first brief skirmish of wit was concluded and the company began to depart, Beatrice merrily offered her hand to Benedick, which he refused "jestingly."[53] She ran "laughing after the others,"

50. Clipping from London newspaper account of Kemble's farewell performance in Enthoven Collection, Victoria and Albert Museum.

51. Actually, Kemble played the part of Benedick again when he temporarily returned to the stage in the spring of 1840 at the request of Queen Victoria.

52. Westland Marston, *Our Recent Actors* (Boston, 1888), p. 132.

53. The reference to Kemble's business here is based on a promptbook in the Theatre Collection of the New York Public Library at Lincoln Center, *NCP .342944. Professor Charles Shattuck describes it as a promptbook compilation made by George Becks. On the last page of the interleaves it bears the notation: "N.B. From Promptbook under Mr. Macready's Direction, T.R.D.L. 1842. Where the bus. of C. Kemble differed from Mr. M—— a note is made of the same." In all references to this promptbook I have used only those notes of business which are specifically marked "C. Kemble." Hereafter I shall cite this promptbook as *NCP .342944. In my references to the staging of *Much Ado* in Kemble's farewell performance, I am assuming that he followed his traditional business. Other sources of information on Kemble's business include another promptbook in the Theatre Collection of the New York Public Library at Lincoln Center, *NCP .285345,

and Benedick the bachelor then challenged Cupid with his proud boasts and taunted Claudio about his love for "Leonato's short daughter"—and Charles Kemble was applauded once more as the most "perfect representative of the witty gentleman."[54]

On this grand evening, "all the second act was exquisitely played."[55] In the elaborate scene of the masquerade the crowd delighted in the familiar Kemble business.[56] Benedick meets Beatrice at the dance and "runs away," but she "follows him." Beatrice tells the masked Benedick that he is "the prince's jester: a very dull fool" and he "walks about much vexed," while she "pursues him." Finally the group of revelers exit leaving Don John and Borachio to work their plot on Claudio, and Benedick "runs off L" with "Beatrice after him" crying, "We must follow the leaders." Apparently the solemnity of the occasion could not dim the veteran performer's habitual spirit and vivacity in this merry scene.[57] In the orchard scene the curtain rose to discover Benedick sitting in a garden seat[58] as he sententiously expressed his "wonder that one man, seeing how much another man is a fool when he dedicates his behaviours to

---

which also belonged to George Becks and which contains explicit references to Charles Kemble (I shall hereafter refer to this promptbook as *NCP .285345); and the Cumberland (c. 1826) and Oxberry (1823) acting editions of *Much Ado,* which both profess to print the stage business for performances at Covent Garden in which Kemble played Benedick.

54. Robson, *The Old Play-Goer,* p. 41.

55. *Examiner,* December 25, 1836.

56. The business described here is from *NCP .342944.

57. Clipping from London newspaper account of Kemble's farewell performance in Enthoven Collection, Victoria and Albert Museum.

58. *NCP .342944; also, *NCP .285345.

love, will, after he hath laughed at such shallow follies in others, become the argument of his own scorn, by falling in love." When "the Prince and Monsieur Love" approached, he withdrew to the arbor, and the audience was momentarily entertained by a quartet composed of Miss Land, Miss Salway, Mr. Collet, and Mr. Ransford singing "Sigh no more, ladies."[59] As Don Pedro, Claudio, and Leonato set their trap, Benedick amused the audience with his listening. Even more, however, he delighted them when he advanced softly to the center of the stage and began his soliloquy. Here "the resolution to take pity on Beatrice and be horribly in love with her was given with the nicest perception of character—as rather a relief than a new resolution."[60] And as he stood in his traditional pose "with his hands linked behind him" and with "a general elevation of his aspect,"[61] "who could resist the sentiment of universal benevolence, of devotion to the interests of the whole human race, with which Mr. Kemble delivered that generous reflection—'The world must be peopled!' His manner at that instant conjured up a long line of Benedicks and Beatrices. It was quite a peep, in the grand style, into futurity."[62]

"Gallants, I am not as I have been," Benedick advises his friends in Act III. On this solemn occasion Charles Kemble must have welcomed Benedick's change from carefree and irrepressible wit who is "all mirth" to "afflicted" lover. One

59. Playbills of this performance noted: "In Act II will be sung Stevens's Glee of 'Sigh No More Ladies,' by Miss Land, Miss Salway, Mr. Collet, and Mr. Ransford." Apparently Balthasar (Mr. Roberts) did not participate in the singing.

60. *Examiner*, December 25, 1836.

61. This traditional Kemble pose is quoted as described by Leigh Hunt, *Dramatic Essays*, ed. Archer and Lowe (London, 1894), p. 206.

62. *Examiner*, December 25, 1836.

reviewer observed: "We do not know whether it was a result of the occasion, but we thought some of the passages of the part—those in which we may say with Don Pedro, Benedick goes in his doublet and hose and leaves off his wit—were given with an unusual mixture of the comic with the really tender, which was delicious."[63] The "serious part of his character" was, of course, "judiciously prefaced" as always by his by-play in the Chapel Scene.[64] At Claudio's very harsh speech to Hero ("Out on thy seeming . . ."), Benedick moved away from his friend to the back of the stage where he joined the Friar and with great concern "surveyed the whole."[65] Then when Hero swooned, as the "chivalric gentleman" he ran to support her. "As the professed woman-hater," he "inspected every feature of her countenance" until at last his suspicion "gave way to his better conviction." In the latter part of this scene the actor's skill as the "tender lover" was, as ever, enhanced by the grace with which he took Beatrice's hand as he confessed his love to her and subsequently by the tender manner in which, when she angrily started to go, dismayed that he would not "kill Claudio," he followed her and pulled her back pleading, "We'll be friends first."[66]

In the last act the challenge of Claudio was "very well delivered" and Benedick's "tremulous change of voice" at

63. *Ibid.*

64. Clipping from London newspaper account of Kemble's farewell performance in Enthoven Collection, Victoria and Albert Museum; *The Times,* April 8, 1840.

65. Kemble's business here is indicated by *NCP .342944, *NCP .285345, and *The Times,* April 8, 1840. The direct quotations are all from *The Times.*

66. Clipping from newspaper account of Kemble's farewell performance, Enthoven Collection, Victoria and Albert Museum; printed stage directions in Cumberland edition (c. 1826).

the words, "You have killed a sweet lady," was admired by at least one observer. In the final scene, however, Kemble was "clearly labouring under strong emotion"; and for both the audience and the performer thoughts of the occasion began to take precedence over the play. Toward the end of the scene, when Benedick was warding off the jokes leveled at him for his change of opinion with respect to marriage, "a wreath and theatrical truncheon were thrown on the stage."[67] The wreath, it seems, was thrown by "the old play-goer," William Robson, who subsequently revealed that he had attached to it some lines in which he promised Kemble that he would hold the impressions made by his performances "pure and untouched" and that he would never see another actor in those parts in which he had so delighted him—a vow, Robson later remarked, "I have kept."[68]

When the curtain fell at the conclusion of the fifth act, the audience stood once more en masse and "with one voice shouted the magic name of KEMBLE."[69] After a few seconds the curtain rose again to reveal the retiring performer, somewhat "pale but firm," surrounded by the entire Covent Garden company plus many other members of the profession who had come to do him honor, including the great American tragedian Edwin Forrest.[70] For ten minutes the furor continued unabated, and then Charles Kemble advanced to the front of the stage and began his farewell speech:

67. Clipping from newspaper account of farewell performance, December 24, 1836, in Harvard Theatre Collection.
68. Robson, *The Old Play-Goer*, p. 47.
69. Clipping from London newspaper account of Kemble's farewell performance, Enthoven Collection, Victoria and Albert Museum.
70. Fitzball, *Thirty-five Years of a Dramatic Author's Life*, II, 53.

> Ladies and Gentlemen, my professional career is ended. Had I consulted only my own inclination in the choice of my last character, it would have been of a graver cast, and more in harmony with the feelings under which I laboured this night. To do anything for the last time is attended with a melancholy sufficient to cast a shade over the most buoyant spirits. How dense is the cloud which now hangs over my mind I have not language to express. . . . From early youth to this my latest hour, I have always received from you your favor and encouragement, and to that alone I ascribe any little merit which your indulgence has allowed me to possess. I only wish it had been a thousand times greater. Your goodness is engraven deeply on my heart never to be obliterated. May all health and happiness attend you, and with heartfelt prayer, I most respectfully and mournfully bid you adieu.[71]

At this point, various reports assure us, there was not a dry eye in the house—including the eloquent actor's. Kemble stepped back, then advanced once more to the lights, "bowed as only he could bow,"[72] and left the stage, to devote himself for the next three years to his new office as Examiner of Plays.

A testimonial dinner given by the Garrick Club on January 10, 1837, and the presentation of a commemorative vase by a group of the actor's friends on March 3, 1840, served as postscripts to the Covent Garden farewell. At the former affair nearly one hundred "authors, actors, patrons, and distinguished ornaments of the drama" joined the toastmaster, Lord Francis Egerton, at the Albion Hotel in offering tributes, including many in song and verse, to the

71. From London newspapers of December 24, 1836. See clippings in Harvard Theatre Collection.

72. Fitzball, *Thirty-five Years of a Dramatic Author's Life*, II, 53.

popular performer.[73] At the latter, which was held privately on the stage of Covent Garden, the Duke of Beaufort presented Charles Kemble with a massive silver vase, designed by the eminent sculptor Francis Chantrey, as a lasting token of the admiration and respect of his many friends. The vase appropriately bore on its cover "a simple and elegant figure of Hamlet," and "round it, in fine relief, the 'Seven Ages of Man,' from Jacques's speech in *As You Like It*."[74] It contained, too, engraved on one side, a laudatory inscription followed by the names of ninety subscribers, including Kemble's fellow actors Macready, Young, Ellen Tree, and Helen Faucit and an impressive list of English nobility who were numbered among the noted actor's special friends.

Two Brief Returns

The presentation of the vase, a little more than three years after Kemble's retirement, had an interesting repercussion. Queen Victoria upon hearing of the event remembered with great pleasure the times that she had seen the famous actor and wished that her Prince Consort might have the opportunity of watching Charles Kemble perform. A few days later the Queen signified to the retired performer that she would be most grateful if he would consent to return to the stage for a few nights at her special request.[75] Kemble, of course, felt highly honored. He immediately accepted the

73. James Robinson Planché, *Recollections and Reflections* (London, 1872), pp. 253 ff.; clipping from London newspaper in Enthoven Collection, Victoria and Albert Museum.

74. Fanny Kemble, *Records of a Girlhood* (New York, 1879), II, 279.

75. *John Bull*, March 29, 1840.

Queen's invitation, and arrangements for four command performances at Covent Garden at the end of March and the beginning of April were quickly made.

Many of Kemble's admirers viewed the prospect of his return to the stage with some alarm. It seemed to them a dangerous trial after several years' absence from the boards at his time of life.[76] The actor's health since his retirement had not been the best. As Fanny had feared, the loss of the nightly excitement which he had experienced for so many years had had an adverse effect on his spirits and his strength.[77] Now should the challenge of the command performances prove beyond his powers, the result would be a sad one indeed.

When, however, the sixty-four-year-old actor stepped upon the Covent Garden stage on March 24, 1840, as Don Felix in *Wonder*, all fears were soon allayed. That night the familiar signs of the Kemble genius were clearly present. One critic sighed: "It seemed as if by a vigorous effect of the will he had shaken forty years off his back, and bounded before us in all the vigour, elasticity, and fervid enthusiasm of youth. Oh! when will our young men learn to be and move the lover like him!"[78] Another exclaimed: "The highborn grace, the delicate shadowing of every variation from the purest love to the bitterest jealousy, the exquisite finish to every line, where could it be equalled?"[79] Kemble's strength and skill, if possible, increased in his subsequent personations of Mercutio, Benedick, and Hamlet. Of his last performance as the Danish prince on April 10 *The Times*

76. *Ibid.*
77. Fanny Kemble, *Records of Later Life* (New York, 1882), p. 47.
78. *John Bull*, March 29, 1840.
79. *The Times*, March 25, 1840.

observed with pleasure: "The most trying of all parts . . . he left to the last"; but "where most was required, the least was missing."[80] When the ordeal was over, many admirers agreed that Kemble was "the master yet."[81] His return had been an unqualified success and a tremendous personal triumph. Fanny Kemble Butler, who had been much concerned about the trial, had to admit that even her father's health had received a "beneficial stimulus from the excitement of his temporary return to the stage."[82]

An attempt by Kemble two years later to return to his former post as manager of Covent Garden met with considerably less success. Since he had left the job in 1832, the Theatre had had a number of different lessees and managers, each of whom had ended his term of office in financial defeat. A French entrepreneur named Laporte had leased Covent Garden immediately after Kemble, but was able to keep going for only about one hundred nights.[83] From 1833 to 1835, Alfred Bunn ruled supreme in an experiment which united Drury Lane and Covent Garden under a single management. This arrangement, however, proved less profitable than Bunn had hoped; and when he failed to receive a reduction in rent, he too gave up his lease.[84] D. W. Osbaldiston was in charge from 1835 to 1837. His unsuccessful plan for making the ill-paying Theatre show a profit was to reduce admission prices in order to compete with the minor houses. Osbaldiston was succeeded by Macready, who was manager from 1837 to 1839, and then by Mme Vestris and her husband, Charles Mathews, who were in

80. *Ibid.*, April 11, 1840.
81. *John Bull*, March 29, 1840; *The Times*, April 11, 1840.
82. Kemble, *Records of Later Life*, p. 196.
83. Bunn, *The Stage*, I, 98–99.
84. *Ibid.*, pp. 269 ff.

control in 1842 when Charles Kemble most unfortunately was tempted to try his hand again.

Mathews and Vestris, in contrast to most of their predecessors, were not anxious to give up the management of Covent Garden. Indeed, they were quite unhappy to lose their lease in the spring of 1842. Mme Vestris's reign at the Theatre, like Macready's, had been marked by many tasteful and artistically excellent productions; but she was not able, any more than her less gifted forerunners, to achieve any financial success. In her first two seasons she suffered heavy losses. Mathews confessed that every payday "was looked forward to with terror," and admited to such unwise and desperate measures as borrowing money at 60 percent interest to meet immediate expenses.[85] In Vestris's third season Adelaide Kemble, Charles's youngest daughter, came to the Theatre's rescue much as Fanny had done twelve years before. Exhibiting "the grace of a Pasta" and "the brilliant execution of a Grisi,"[86] the young soprano enjoyed a triumphant debut in Bellini's opera *Norma* on November 2, 1841. Nevertheless, the added expense of equipping the company for opera and the fact that on the nights when Adelaide did not appear the house was virtually empty[87] meant that the Theatre ended this season too in the red. At this point the stockholders took action. When Vestris and Mathews were unable to meet alleged arrears of rent amounting to fourteen thousand pounds, they canceled their lease, took the Theatre out of their hands, and, according to Mathews, confiscated their scenery, ward-

85. Charles Mathews, *The Life of Charles James Mathews,* ed. Charles Dickens (London, 1879), II, 91, 97.

86. *Theatrical Journal,* November 6, 1841.

87. Kemble, *Records of Later Life,* p. 295.

robes, and properties.[88] Then turning to their fellow proprietor, the shareholders of Covent Garden entreated Charles Kemble to take control of the forsaken concern once more, promising "that no responsibility or liability whatever should rest upon or be incurred by him, and that if the thing did not turn out prosperously, it should be put an end to, and the theatre immediately closed."[89]

Fanny and all the rest of his family strongly remonstrated against the move[90]—and poor Kemble, remembering the past, should certainly have known better; but despite advice and personal experience, the aged performer foolishly agreed to lend his name and talents to Covent Garden Theatre once again. In fact, in the spring of 1842 he looked forward with obvious delight to the prospect of resuming his old duties in September. Kemble had never found retirement conducive to good spirits; and since he had resigned his office as Examiner of Plays to his son John Mitchell in February, 1840, time had weighed heavily on his hands. In a letter of April 17, 1842, Fanny Butler, who with her husband and children was visiting in England, disclosed to a friend:

> My father appears to be quite well, and in a state of great pleasurable excitement and activity of mind, having (alas! I regret to say) accepted once more the management of Covent Garden. . . . He is in the Theatre from morning till night, as happy as the gods, and apparently, just now, as free from all mortal infirmity. It is amazing, to be sure, what the revival of the one interest of his life has done to his health.[91]

88. Mathews, *Life of Mathews*, II, 105.
89. Kemble, *Records of Later Life*, p. 365.
90. *Ibid.*
91. *Ibid.*, p. 309.

By the fall, however, the bad luck that was destined to attend Kemble's managerial return had already begun to appear. For one thing, during the summer his daughter Adelaide, the mainstay of the Theatre, had decided to give up her career for marriage; 1842–43, she declared, would definitely be her last season. Then after the opening of Covent Garden had been announced for September 3, the talented young soprano became ill; and the Theatre had to postpone its first night for another week. The opening on September 10 seemed propitious enough. Adelaide Kemble in her favorite opera *Norma* was hailed with tremendous cheers; and the London critics, noting his "restoration," extended to "King Charles" best wishes for a "prosperous reign."[92] Kemble's daughter repeated her popular roles of the previous season in *La Sonnambula* and *The Marriage of Figaro* in the next few weeks, and on October 1 performed for the first time in Rossini's *Semiramide*. "No opera within our recollection made so powerful an impression," the *Theatrical Journal* remarked on the latter occasion. "Thunders of applause" greeted the young prima donna, as well as showers of bouquets at her feet.[93] Despite Adelaide's acclaim, however, Charles Kemble had already begun to experience the difficulty encountered the year before by Mathews and Mme Vestris. On the off nights when the grand Anglo-Italian opera was not scheduled, a depressing quiet prevailed at Covent Garden. Fanny sadly noted in a letter of October 8:

> My father has a violent lumbago; so I am sorry to say, has the theatre, which in spite of my sister's exertions can

92. *The Times*, September 12, 1842; *Theatrical Journal*, September 3, 1842.

93. *Theatrical Journal*, October 8, 1842.

> hardly keep upon its legs. . . . Great as her success is, it will not make the nights pay on which she does not sing, when it is absolutely empty. What they will do when she goes I cannot . . . conceive.[94]

At the end of October, in an effort to escape the deficit of these off nights, it was announced that thereafter opera would be provided four times a week;[95] and in an attempt to find a popular alternative for Adelaide's performances, Charles Kemble brought out a magnificent new production of *The Tempest*. Macready had staged a version of *The Tempest* in 1838 which, in terms of *mise en scene,* was expected long to be unequaled, much less surpassed. But the stage effects and scenic grandeur of Kemble's revival reportedly left Macready's production "in the shade."[96] In the first scene, for example, Kemble introduced a real ship,

> —no painted profile, but an actual hull, completely rigged and appointed in every respect, her deck covered with sailors, hauling, shouting, and executing the orders of the rude boatswain. . . . At every roll of the monstrous sea, the struggling vessel seemed to plunge into the hideous vale of water till the spectators held their breath, expecting every moment to see her engulphed. A manoeuvre is executed by the crew, and the vessel slowly veering, presents to the audience her opposite side, and afterwards her high, antique looking stern, upon which three lanterns are hung. Each of these changes of positions elicited reiterated bursts of applause from the audience.[97]

94. Kemble, *Records of Later Life,* p. 361.
95. *Theatrical Journal,* October 29, 1842.
96. Ernest Bradlee Watson, *Sheridan to Robertson* (Cambridge: Harvard University Press, 1926), p. 260.
97. *Theatrical Journal,* November 19, 1842.

The cost of getting up the elaborate *Tempest* production, like that of the new opera *Semiramide*, was tremendous—far greater, it turned out, than the modest houses it attracted could repay. But the most unfortunate result of the project was that the constant strain and anxiety of personally superintending the affair proved more than Charles Kemble could bear. By the end of November the aged manager was confined to his bed with little prospect of a speedy recovery.[98] It now seemed clear to the other proprietors and to Kemble as well that his return had been a decided mistake. The shareholders called together the members of the company for a meeting in the Green Room and announced that Charles Kemble could no longer serve as manager and advised them that unless they wished to continue on a sharing basis until after Christmas when Alfred Bunn agreed once more to take the lease, Covent Garden, for the time being, would close.[99]

Somehow Covent Garden struggled to keep open as a legitimate theatre for five more years; but after Charles Kemble left, affairs there generally went from bad to worse. The actors, following the announcement of Kemble's withdrawal, managed to continue until the holidays by sharing receipts and losses, after turning over the first twenty pounds nightly to the stockholders; and they were greatly aided by Adelaide Kemble's generous offer to play without salary until her farewell. After Christmas the season staggered along under Bunn until April 29, marked largely by empty seats and a failure to perform the program announced.[100] In subsequent years several more enterprising

98. *Ibid.*, November 26, 1842.
99. *Ibid.*, December 3, 1842.
100. *Ibid.*, May 6, 1843.

lessees and managers tried to save the famous Theatre, but without success. Finally in 1847 Covent Garden, "the throne of the Kembles,"[101] underwent drastic structural alterations, after which it was converted permanently into an opera house.

With his departure from Covent Garden in the winter of 1842, Charles Kemble's professional career was pretty well ended. The actor did, however, occasionally give public readings, mostly from his favorite Shakespearean plays, for the next six years. In April, 1844, he was called upon to read *Cymbeline* before Her Majesty Queen Victoria and the Court at Buckingham Palace, and in May of that year he gave an especially popular series of readings at Willis's Rooms in London, which he repeated the following year. When he was asked to give a recitation of *Antigone* at Buckingham Palace in February, 1848, however, Kemble was forced to reply that his deafness would no longer enable him to do so. At that time he finally renounced the idea of reading again, and turned over to his daughter Fanny the Shakespearean texts that he had carefully and laboriously edited to bring the plays within the two-hour limit usually required for reading performances.[102]

Kemble's last years were relatively peaceful, though he was, of course, periodically troubled by the infirmities of old age. Severe deafness, which according to Fanny was occasioned by a broken nose suffered during a fall while ice skating,[103] considerably limited the performer's social life. Nevertheless, the genial actor delighted in spending endless hours at the Garrick Club, where his fellow members

101. *Ibid.*, September 3, 1842.
102. Kemble, *Records of Later Life*, pp. 614, 653.
103. Kemble, *Records of a Girlhood*, III, 160.

would address him through a speaking trumpet and he would entertain them with an inexhaustible fund of anecdotes. On one occasion, Edmund Yates recalled with amusement, the members were sitting in the library of the club with Kemble when "a tremendous thunderstorm broke over the house."

> It raged with extraordinary fury, one clap exploding with terrific noise immediately above us like a volley of artillery. We looked round at each other almost in horror; when Charles Kemble, who was calmly reading, lifted his eyes from his book, and said in his trumpet-tone: "I think we are going to have some thunder; I feel it in my knees."[104]

One of his last public appearances was at a farewell dinner given for Macready on March 1, 1851. Macready noted how the members of the theatrical profession paused in their celebration of his retirement to pay the aged Kemble honor that night. It seems that when Charles Kemble rose to offer his toast, the whole company stood and greeted him with tremendous applause and cheers.[105]

Concern for two of his children provided the main worry of Kemble's later life.[106] Fanny's marriage to Pierce Butler was not a happy one; and although her father constantly counseled "mutual forbearance,"[107] there were repeated separations and reconciliations, and finally a permanent

104. Edmund Yates, *Recollections and Experiences* (London, 1884), II, 5.

105. William Macready, *Reminiscences and Selections from His Diaries and Letters*, ed. Frederick Pollock (New York, 1875), p. 645.

106. Charles Kemble's wife had died in England in September, 1838, while he was with Adelaide in Milan, Italy.

107. Charles Kemble, letter to Pierce Butler, May 2, 1844, cited by Butler in *Mr. Butler's Statement, Originally Prepared in Aid of His Professional Counsel* (Philadelphia, 1850), p. 122.

separation in 1845, followed by a much publicized divorce in 1849. Kemble's younger son Henry, some years after an unfortunate affair with the heiress Mary Ann Thackeray which provided Henry James with the plot for *Washington Square*, suffered a mental collapse. Much to his father's dismay, poor Henry finally had to be confined to William Stilwell's private lunatic asylum at Hillingdon, Middlesex, where in 1854 William Thackeray visited him and suggested, in a letter of October 17, that he was completely and hopelessly insane.[108]

At the time of Kemble's severe illness in 1840 his friend William Bodham Donne had remarked, after noting that the performer's condition appeared to be hopeless, "It seems impossible for an actor to retire without dying."[109] Kemble, of course, soon recovered; and in subsequent years he proceeded to refute Donne's observation. Indeed, Charles Kemble lived for eighteen years after his formal farewell to the stage. It was not until November 12, 1854, that the final curtain descended on the famous actor and English newspapers sadly announced to the world that a great man of the theatre and the last of the Kembles was dead.

108. Thackeray's letter is quoted by Bruce Dickins, "The Story of 'Washington Square,'" *Times Literary Supplement,* October 13, 1961.

109. William Bodham Donne, letter to R. C. Trench, July 14, 1840, *William Bodham Donne and His Friends,* ed. Catharine B. Johnson (New York: Dutton, 1905), p. 65.

Bibliography

Charles Kemble's Plays

The Brazen Bust. Larpent MS 1771. Huntington Library. Never published. First performed at Covent Garden Theatre, May 29, 1813.

The Child of Chance. Larpent MS 1723. Huntington Library. Originally called *Love's Errors; or, The Child of Chance*. Never published. First performed at the Haymarket Theatre, July 8, 1812.

Henry VI: A Tragedy in Five Acts Condensed from Shakespeare. Published in *The Works of William Shakespeare*, ed. Henry Irving and Frank A. Marshall. 8 vols. London, 1890.

Kamchatka; or, The Slave's Tribute. Larpent MS 1691. Huntington Library. Originally called *The Day of Tribute*. Never published. First performed at Covent Garden Theatre, October 16, 1811.

Plot and Counterplot; or, The Portrait of Michael Cervantes. London, 1808.

The Point of Honour. London, 1800.

Proof Presumptive; or, The Abbey of San Marco. Larpent MS 2049. Huntington Library. Originally called *Proof Presumptive; or, The Secret Marriage*. Never published.

First performed at Covent Garden Theatre, October 20, 1818.

The Wanderer; or, The Rights of Hospitality. London, 1808.

Manuscripts, Excluding Kemble's Plays

British Museum:

Ad. MSS 23156–23160. "Covent Garden Theatre Diary, 1821–1831."

Ad. MSS 23163–23166. "Covent Garden Theatre: Pay-book, 1822–1828."

Ad. MS 23167. "Covent Garden Theatre: General Ledger, 1822–1829."

Ad. MS 27706. Musical score for *The Brazen Bust.*

Ad. MS 29641. "Covent Garden Theatre: Receipts and Payments, 1822–1826."

Ad. MS 29643. "Letterbook of Henry Robertson, Secretary to the Management, Covent Garden Theatre."

Ad. MSS 31972–31975. "Professional Memoranda of John Philip Kemble, 1788–1815."

Ad. MS 31976. "Professional Memoranda of Charles Kemble, March–July, 1822.

Ad. MS 33964. F. 66, letter to Charles Kemble, 1849; f. 68, letter to Charles Kemble, 1851; f. 131, letter to Charles Kemble from F. J. Talma, 1814; f. 245, letter to Charles Kemble from G. Colman, Jr., 1826.

Ad. MS 38071. F. 59, letter from Charles Kemble to Stationery Office, 1837.

Ad. MS 39577. F. 37, letter from Charles Kemble to I. Pocock, 1822.

Ad. MS 39809. F. 4, letter from Charles Kemble [to C. Mallet], 1828.

Ad. MS 41771. F. 57, letter from Charles Kemble to Sir G. T. Smart, 1826.

Harvard Theatre Collection:

Letter from Charles Kemble to Messrs. Londham Parke and Company, August 13, 1829.

Letter from Charles Kemble to Brunton, July 8, 1809.

Letter from Charles Kemble to Robbins, May 11, 1827.

Letter from Charles Kemble, February 21, 1824.

Letter from Charles Kemble, February 7, 1823.

Letter from Charles Kemble to Miss M. Tree, January 13, 1823.

Letter from Charles Kemble to Edward Gandy, December 15, 1824.

Letter from Edward Gandy to Charles Kemble, December 17, 1824.

Letter from Charles Kemble to John Taylor, December 24, 1828.

Letter from Charles Kemble to Poole, November 1, 1825.

Letter from Sheridan Knowles to Charles Kemble, June 19, 1832.

Letter from Charles Kemble to Fanny Kemble, November 1, 1850.

Receipt for salary, October 5, 1829–June 3, 1830, signed by Charles Kemble.

"Report of J. H. Edwards as to the Performances at the Surrey and New Strand Theatres, February 2, 1832."

"Report of F. H. Ingersoll as to the Performances at the Tottenham Theatre, November–December, 1830.

Gabrielle Enthoven Collection, Victoria and Albert Museum:

Letter from Charles Kemble to Alexander Mundell, Esq., November 6, 1808.

Letter from Charles Kemble [to an official at Drury Lane Theatre], June 17, 1812.

Letter from Charles Kemble to Charles Mathews, May 14, 1824.

Letter from Charles Kemble, G. H. Robbins, and John White to C. M. Westmacott, February 23, 1830.

Letter from Charles Kemble to the Duchess of St. Albans, April 15, 1832.

"Stanzas Written on Seeing Mr. Charles Kemble in the Pantomime of Obi," signed "Azuria," July 24, 1800.

Garrick Club:

Letter from Charles Kemble to Sir George Smart, April 15, 1846.

Letter from Charles Kemble, March 25, 1835.

London County Council:

"Articles of Agreement between Henry Harris . . . and John Saltren Willett of Park Street, West, John Forbes of Winkfield Place, and Charles Kemble of Gerrard Street, West," March 11, 1822.

Folger Shakespeare Library:

M.b. 15. "Diary of Jane Porter, 1801–1803."

W.b. 67. (79) Letter from Charles Kemble to Thomas Hill, May 6, 1803.

(80) Letter from Charles Kemble, March 25, 1824.

Shakespeare Memorial Theatre Library, Stratford-on-Avon:
Letter from Charles Kemble to Alfred Bunn, August 1, 1834.
Letter from Charles Kemble to William C. Lucy, September 19, 1844.
Letter from Charles Kemble to William C. Lucy, September 22, 1844.
Letter from Charles Kemble to William C. Lucy, October 27, 1844.

Private Theatre Collection of Roy Plomley, London:
Letter from Charles Kemble to Richard Milliken, December 11, 1829.
Receipt for salary, October 5, 1829–May 28, 1830, signed by Frances Ann Kemble.

Books and Articles

Archer, William. *William Charles Macready*. London, 1890.

Armstrong, William A. "Madame Vestris: A Centenary Appreciation," *Theatre Notebook*, XI (October–December 1956), 11–18.

Baker, H. Barton. *History of the London Stage: 1576–1903*. London: G. Routledge and Sons, 1904.

Baker, Herschel. *John Philip Kemble: The Actor in His Theatre*. Cambridge: Harvard University Press, 1942.

Biographia Dramatica; or, A Companion to the Playhouse. 3 vols. London, 1812.

Boaden, James. *Memoirs of the Life of John Philip Kemble, Esq., Including a History of the Stage from the Time of Garrick to the Present Period*. 2 vols. London, 1825.

Boaden, James. *Memoirs of Mrs. Siddons, Interspersed with Anecdotes of Authors and Actors.* 2 vols. London, 1827.

Borgerhoff, J. L. *Le Théâtre anglais à Paris sous la Restauration.* Paris: Hachette, 1912.

Bowers, Claude G. *The Party Battles of the Jackson Period.* Boston: Houghton Mifflin Company, 1928.

Browning, Robert. *Life and Letters of Robert Browning.* Ed. Mrs. Sutherland Orr. 2 vols. Boston, 1891.

Bunn, Alfred. *The Stage: Both Before and Behind the Curtain.* 3 vols. London, 1840.

Burnim, Kalman A. *David Garrick Director.* Pittsburgh: University of Pittsburgh Press, 1961.

Butler, Frances Anne Kemble. *Journal.* 2 vols. Philadelphia, 1835.

Butler, Pierce. *Mr. Butler's Statement, Originally Prepared in Aid of His Professional Counsel.* Philadelphia, 1850.

Byrne, M. St. Clare. "The Stage Costuming of 'Macbeth' in the Eighteenth Century." In *Studies in English Theatre History in Memory of Gabrielle Enthoven.* London: The Society for Theatre Research, 1952, pp. 52–64.

Charles Kemble's Shakespere Readings: Being a Selection of the Plays of Shakespere as Read by Him in Public. Ed. R. J. Lane. 3 vols. London, 1870.

Clarke, Mary Cowden. *My Long Life.* New York, 1896.

Dickins, Bruce. "The Story of 'Washington Square,'" *Times Literary Supplement,* October 13, 1961.

Dieulafoy, Michel. *Le Portrait de Michel Cervantes.* Paris, An XI de la République.

Donne, William Bodham. *Essays on the Drama.* London, 1858.

Doran, [John]. *Their Majesties Servants: Being an Annual of the English Stage from Thomas Betterton (1635–1779) to Edmund Kean (1787–1833).* 3 vols. London, 1888.

Downer, Alan S. *The Eminent Tragedian William Charles Macready*. Cambridge: Harvard University Press, 1966.

Driver, Leota S. *Fanny Kemble*. Chapel Hill: University of North Carolina Press, 1933.

Durang, Charles. *The Philadelphia Stage from the Year 1749 to 1855*. Philadelphia, n.d.

Eddison, Robert. "Souvenirs du Théâtre anglais à Paris, 1827," *Theatre Notebook*, IX (July–September, 1955), 99–103.

Fitzball, Edward. *Thirty-five Years of a Dramatic Author's Life*. 2 vols. London, 1859.

FitzGerald, Edward. *Letters to Fanny Kemble, 1871–1883*. Ed. Aldis Wright. New York, 1895.

Fowell, Frank. *Censorship in England*. London: Frank Palmer, 1913.

Frith, W. P. *My Autobiography and Reminiscences*. New York, 1888.

Ganzel, Dewey. "Patent Wrongs and Patent Theatres: Drama and the Law in the Early Nineteenth Century," *PMLA*, LXXVI (September 1961), 384–96.

Genest, John. *Some Account of the English Stage: From the Restoration in 1660 to 1830*. 10 vols. Bath, 1832.

The Georgian Era: Memoirs of the Most Eminent Persons, Who Have Flourished in Great Britain, from the Accession of George the First to the Demise of George the Fourth. 4 vols. London, 1832.

[Greffulhe]. *A Budget of Blunders*. Philadelphia, 1811.

Hackett, James Henry. *Notes, Criticisms and Correspondence upon Shakespeare's Plays and Actors*. New York, 1863.

Harris, Henry. *A Letter to John White, Esq*. London, August 14, 1829.

Harris v. *Kemble. The Vice Chancellor's Report.* London, April 12, 1827.

Harris v. *Kemble. The Lord Chancellor's Report.* London, May 19, 1829.

Harris v. *Kemble. Journals of the House of Lords,* LXI (1829), LXII (1830), LXIII (1831).

Hazlitt, William. *Complete Works.* Ed. P. P. Howe. 21 vols. London: J. M. Dent and Sons, 1930.

Hill, Benson Earle. *Playing About; or, Theatrical Anecdotes and Adventures with Scenes of General Nature, from the Life in England, Scotland, and Ireland.* 2 vols. London, n.d.

Holcroft, Thomas. *The Life of Thomas Holcroft.* Ed. Elbridge Colby. 2 vols. London: Constable and Company, 1925.

Hone, Philip. *Diary.* Ed. Allan Nevins. New York: Dodd, Mead and Company, 1936.

Hunt, Leigh. *Dramatic Criticism, 1808–1831.* Ed. Laurence Huston Houtchens and Carolyn Washburn Houtchens. New York: Columbia University Press, 1949.

———. *Dramatic Essays.* Ed. William Archer and Robert Lowe. London, 1894.

Ireland, Joseph N. *Records of the New York Stage.* 2 vols. New York, 1867.

Irving, Pierre. *The Life and Letters of Washington Irving.* 3 vols. New York, 1883.

James, Reese D. *Old Drury of Philadelphia.* Philadelphia: University of Pennsylvania Press, 1932.

Kemble, Frances Ann. *Records of a Girlhood.* 3 vols. London, 1879.

———. *Records of Later Life.* New York, 1882.

———. *Further Records, 1848–1883.* 2 vols. London, 1890.

Kotzebue, August Friedrich Ferdinand von. *Eduard in Schottland.* London, 1836.

Lacy, Walter. "Old and Young Stager." In *The Green Room,* Ed. Clement Scott. London, n.d.

Leggett, William. "Charles Kemble's Hamlet." In *The American Theatre as Seen by Its Critics, 1752–1934,* Ed. Montrose J. Moses and John Mason Brown. New York: W. W. Norton and Company, 1934.

Leslie, Charles Robert. *Autobiographical Recollections.* Ed. Tom Taylor. Boston, 1860.

L'Estrange, Rev. A. G. *The Literary Life of the Rev. William Harness.* London, 1871.

Mackintosh, Donald T. "New Dress'd in the Habits of the Times," *Times Literary Supplement,* August 25, 1927.

Macready, William Charles. *Reminiscences, and Selections from His Diaries and Letters.* Ed. Frederick Pollock. New York, 1875.

Marston, Westland. *Our Recent Actors.* Boston, 1888.

Mathews, Charles. *The Life of Charles James Mathews: Chiefly Autobiographical with Selections from His Correspondence and Speeches.* Ed. Charles Dickens. 2 vols. London, 1879.

Mercier, L. S. *Le Déserteur.* Paris, 1770.

Mitford, Mary Russell. *The Life of Mary Russell Mitford, Authoress of Our Village, etc.: Related in a Selection from Her Letters to Her Friends.* Ed. the Rev. A. G. L'Estrange. 2 vols. New York, 1870.

Morse, John T. *Life and Letters of Oliver Wendell Holmes.* 2 vols. London, 1896.

Nicholson, Watson. *The Struggle for a Free Stage in London.* Boston: Houghton Mifflin and Company, 1906.

Nicoll, Allardyce. *A History of Early Nineteenth Century*

Drama: 1800–1850. 2 vols. Cambridge: Cambridge University Press, 1930.

Odell, George C. D. *Annals of the New York Stage*. 15 vols. New York: Columbia University Press, 1927–49.

———. *Shakespeare from Betterton to Irving*. 2 vols. New York: C. Scribner's Sons, 1920.

Oulton, W. C. *A History of the Theatres of London: Containing an Annual Register of New Pieces, Revivals, Pantomimes and with Occasional Notes and Anecdotes, Being a Continuation of Victor's and Oulton's Histories from the Year 1795–1817 Inclusive*. 3 vols. London, 1818.

Oxberry, W. *Dramatic Biography and Histrionic Anecdotes*. 6 vols. London, 1825–26.

Philo-Dramaticus: A Letter to C. Kemble and R. W. Elliston, Esqrs., on the Present State of the Stage. London, 1825.

Pierce, Edward L. *Memoir and Letters of Charles Sumner*. 3 vols. Boston, 1877.

Planché, James Robinson. *Dramatic Costume: Costume of Shakespeare's Historical Tragedy of King John*. London, 1823.

———. *Dramatic Costume: Costume of Shakespeare's Historical Play of King Henry the Fourth, Parts I and II*. London, 1824.

———. *Dramatic Costume: Costume of Shakespeare's Comedy As You Like It*. London, 1825.

———. *Dramatic Costume: Costume of Shakespeare's Tragedy of Hamlet*. London, 1825.

———. *Dramatic Costume: Costume of Shakespeare's Tragedy of Othello and Comedy of the Merchant of Venice*. London, 1825.

———. *Recollections and Reflections*. London, [1872].

Ray, Gordon N. *Thackeray: The Uses of Adversity, 1811–1846.* New York: McGraw Hill Book Company, [1955].

"Report of the Select Committee on Dramatic Literature of the House of Commons." *Great Britain Parliamentary Reports*, VII (1831–32).

Rice, Charles. *The London Theatre in the Eighteen Thirties.* Ed. Arthur Colby Sprague and Bertram Shuttleworth. London: Society for Theatre Research, 1950.

Robinson, Henry Crabb. *The London Theatre, 1811–1866: Selections from the Diary of Henry Crabb Robinson.* Ed. Eluned Brown. London: Society for Theatre Research, 1966.

Robson, William. *The Old Play-Goer.* London, 1846.

Sellier, Walter. *Kotzebue in England.* Leipzig: Druck von O. Schmidt, 1901.

Sprague, Arthur Colby. *Shakespeare and the Actors: The Stage Business in His Plays: 1660–1905.* Cambridge: Harvard University Press, 1944.

———. *Shakespeare's Histories: Plays for the Stage.* London: Society for Theatre Research, 1964.

———. *Shakespearian Players and Performances.* Cambridge: Harvard University Press, 1953.

Story, Joseph. *Life and Letters.* Ed. William Story. 2 vols. Boston, 1851.

Taylor, John. *Records of My Life.* 2 vols. London, 1832.

Thackeray, William Makepeace. *The Letters and Private Papers of William Makepeace Thackeray.* Ed. Gordon Ray. 4 vols. Cambridge: Harvard University Press, 1945.

Thompson, L. F. *Kotzebue: A Survey of His Progress in France and England.* Paris: Champion, 1928.

Vandenhoff. *Leaves from an Actor's Notebook.* New York, 1860.

Walpole, Horace. *Letters*. Ed. Peter Cunningham. 9 vols. London, 1859.

Watson, Ernest Bradlee. *Sheridan to Robertson: A Study of the Nineteenth Century London Stage*. Cambridge: Harvard University Press, 1926.

Wemyss, Francis Courtney. *Twenty-Six Years of the Life of an Actor and Manager*. 2 vols. New York, 1847.

William Charles Macready's King John. Ed. Charles H. Shattuck. Urbana: University of Illinois Press, 1962.

Wyndham, Henry Saxe. *The Annals of Covent Garden Theatre from 1732 to 1897*. 2 vols. London: Chatto and Windus, 1906.

Yates, Edmund. *Recollections and Experiences*. 2 vols. London, 1884.

Young, Julian Charles. *A Memoir of Charles Mayne Young, Tragedian, with Extracts from His Son's Diary*. London, 1871.

Newspapers and Periodicals

In addition to those cited below I have used scattered issues of many other newspapers and periodicals in the Harvard Theatre Collection, the Enthoven Collection, and the Garrick Club.

Boston *Weekly Gazette*, April, May, and September 1833.

Boston *Weekly Messenger and Massachusetts Journal*, April and May 1833.

Drama; or, Theatrical Pocket Magazine (London), 1821–25.

Dramatic Magazine (London), 1830–31.

Johnson's Sunday Monitor and British Gazette (London), 1805–13.

London *John Bull*, August and September 1823.

London *Morning Chronicle*, 1800–1812.

London *Morning Herald*, August and September 1823; October and November 1830.

London *Times*, 1794–1832; 1842; November 1854.

Monthly Mirror: Reflecting Men and Manners, with Strictures of Their Epitome, the Stage (London), December 1795–December 1806.

New York *American*, 1832.

Theatrical Inquisitor (London), 1812–21.

Theatrical Journal (London), 1841–42.

Theatrical Observer (London), 1821–32.

Thespian Magazine (London), 1794–98.

Promptbooks

Hamlet

Folger, *Hamlet* 44. A promptbook which apparently belonged to the American actor J. B. Roberts, whose name appears on the title page. On the page opposite the beginning of the text it bears the note: "Marked from Mr. C. Kemble's promptbook." It may have been copied from Kemble's promptbook during his American visit in 1832–34. It is a Cumberland edition with interleaves and includes stresses marked for Hamlet's speeches, cuts, restorations, diagrams, and much stage business.

King John

Folger, *King John* 10. A promptbook, marked in John Kemble's hand, which was used for productions at Covent Garden Theatre in which Charles Kemble played Faulconbridge to his brother's John. It is a Kemble edition (1804) with interleaves watermarked

1807, and contains calls, stage business, maps, cues for effects, and timings.

Thomas Barry's promptbook, Walter Hampden Memorial Library, The Players. "Tho Barry, Park, N.Y. 1832" is marked on the cover. A promptbook used for performances at the Park Theatre in New York in 1832 in which Charles Kemble played Faulconbridge, with Fanny Kemble as Constance and Barry as King John. It is a Cumberland edition and includes calls, some stage business, cues for effects, and notes by Barry on the playing of John.

Much Ado About Nothing

New York Public Library, *NCP .342944. Professor Shattuck describes this promptbook as a compilation made by George Becks. It is a Cumberland edition with interleaves, and on the last page of the interleaves it bears the notation: "N.B. From Promptbook under under Mr. Macready's Direction, T.R.D.L. 1842. Where the bus. of C. Kemble differed from Mr. M—— a note is made of the same." It contains many specific references to the business of C. Kemble.

New York Public Library, *NCP .285345. A promptbook which belonged to George Becks. It is a French issue of a Booth-Hinton edition. Its markings include a number of explicit references to the business of C. Kemble.

Index